a landscape of architecture, history and fiction

Architecture can be analogous to a history, a fiction and a landscape. We expect a history or a novel to be written in words, but they can also be cast in concrete or seeded in soil. The catalyst to this tradition was the simultaneous and inter-dependent emergence in the eighteenth century of new art forms: the picturesque landscape, the analytical history and the English novel. Each of them instigated a creative and questioning response to empiricism's detailed investigation of subjec-tive experience and the natural world, and together they stimulated a design practice and lyrical environmentalism that profoundly influenced subsequent centuries.

Associating the changing natural world with journeys in self-understanding, and the design process with a visual and spatial autobiography, this book describes journeys between London and the North Sea in successive centuries, analysing an enduring and evolving tradition from the picturesque and romanticism to modern-ism. Creative architects have often looked to the past to understand the present and imagine the future. Twenty-first-century architects need to appreciate the shock of the old as well as the shock of the new.

Jonathan Hill is Professor of Architecture and Visual Theory at the Bartlett School of Architecture, University College London (UCL), UK, where he directs the MPhil/PhD Architectural Design programme. Jonathan is the author of *The Illegal Architect* (1998), *Actions of Architecture* (2003), *Immaterial Architecture* (2006) and *Weather Architecture* (2012); editor of *Occupying Architecture* (1998) and *Architecture – the Subject is Matter* (2001); and co-editor of *Critical Architecture* (2007).

A LANDSCAPE OF ARCHITECTURE, HISTORY AND FICTION

Jonathan Hill

Routledge
Taylor & Francis Group

LONDON AND NEW YORK

First published 2016
by Routledge
2 Park Square, Milton Park, Abingdon, Oxon OX14 4RN

and by Routledge
711 Third Avenue, New York, NY 10017

Routledge is an imprint of the Taylor & Francis Group, an informa business

British Library Cataloguing-in-Publication Data
A catalogue record for this book is available from the British Library

Library of Congress Cataloging-in-Publication Data
Hill, Jonathan, 1958–
    A landscape of architecture, history and fiction / Jonathan Hill.
        pages cm
    Includes bibliographical references and index.
    1. Architecture–Philosophy. 2. Architecture–Human factors.
    3. Architecture and society–History–18th century. I. Title.
    NA2540.H55 2015
    720.1–dc23   2015019479

ISBN: 978-1-138-85228-0 (hbk)
ISBN: 978-1-138-85229-7 (pbk)
ISBN: 978-1-315-72364-8 (ebk)

Typeset in News Gothic
by Keystroke, Station Road, Codsall, Wolverhampton

Printed and bound in Great Britain by
TJ International Ltd, Padstow, Cornwall

CONTENTS

FIGURES

COVER

Denys Lasdun, UEA, 1968. View of the ziggurats from the River Yare. Courtesy of Richard
  Einzig/Arcaid Images.

CHAPTER 1

figures

CHAPTER 2

CHAPTER 3

ACKNOWLEDGEMENTS

A Landscape of Architecture, History and Fiction developed from my teaching and research at the Bartlett School of Architecture, UCL. I particularly wish to thank Matthew Butcher and Elizabeth Dow, my teaching partners in MArch Unit 12, for stimulating and generous discussions. My colleagues in the MPhil/PhD Architectural Design programme offered invaluable encouragement, especially Dr Ben Campkin, Professor Nat Chard, Professor Murray Fraser, Dr Penelope Haralambidou, Dr Yeoryia Manolopoulou, Dr Sophia Psarra, Dr Peg Rawes and Professor Jane Rendell. Also at the Bartlett, I wish to thank Laura Allen, Professor Adrian Forty, Dr Anne Hultzsch, Dr Guan Lee, Dr Jan Kattein, Chee-Kit Lai, Professor C. J. Lim, Dr Barbara Penner, Dr Tania Sengupta, Professor Bob Sheil, Mark Smout and Dr Nina Vollenbröker. Dialogue with an exceptional group of MArch and PhD students has influenced the character of this book, including Rodolfo Acevedo Rodriguez, Alessandro Ayuso, Steve Baumann, David Buck, Graham Burn, James Church, Omar Ghazal, Colin Herperger, Alastair King, Felipe Lanuza Rilling, Ifigeneia Liangi, Tom Noonan, David Potts, Camila Sotomayor, Catrina Stewart, Louis Sullivan, Kieran Wardle, Gabriel Warshafsky, Owain Williams, Dan Wilkinson, Danielle Willkens, Alan Worn and Tim Zihong Yue. Supported by the Bartlett Architecture Research Fund, the image permissions were acquired with considerable care and diligence by Catalina Mejia Moreno.

I very much appreciate the advice of the many people who have assisted my research. These include Stephen Astley and Susan Palmer, respectively the Curator of Drawings and Head of Library Services at Sir John Soane's Museum, London; Roger Bond, Director of Estates and Buildings, UEA; Dominic Bradbury; Professor Peter Brimblecombe, UEA; Dr Barnabas Calder, University of Liverpool; Katherine Clarke, muf architecture/art; Colin Harris, Superintendent, Special Collections Reading Rooms, Bodleian Library, Oxford; Kurt Helfrich, Fiona Orsini and Suzanne Walters, RIBA Drawings and Archives Collections; Kathryn Holeywell, UEA; Christine Hiskey and Dr Suzanne Reynolds, respectively the Archivist and Manuscript Curator at Holkham Hall, Norfolk; Dr Amy Kulper, University of Michigan; James Lasdun; Lady (Susan) Lasdun; Hal Moggridge, Colvin & Moggridge Landscape Architects; Dr Andrew Moore, Keeper of Art and Senior Curator, Norwich Castle Study Centre; Dr Joyce Townsend, Senior Conservation Scientist, Tate, London; and David Yaxley, Archivist, Houghton Hall. I am also indebted to Dr Ana Araujo, Architectural Association School of Architecture; Morag Bain; Carolyn Butterworth, University of Sheffield; Barbara-Ann Campbell-Lange, Architectural Association School of Architecture; Dr Emma Cheatle, University of

Brighton; Ben Clement and Sebastian de la Cour; Dr Willem de Bruijn; Professor Mark Dorrian, University of Edinburgh; Paul Fineberg; Professor William Firebrace, State Academy of Fine Arts, Stuttgart; Catherine Harrington; Emma Jones; Professor Perry Kulper, University of Michigan; Dr Constance Lau, University of Westminster; Dr Lesley Lokko, University of Johannesburg; Ganit Mayslits Kassif; Jean Oh; Ulrike Passe, Iowa State University; Rahesh Ram, University of Greenwich; Neil Rawson; and Ro Spankie, University of Westminster.

A Landscape of Architecture, History and Fiction is my seventh book to be published by Routledge, and I am especially grateful to Fran Ford for her continuing support. I also wish to thank Jennifer Birtill, Christina O'Brien and Trudy Varcianna for their care in preparing this book.

ILLUSTRATIONS

Considerable effort has been made to trace copyright holders of images. The author and publishers apologise for any errors and omissions, and, if notified, will endeavour to correct these at the earliest available opportunity.

introduction

The catalyst for this book was a fascination for a place: a four-mile long sandy beach flanked by dunes and adjacent to one of the grandest early eighteenth-century English estates, created while the turbulent and threatening sea was moving inland. The estate's dual orientation established a dialogue between culture and nature – London and Rome to the south and the sea to the north – and also between differing conceptions of nature, which was celebrated to a more profound degree than in earlier centuries and associated with journeys in self-understanding.

The initial aim of this book is to identify the simultaneous and interdependent emergence of new art forms, each of them a creative and questioning response to empiricism's detailed investigation of subjective experience and the natural world: the picturesque landscape, the analytical history and the English novel, which its early advocates conceived as a fictional autobiography and characterised as a history not a story. The conjunction of art forms instigated a new design practice in which architecture is analogous to a landscape, a history, and a fiction, stimulating a lyrical environmentalism that profoundly influenced subsequent centuries.

Associating the changing natural world with subjective and social experience, and the design process with a visual and spatial autobiography, this book describes journeys between London and the North Sea in successive centuries. Its focus is an enduring and evolving tradition from the picturesque and romanticism to modernism, which has the 'living' ruin as its emblem and model. A hybrid of nature and culture, architecture and landscape, and a recurring temporal metaphor in gardens, histories and novels, the ruin represents growth as well as decay, potential as well as loss, and the future as well as the past.

Integrating the analysis of architecture, art, literature, agriculture, landscape, industry, politics and social life, the detailed, holistic and evocative comparison of specific times and places is my research method. The first chapter begins with John Evelyn's seventeenth-century account of London's polluted atmosphere, which initiated centuries of poetic and practical responses to anthropogenic climate change. While in London, the chapter sets the scene for the artistic, literary and philosophical transformations in early eighteenth-century Britain, before following Evelyn's advice to discover the clear air of a country estate, journeying north to analyse William Kent's Arcadian designs for two neighbouring Norfolk estates: Houghton, the home of Sir Robert Walpole, the first British Prime Minister, and Holkham, the coastal estate that initiated this book.

The second chapter begins with J.M.W. Turner's painting of the paddle steamer *Ariel* in a turbulent night-time snow storm off the East Anglian coast, which depicts the complex interweaving of intense natural and man-made energies as the era's most formidable machine, the steam engine, is vulnerable to the power of the sea. The chapter then returns to London, focusing on the contrasting responses to the city's polluted atmosphere of Turner and his close friend John Soane, who conceived 12–14 Lincoln's Inn Fields as a fictional autobiography and picturesque garden, portraying it as a romantic ruin in a novelistic history of his home.

The third chapter begins in mid twentieth-century London, when a threatened national identity reaffirmed the association of a people with a place, and British modernism was identified with the picturesque and romanticism, encouraging architects to counter an earlier, didactic and universal modernism by embracing history, landscape and environmentalism. Leaving London, the chapter travels north to a late eighteenth-century Norfolk estate where the architect Denys Lasdun and landscape architect Brenda Colvin designed the new University of East Anglia in the 1960s. In the symbiosis of geography and history in an island nation, Lasdun and Colvin acknowledged that British architecture is both interdependent with landscape and a form of landscape architecture. Associating designs with stories and histories, Lasdun remarked that each architect must devise his or her 'own creative myth', a set of ideas, values and inspirations that inform design, concluding: 'My own myth . . . engages with history'.[1] The most creative architects have often looked to the past to imagine a future, studying an earlier architecture not to replicate it but to understand and transform it, revealing its relevance to the present.

The conclusion considers the contemporary relevance of this evolving tradition with particular regard to the influence of digital media and anthropogenic climate change on architectural design in Britain and the many other nations where 'romantic modernism' remains of abiding importance. Acknowledging that people are natural as well as cultural beings, and that each urban or rural landscape is teeming with life forms that are not simply subject to humanity, the conclusion considers an expanded conception of architectural authorship that includes natural as well as cultural influences. In conceiving a design as both a history and a novel, this book places architecture and landscape at the centre of cultural and social production, and emphasises their ability to engage and stimulate ideas, values and emotions that influence and inform individuals and societies.

1 Denys Lasdun, 'The Architecture of Urban Landscape', pp. 137, 139.

1

a hellish cloud
and a sublime sea

1 Evelyn, *Fumifugium*, p. 18.

2 Brimblecombe, 'Interest in Air Pollution', p. 123.

A 'Hellish and dismall Cloud of SEA-COALE' blankets London, complained John Evelyn in 1661.[1] Coals then had sulphur levels twice that of ones used centuries later. On combustion, sulphur oxidised to introduce sulphur dioxide into the air and a secondary oxidation created sulphuric acid.[2] Fog, coal smoke and industrial fumes turned the sky into a darkly odorous smog, blackening buildings, corroding metals, killing plants, lodging in lungs, and making streets and squares unbearable. A new building had a shadow of soot even before the end of its construction.

Evelyn's *Fumifugium: Or, The Inconveniencie of the Aer and Smoak of London Dissipated*, 1661, was the first book to consider the city's polluted atmosphere as a whole, as well as the first to recognise mitigation and adaptation as responses to human-induced – anthropogenic – climate change, three centuries before these principles were widely accepted. Opening with a dedication to King Charles II, Evelyn conceived *Fumifugium* in response to a 'pernicious Accident' in the royal palace of Whitehall. A 'presumptuous Smoake . . . did so invade the Court' that 'Men could hardly discern one another' in the same room.[3]

3 Evelyn, *Fumifugium*, pp. 1–2.

Evelyn distinguishes between London's agreeable setting and the ruinous effects of its polluted atmosphere. A keen admirer of Francis Bacon – the father figure of empiricism – Evelyn advocates modern science but also acknowledges the medical tradition of ancient Greece, which considers health and disease holistically and the interdependence of the body, soul and environment. Recalling the principle that the air – the breath – is 'the *Vehicle* of the *Soul*, as well as that of the Earth', he recounts Hippocratic opinion that the character of a people depends upon the air they inhale.[4] Convinced that London's atmosphere is unhealthy, he notes the comparative clarity of the sky on Sunday when industries are idle, and mistakenly assumes that domestic fires contribute little pollution. Offering a 'Remedy' for the '*Nuisance*', he proposes a number of practical and poetic measures, including the relocation of coal-burning trades, butchers and burials to the east of the city so that the prevailing westerly winds would carry the smoke away from London and the rivers and ground-water would be unsullied.[5] Prisons are also to be removed, indicating that his purpose is moral as well as medical.[6]

4 It is uncertain whether the influential treatises attributed to him were actually written by Hippocrates, who was born in the fifth century BC. Evelyn, *Fumifugium*, pp. 18, 11–13.

5 Evelyn mentions *A Discourse on Sympathetic Powder*, 1658, in which Kenelm Digby was probably the first person to attempt to explain the detrimental effect of atmospheric pollution on health, noting that the airways to the lungs are narrowed in pulmonary diseases. Evelyn, *Fumifugium*, pp. 3, 28, 34–37.

6 Evelyn, *Fumifugium*, pp. 42–43.

7 Evelyn, *Fumifugium*, pp. 47, 49.

Emphasising the allegorical and poetic as well as practical significance of his treatise, Evelyn proposes that the edges of London are to be forested with trees and planted with fragrant shrubs so that wood could replace coal as the principal fuel and the whole city would be sweetly perfumed.[7] Noting Evelyn's detailed attention to aesthetics, climate, natural history, horticulture and human experience, Mark Laird writes that 'he reflected on how gardens gratify all five senses through tinctures, redolent scents, delight of touch, fruit gusto, and warbling birds and

FUMIFUGIUM:

O R

The Inconveniencie of the A E R

A N D

SMOAK of LONDON

D I S S I P A T E D.

T O G E T H E R

With some R E M E D I E S humbly

P R O P O S E D

By *J. E.* Esq;

To His Sacred M A J E S T I E,

A N D

To the P A R L I A M E N T now Assembled.

Published by His Majesties Command.

Lucret. l. 5.

*Carbonúmque gravis vis, atque odor insinuatur
Quam facile in cerebrum?*

L O N D O N,

Printed by *W. Godbid* for *Gabriel Bedel*, and *Thomas Collins*,
and are to be sold at their Shop at the *Middle Temple* Gate
neer *Temple-Bar*. *M. DC. LXI.*

John Evelyn, *Fumifugium: or The Inconveniencie of the Aer and Smoak of London Dissipated*, 1661. Frontispiece. Courtesy of the British Library.

echoes'.[8] Evelyn's remedy – a perfumed botanical garden – would have implied good health due to the known medicinal properties of certain plants and also promoted associations with Heaven and the Garden of Eden.[9] Carolyn Merchant acknowledges that 'The Recovery of Eden story is the mainstream narrative of Western culture. It is perhaps the most important mythology humans have developed to make sense of their relationship to the earth.'[10]

[8] Laird refers to Evelyn's 'Elysium Britannicum, or, The Royal Gardens in Three Books', which was written between the 1650s and 1690s, and only published in 2001. Laird, p. 329.

[9] Jenner, pp. 544–546.

[10] Merchant, p. 2.

In a publication such as *Sylva Sylvarum: Or A Natural History, in Ten Centuries*, 1627, Bacon set the tone for investigations later in the seventeenth century, promoting reasoned analysis of the natural world. Bacon's advice that the philosopher required a garden – as well as a library and a laboratory – influenced Evelyn's enduring fascination for horticulture and led him to cultivate an analogy between the domestic and urban scales. Recording seasonal and yearly changes, he avidly tended his garden at Sayes Court, Deptford, which included an arbour and medicinal plants, like his proposition for London. The need for a 'Remedy' was most apparent in winter, when cold stagnant weather prevented the dispersal of pollutants, leading Evelyn to observe 'the havock which a rude season has made in my poor Gardens'.[11]

Mark Jenner notes that contemporary imagery equated the monarch with the illuminating sun and the interregnum – between the execution of Charles I in 1649 and accession of Charles II in 1660 – as 'the obscuring cloud'.[12] Recalling Hippocrates and an Old Testament verse, and associating the sun with a clear sky, Evelyn eulogises 'our Illustrious *CHARLES*, who is the very Breath of our Nostrils, in whose health all our happiness resides'.[13] In January 1662, at the King's request, Evelyn prepared a parliamentary bill but there was no public demand for a reduction in urban pollution and the legislation progressed no further.[14]

Fumifugium concentrates on London's atmosphere but Evelyn also derides its misshapen houses, narrow streets, uneven paving and irregular drainage.[15] Returning to these concerns after the Great Fire of 1666, he once again called for the removal of odorous trades and industries. Proposing that the city should be rebuilt in a manner inspired by Rome with broad streets and regular frontages, Evelyn's regard for classical architecture depended on its grounding in scientific and geometric principles that, he believed, assured its beauty, and recalled Hippocrates' influence on Renaissance architects who emphasised the health benefits of gentle air movement in contrast to the narrow lanes and stagnant air of a medieval city. But the Great Fire's only significant consequence was that sturdier brick construction replaced timber. Property rights and the economic intricacies of London's industries, as well as popular identification of a fire with a home, undermined Evelyn's proposals to transform London's material form and immaterial air.

Extending a metaphor that he explored in *Fumifugium*, Evelyn considered the sun to be an appropriate emblem for the intellectual enlightenment of the Royal Society, which was founded in 1660 after Christopher Wren's inaugural lecture and received a royal charter two years later with the purpose to advance

11 Evelyn, 'An Abstract of a Letter', p. 559, reporting on the winter of 1683. Refer to Laird, pp. 28-61.

12 Jenner, pp. 542–543.

13 Jenner notes that this 'is a quotation from *Lamentations* 4.20 and refers to the Lord's Annointed'. Evelyn, *Fumifugium*, p. 44; Jenner, pp. 543–544.

14 Jenner, p. 549; Smith, 'John Evelyn and London Air', p. 186.

15 Evelyn, *Fumifugium*, p. 8. Refer to Li, p. 45.

scientific knowledge through empirical investigation. The Royal Society was first accommodated in Gresham's College in the heart of the city, where Wren was Professor of Astronomy, and after the Great Fire moved to Arundel House just to the west. Evelyn was elected a Fellow of the Royal Society in 1661, as was John Locke seven years later.

Beginning in the mid-seventeenth century and extending into the subsequent century, the Enlightenment – the natural light of reason – was founded

William Kent, Elysian Fields, Stowe, c.1735. The bust of John Locke in the Temple of British Worthies. Photograph, Jonathan Hill.

on the assumption that humanity and nature are subject to the same laws of divine reason, can be understood by reason and progress by reason. Derived from e*mpeiria*, the ancient Greek term for experience, the principal British contribution to Enlightenment theory was empiricism, which promoted reason but made it specific rather than generic. Empirical investigation was applied extensively, notably to the natural world and the operations of the mind.

In *An Essay Concerning Human Understanding*, 1690, Locke describes diverse beliefs to emphasise that ideas and values are provisional not universal, and indicates that his travels enabled him to reach this conclusion. Countering the Platonist and Cartesian traditions in which knowledge is acquired by the mind alone, Locke states that personality and morality develop through a dialogue between the environment, senses and mind. Dismissing the search for ultimate truth, he accepts that there are limits to what we can know and argues that conclusions must be in proportion to the evidence: 'Our business here is not to know all things, but those which concern our conduct.'[16] A model of empirical education – a person learning through experience in a measured and reasonable manner – is at the heart of *An Essay Concerning Human Understanding*, which Locke confirms in *A Letter Concerning Toleration*, 1689, and *Some Thoughts Concerning Education*, 1693. The Lockean self is self-controlled, punctual, industrious and drawn to self-improvement and socially acceptable pleasures.[17] The personal liberty and responsible behaviour that Locke conjoins in *An Essay Concerning Human Understanding* mirror the political freedoms of a citizen in a civil society that he describes in *Two Treatises of Government*, 1690.

Offering an evocative metaphor, Locke states that the mind begins as a 'white Paper', an empty cabinet, which experience furnishes with understanding.[18] To explain this metaphor, he distinguishes between the simple ideas of sensations, over which the mind has no control, and complex ideas, which the mind creates by selecting and combining simple ideas. Memory and judgement allow complex ideas to develop and for one to be associated with another, but Locke also values the continuing return to the simple ideas of sensations as a necessary means to affirm, adjust or deny complex ideas. Valuing all the senses, he gives special attention to vision, associating it with illumination and understanding.[19] The assumption that ideas and opinions must be developed and tested through experience is fundamental to empiricism and its influence on landscape and architecture.

As morality and standards of behaviour are acquired not innate, an extensive association of ideas can foster good judgement and nourish a responsible mind. Wishing not to deny creativity but to contain it, Locke assumes that understanding grounded in experience is more likely to resist the inappropriate association of ideas,

16 Locke, *An Essay Concerning Human Understanding*, bk 1, ch. 1, p. 46. Refer to Porter, *Enlightenment*, p. 9.

17 Taylor, pp. 159–176.

18 Locke, *An Essay Concerning Human Understanding*, bk 2, ch. 1, p. 104.

19 Locke, *An Essay Concerning Human Understanding*, bk 2, ch. 2, pp. 119–121.

which, he concludes, result from shock more often than habit and may lead to unfortunate consequences such as unhappiness or even madness.[20] In a famous reference to Socrates awake and asleep, Locke even acknowledges that one person may have different mental states and more than one personality: 'If the same *Socrates* waking and sleeping do not partake of the same consciousness, *Socrates* waking and sleeping is not the same Person.'[21]

Locke was very influential but other empiricists soon discarded his assumption that there can be a direct relationship between the observer and the observed, recognising that this ignores the observer's role in shaping experience. As empirical investigation without prior concepts is impossible, we cannot simply see objects as they are. For example, the microscope and telescope are ideas as well as instruments of empirical science, influencing what is investigated as well as how.

An Essay Concerning Human Understanding was also criticised as an attack on faith. Locke asserts that reason and faith are compatible because they are relevant to different concerns and need not interfere with each other.[22] The resurrection, for example, is a question of faith. The consequence of this distinction was to focus attention on scientific investigation rather than spiritual contemplation. The authority of the emerging secular elite was increased and that of the Church diminished, although the political upheavals that stimulated Locke's philosophical production emphasised religion's continuing role in English society.

Strikingly different characters as siblings often are, Charles II's brother succeeded him as James II in 1685. A rebellion led by James, Duke of Monmouth, Charles II's eldest illegitimate son, was swiftly rebuffed. But in 1688 the birth of a Catholic son to James II and his wife, Mary of Modena, demoted Mary and Anne, the Protestant daughters of his first marriage. A confrontation with the absolutist Catholic monarch led the dominant Protestant parliamentary grouping, the Whigs, to invite invasion. On the eve of the Glorious Revolution, the October wind that kept the Dutch fleet in harbour was deemed to be Papist and the strong east wind that followed in early November was praised as Protestant, establishing Mary and her husband, William of Orange, as constitutional monarchs with the overriding power of parliament affirmed. A contemporary satire, presented as a dialogue between two Kings, has James despising William as 'A marble Caesar pinioned to a throne, / The people regnant, and the monarch stone.'[23] However, continental Europeans, as well as the English themselves, perceived England to be the model of a progressive society, writes John Brewer:

> *Foreign visitors and commentators emphasized England's liberty and modernity.*
> *Its vigorous political culture, epitomized by the most fully developed European*

20 The chapter 'Of the Association of Ideas' appears in the fourth edition of 1700, although it was written somewhat earlier. Locke, *An Essay Concerning Human Understanding*, bk 2, ch. 33, pp. 394–401. Refer to Ballantyne, pp. 144–145; Forty, *Words and Buildings*, pp. 208–209; Hunt and Willis, 'Introduction', pp. 37–38; Taylor, pp. 159–176; Tuveson, p. 75.

21 Locke, *An Essay Concerning Human Understanding*, bk 2, ch. 27, p. 342.

22 Locke, *An Essay Concerning Human Understanding*, bk 4, ch. 18, p. 696.

23 Charles Blount, 'A Dialogue between King William and the late King James', 1690, quoted in Cameron, p. 49. Refer to Ayres, *Classical Culture*, p. 8.

newspaper press, the absence of prior censorship (the Licensing Act had lapsed in 1695), the existence of religious toleration and of freedom to worship, the concern for subjects' rights and the openness of society all impressed foreigners because they were conspicuous by their absence elsewhere.[24]

24 Brewer, pp. xxiv–xxviii.

Stimulating reaffirmations of democracy and liberty in the spirit of 1688, fear of the restoration of the Stuart monarchy lingered for over 50 years until the second unsuccessful Jacobite uprising in 1745. Tory ministers held power between 1700 and 1714 but Queen Anne's death and the ascent of the first Hanoverian monarch, George I, returned the Whigs to power seven years after the union of England and Scotland. While the Whigs promoted religious toleration and the collaboration of parliament and monarch, the Tories supported the high Church establishment and the supreme power of the Crown. A coalition of factions rather than a coherent organisation, the Whigs dominated cultural and social life as well as the government and included Locke, who only returned to England in 1688. But the transformations in British society were not exclusively due to Whig influence. For example, among literary figures, Alexander Pope was a Tory and Joseph Addison claimed to be neutral. Anthony Ashley Cooper, third Earl of Shaftesbury, has often been associated with the Whig ascendancy but he was loyal to his principles rather than a particular party.

Robert Walpole, a Whig, is familiarly described as Britain's first Prime Minister, holding the position for over 20 years. But the title was not then official and his contemporaries used it pejoratively, criticising him for holding too much power and influence. In theory, the monarch still made ministerial appointments but Walpole's power was due principally to the House of Commons.[25] In 1739 he remarked:

25 Kemp, pp. 7, 77–78; Speck, pp. 12–13.

A Seat in this House is equal to any Dignity deriv'd from Posts or Titles, and the Approbation of this House is preferable to all that Power, or even Majesty itself, can bestow: therefore when I speak here as a Minister, I speak as possessing my Powers from his Majesty, but as being answerable to this House for the Exercise of those Powers.[26]

26 Walpole, quoted in Kemp, p. 77.

Walpole retired three years later because he had lost the confidence of the Commons not the King, only then becoming a peer as the Earl of Orford. Nearly all of his cabinet colleagues sat in the House of Lords and it was unusual for the leading government minister to be a commoner rather than a peer. But Walpole remained in the Commons while he was Prime Minister because of the power that resided there and it gained status from his presence. While the Commons could initiate financial bills, the Lords could only pass or reject them. Early eighteenth-century governments focused on taxation, the military and foreign affairs; they did not have the wider powers and concerns of later centuries.

Walpole's power and status significantly depended on his understanding of contemporary credit systems and the nation's finances. Especially after 1688, common strategic and trading concerns tied England to the United Provinces of the Netherlands, which Walpole understood better than any other European country because of its strong trading links with Norfolk, his home county in England's most easterly region.[27] Adopting Dutch models, the Bank of England was founded in 1694 and long-term bonds were traded on the Stock Exchange, allowing the government to fund large-scale projects at reduced rates.[28]

The monarchy was weaker than in other European nations, encouraging the landowning class to expand beyond the aristocracy and the mutual co-existence of agriculture and trade. Together, political and financial reforms stimulated investment and speculation in Britain and its colonial empire, encouraging an expanding mercantile class and the nation's early industrialisation in the second half of the eighteenth century, which also depended on empirical science, efficient agriculture, abundant coal and iron, and close proximity to ports.

The majority of the working population and minor gentry were Tories who believed that the Whig government's only aim was to serve itself and its supporters.[29] To some extent they were right. During his long premiership, Walpole used his power and patronage to significantly increase his wealth, placing friends, allies and family members in important positions and denying his rivals, both Whigs and Tories.[30] Frequently satirised and mocked, in Jonathan Swift's *Gulliver's Travels*, 1726, he is Flimnap, the scheming treasurer of Lilliput, and in John Gay's *The Beggar's Opera*, 1728, he is simply a thief.[31] Even his nickname – The Great Man – was not necessarily flattering. J. H. Plumb remarks that Walpole 'was frequently regarded as obscene in an age when men and women were not prudes', while William Speck writes that he 'projected the image of a gross Norfolk squire, boasting that he read letters from his gamekeeper before those of his Cabinet ministers, and rarely read books' although he had an extensive library.[32] Even an admirer, Queen Caroline, the wife of King George II, noted 'that gross body, those swollen legs, and that ugly belly'.[33] But Walpole's demeanour was not unusual. Englishmen relished their cantankerous and contrary behaviour, which they explained by reference to the fickle and variable weather of an island nation.[34]

Due to government business as well as social and cultural life, Walpole spent much of the year in London, which dominated the nation unlike any other European capital. At the start of the eighteenth century around 675,000

27 Plumb, *Sir Robert Walpole: The King's Minister*, p. 23.

28 Ferguson, p. 23; Speck, p. 12.

29 Plumb, *Sir Robert Walpole: The Making of a Statesman*, p. 31.

30 One of the most lucrative government positions, Walpole's terms as Paymaster General significantly added to his fortune; a previous incumbent, James Brydges, accumulated £600,000 between 1705 and 1713 and later became first Duke of Chandos. Porter, *English Society in the Eighteenth Century*, p. 59.

31 Swift, p. 39.

32 Plumb, *Sir Robert Walpole: The Making of a Statesman*, p. xii; Speck, p. 12. For a discussion of Walpole's library at Houghton, refer to Moore, 'The Making of Britain's First Prime Minister', pp. 39–42.

33 Queen Caroline, quoted in Speck, p. 12.

34 Porter, *English Society in the Eighteenth Century*, p. 10.

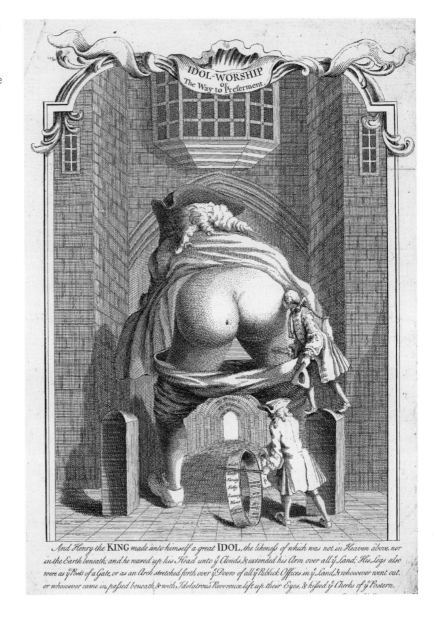

And Henry the KING made unto himself a great IDOL, the likeness of which was not in Heaven above, nor in the Earth beneath; and he reared up his Head unto ỹ Clouds, & extended his Arm over all ỹ Land: His Legs also were as ỹ Posts of a Gate, or as an Arch stretched forth over ỹ Doors of all ỹ Publick Offices in ỹ Land, & whosoever went out, or whosoever came in, passed beneath, & with Idolatrous Reverence lift up their Eyes, & kissed ỹ Cheeks of ỹ Postern.

people crowded together in the city, which was as populous as Paris even though England's population was barely a third that of France. Coal consumption continued to rise, doubling from 800,000 tons in 1700 to 1,500,000 tons in 1750. As London's population remained nearly the same, the increase was due principally to rising demand from the city's many trades and industries.

In the 1680s the average life span in England was 30, while it was 42 by the 1750s.[35] Prosperous members of society lived longer; Walpole died in his sixties, as did his young relative Thomas Coke and their architect William Kent.[36] The high mortality rate in this period, when there were more deaths than births in London, meant that immigrants from English counties and foreign countries maintained the population. At all levels of society, many of London's inhabitants were new to the city. In 1690 three-quarters of the city's apprentices were not born there, as were most members of the elite Whig social club, the Kit-Cat.[37]

Just as political power was increasingly concentrated in parliament, cultural influence moved away from the royal court to assembly rooms, learned societies, literary journals and dining clubs. In 1703 Walpole joined the Kit-Cat, which was named after the mutton pie maker Christopher Catling, a Norfolk pastry cook and the proprietor of the *Cat and Fiddle* in Gray's Inn Lane where the Club first met.[38] Ophelia Field remarks: 'As pies and puddings were considered the best of English cookery, the Club's favourite dish would have signified the founders' self-consciously English, as opposed to French, tastes.'[39] Active from around 1696 to 1722, the Kit-Cat included aristocrats such as Richard Boyle, third Earl of Burlington, and Richard Temple, first Viscount Cobham, alongside writers, drama-tists and architects including Joseph Addison, Richard Steele, William Congreve and John Vanbrugh.[40] Godfrey Kneller's portraits of its members depicted peers and commoners as though they were equals, shocking many of their contemporar-ies. The sitters were notably rotund and well fed. Alongside the pleasures of food, wine and male company, the Club's purpose was political, social and cultural patronage and influence.

As the Kit-Cat's convenor and London's most prestigious publisher, Jacob Tonson reflected publishing's high status at the start of the eighteenth century, when the English book-buying public was an elite. Influenced by Locke and Shaftesbury, Addison and Steele stimulated notions of polite society in the pages of *The Tatler*, 1709–1711, and *The Spectator*, 1711–1714, which Tonson pub-lished.[41] Considerate behaviour was not new but the emphasis on politeness was more than just a reaffirmation of earlier values. Reacting to the moral ambiguity and debauchery associated with the restoration of the Stuart monarchy, politeness was a means to establish social and moral standards appropriate to commercial activity, learned discourse and the political consequences of 1688. Sensitive to people, places and situations, polite behaviour avoided disruptive disagreements and oiled the flow of knowledge, politics and trade.[42] The fashion for social engage-ment stimulated consumer demand for places and goods, whether coffee houses, gardens, guidebooks or clothes.

35 Black, *Eighteenth-Century Britain*, p. 13.

36 Coke's grandmother, Lady Anne Walpole, was married to Colonel Horatio Walpole, her second husband and the uncle of Sir Robert Walpole.

37 Field, pp. 10, 255; George, pp. 37–41.

38 The proprietor's surname was Cat or Catling.

39 Field, p. 35. Refer to Brewer, pp. xxiv–xxviii, 40–49.

40 Kent was not a member but a number of his clients were, including Walpole, General James Dormer, Burlington and Cobham, for whom he designed interiors, buildings and gardens at Houghton, Chiswick, Rousham and Stowe respectively. The Club was in decline by the time that Coke was old enough to be a member.

41 Printed jointly with Sam Buckley.

42 Carter, pp. 25, 27, 63; Phillipson, p. 235.

Politeness was intended to reassure strangers as well as friends, and women as well as men. Believing that female company was detrimental to learned conversation, Shaftesbury praised 'the Liberty of *the Club*, and of that sort of Freedom which is taken amongst *Gentlemen* and *Friends* who know one another perfectly well'.[43] But *The Spectator* patronisingly encouraged conversation with women because 'where that was wholly denied, the Women lost their Wit and the Men their good Manners'.[44] Addison and Steele's readership was mostly middle class, unlike the Kit-Cat, and polite society developed incrementally, only coming to fruition in the mid-eighteenth century.[45] The behaviour of Walpole and other Club members was largely unaffected.

Beginning in the late sixteenth century and increasing by the 1640s, devout Christians, especially Protestants, prepared diaries in which they assessed their daily spiritual progress.[46] Addison recommended that his readers maintain a diary, extending a literary practice favoured by Evelyn and Locke, who placed great emphasis on activities that led to personal development. People have written about themselves for millennia but the formation of modern identity is associated with a type of writing that Michel Foucault describes as a 'technology of the self', the process of self-examination by which moral character and behaviour are constructed and maintained in conjunction with other social forces.[47] Objectivity may be an aspiration but no diary is entirely truthful and the diarist cannot fail to edit and reinvent life while reflecting upon it, altering the past as well as influencing the future. As Paul de Man remarks:

> We assume that life produces the autobiography as an act produces its consequences, but can we not suggest, with equal justice, that the autobiographical project may itself produce and determine the life and that whatever the writer does is in fact governed by the technical demands of self-portraiture and thus determined, in all its aspects, by the resources of his medium?[48]

Addison and Steele encouraged diary writing, a conversational literary style and engagement with contemporary culture. But the Kit-Cat's attempt to direct the course of English literature was undermined by a new literary development that its members did not foresee. Empiricism gave greater emphasis than before to the distinction between fact and fiction.[49] In valuing direct experience, precise description and a sceptical approach to 'facts', which needed to be repeatedly questioned, the empirical method created a fruitful climate in which the everyday realism of a new literary genre – the novel – could prosper as 'factual fiction'.[50] In contrast to the epic or romance, which incorporated classical mythologies,

43 Shaftesbury, *Characteristicks*, vol. 1, p. 45. Refer to Carter, p. 66; Cowan, p. 138.

44 Steele, in Addison and Steele, vol. 1, 1 May 1711, no. 53.

45 In the second half of the eighteenth century, a concern for sensibility accompanied a concern for politeness. They were somewhat similar but sensibility gave further emphasis to inner feelings and moral purpose. Refer to Brewer, pp. 100, 117; Carter, p. 28.

46 Webster, 'Writing to Redundancy', p. 50.

47 Foucault mentions 'four types of technologies' that 'hardly ever function separately': technologies of production, sign systems, power and the self. Foucault, 'On the Genealogy of Ethics', p. 369; Foucault, 'Technologies of the Self', 18–19.

48 De Man, p. 69.

49 Davis, pp. 67–68.

50 Davis, p. 213. Refer to Watt, p. 62.

the novel concentrated on the lives of everyday people in eighteenth-century society and the individualism it professed. The detailed description and analysis that empiricism demanded was applied to the novel, which emphasised specific times, peoples and places and sought justification through a combination of reasoned explanation and intuitive experience. Daniel Defoe's *Robinson Crusoe*, 1719, is often described as the first English novel. But in suggesting that the objects referred to in his novels are 'emblems', Cynthia Wall argues that the detailed description of visual characteristics only developed incrementally in eighteenth-century fiction as emblems, associations and analogies became less consistently understood by an expanding readership.[51]

Recognising a difference in style as well as content, Congreve remarked that in contrast to 'the lofty Language, miraculous Contingencies and impossible Performances' of the romance, novels are 'of a more familiar nature' and 'delight us with Accidents and odd Events . . . which not being so distant from our Belief bring also the pleasure nearer us'.[52] The uncertainties and dilemmas of identity, as in Locke's assertion that '*Socrates* waking and sleeping is not the same Person', were ripe for narrative account.[53] Countering Locke's call for moderation and restraint, subjectivity was exploited for its creative potential. Significantly, *Robinson Crusoe* is a fictional autobiography, as is Defoe's other famous novel *Moll Flanders*, 1722. In each case, the principal character is complex and conflicted, and one voice among others in a changing society.

Focusing on the fate of individuals, the early novels – fictional autobiographies – developed in parallel with the early diaries – autobiographical fictions. Ian Watt argues that 'Defoe's heroes pursue money' and property above all else, reflecting the secularist sentiments and economic individualism of a mercantile readership.[54] Emphasising the potential for social mobility in a capitalist economy, the hero's aim is prosperity whatever the means, whether by trade, crime or prostitution, as in Defoe's *Robinson Crusoe*, *Moll Flanders* and *Roxana,* 1724, respectively. However, Liz Bellamy remarks that 'Money is presented as a means of attaining a virtuous life, through retirement from the sphere of dishonest action' and Michael McKeon emphasises 'the spiritualizing presence that overshadows and infiltrates much of Robinson Crusoe's adventures'.[55] Indicating a debt to the spiritual diary that informed the novel's development, Leon Guilhamet concludes: 'The Whig novel takes as the paradigm of human life the scriptural pattern, beginning with creation or birth. It includes temptation, fall or disobedience, exile, captivity, deliverance, and repentance.'[56]

While romances were published as expensive folios and appealed mostly to wealthy landowners, novels were affordable to the middle class. The price

51 Wall, p. 110, refer to pp. 39, 113–114. Refer to Hultzsch, pp. 92–96; Varey, pp. 139–140.

52 Congreve, pp. 5–6. Refer to Davis, pp. 103–104.

53 Locke, *An Essay Concerning Human Understanding*, bk. 2, ch. 27, p. 342.

54 Watt, p. 63.

55 Bellamy, p. 193; McKeon, pp. 2–3.

56 Guilhamet, p. 200, refer to pp. 198–199.

of a book in relation to an average income was much higher than today and a novel could cost more than a labourer's weekly wage. Illiteracy as well as finance limited the readership; poor children often left school before they were seven, and three-quarters of the population could not read.[57] But challenging the assumption that *Robinson Crusoe* was the first English novel, Lennard J. Davis identifies earlier novels that were serialised for less prosperous readers and questions Watt's 'decision to begin at the moment when novels began to be more widely accepted by the middle-class reader'.[58] Acknowledging that early eighteenth-century London was known for a newly flourishing newspaper trade, and recognising the influence of one literary practice on another, Davis also notes that Defoe was a journalist before he became a novelist and already proficient in 'fictionalizing fact'.[59]

Defoe describes *Roxana* as 'laid in Truth of *Fact*' and thus 'not a Story, but a History', a claim echoed by other novelists throughout the eighteenth century.[60] He also characterises *Moll Flanders* as 'a private History' but invites 'the Reader to pass his own Opinion upon the ensuing Sheets, and take it as he pleases'.[61] Even *Gulliver's Travels* is teasingly presented as true. The frontispiece to the first edition depicts a portrait of Lemuel Gulliver, a ship's surgeon and captain, who

57 Watt, pp. 35–42.

58 Davis, pp. 102–103; Watt, p. 42.

59 Davis, pp. 166–173.

60 Defoe, *Roxana*, p. 21.

61 Defoe, *Moll Flanders*, p. 3. Refer to Downie, pp. 30–45.

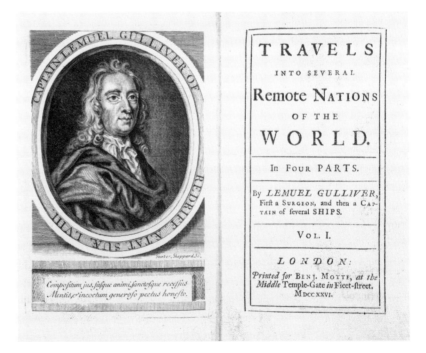

Jonathan Swift, *Gulliver's Travels*, 1726. Frontispiece and title page depicting the portrait of Lemuel Gulliver. Courtesy of Private Collection/Bridgeman Images.

claims to verify his story in a number of ways, including by reference to the sting-ers of three gigantic Brobdingnagian wasps donated to Gresham College, the first home of the Royal Society.

History's uncertain status at that time supported authors' claims that the first novels were in fact histories. Describing actual events and others of his own invention, Giorgio Vasari's *Le vite de' piu eccellenti pittori, scultori e architettori* (The Lives of the Most Eminent Painters, Sculptors and Architects), 1550, was the first significant history of art and architecture, initiating a new discipline. In the sixteenth century, history's purpose was to offer useful lessons; accuracy was not necessary. In subsequent centuries, empiricism's emphasis on the distinction between fact and fiction began to transform historical analysis, diminishing the humanist emphasis on literary sources. Indebted to Bacon, Giambattista Vico's *La scienza nuova*, 1725, is the best-known early modern history. Rather than Vasari's focus on individual achievements, the modern historian employed a methodical and comparative method to characterise changing cultural, social, political and economic processes in which the deeds of specific protagonists were contextual-ised. But most eighteenth-century histories and novels were not yet so distinct from each other and they inherited some of the rhetorical approach of earlier histories, implying that the truth does not always depend on facts alone.[62]

Even after the success of his novels, Defoe continued to work as a journalist and travel writer, completing *A Tour through the Whole Island of Great Britain* in 1726, in which he contrasts the capital to the counties. The polluted air of his 'monstrous city' affected the Kit-Cat as it did other aspects of London life.[63] In 1702 the Club moved its summer meetings to enjoy the higher ground of Hampstead's 'airy head' and in the following year acquired a new venue at Barn Elms, seven miles to the west of London.[64] Field concludes that 'The westerly migration from the stink of London into fresher air represented . . . the Club's rising status since the 1690s.'[65]

London teemed with nature. Rats, mice, pigeons and other scavenging birds were drawn to the city's refuse tips, cesspits and grain stores. The plants that prospered on such fluctuating surfaces were capable of rapid germination and growth, such as knotgrass, thistles and nettles.[66] Poorer housing dominated the east and south of the city, while elegant squares were created to the west, away from the port and to suit the prevailing wind. Upon returning from the Grand Tour in 1718, Coke lived in Great Russell Street, Bloomsbury, one of the new residen-tial districts begun in the late seventeenth century. His home, Thanet House, was then at the edge of London's dense urban core and close to open fields, and had a generous garden noted for honeysuckle.[67] In around 1714, Walpole moved to

62 Garnham, pp. 1–10; Hawes, pp. 64–67.

63 Defoe, *A Tour through the Whole Island of Great Britain*, p. 316.

64 Richard Blakemore's *The Kit-Cats, A Poem*, 1708, quoted in Field, p. 113.

65 Field, p. 114.

66 Williamson, *An Environmental History of Wildlife in England*, pp. 60–61.

67 Coke married Margaret Tufton in 1718. His father-in-law, Thomas Tufton, sixth Earl of Thanet, had acquired the lease of the house in 1693. Refer to James, p. 210.

Orford House in Chelsea, then a riverside village to the west of London. Nearly 20 years later, George II offered him a property close to Parliament. Walpole accepted on the condition that 10 Downing Street became the residence of the First Lord of the Treasury, his principal title, and commissioned Kent to remodel the house. As many of the Kit-Cat's members were wealthy landowners, a London residence to the west of the city was accompanied by the clear air of a country estate, the virtues of which Evelyn had already acknowledged:

> But, it is manifest, that those who repair to London, no sooner enter into it, but they find a universal alteration to their Bodies, which are either dryed up or enflamed, the humours being exasperated and made apt to putrifie, their sensories and perspiration so exceedingly stopped, with the loss of Appetite, and a kind of general stupefaction, succeeded with such Catharrs and Dissillations, as do never, or very rarely quit them, without some further Symptoms of dangerous Inconveniency so long as they abide in the place; which yet are immediately restored to their former habit; so soon as they are retired to their Homes and they enjoy fresh Aer again.[68]

68 Evelyn, *Fumifugium*, p. 24.

Walpole and Coke were Norfolk neighbours as well as relatives. The Prime Minister resided at Houghton in the northwest of the county while Coke's coastal estate was a 10-mile ride to the northeast at Holkham. London was over 100 miles distant. Prey to highwaymen, even a simple journey could be dangerous as well as uncomfortable, as Walpole's youngest son, Horace, observed: 'One is forced to travel, even at noon, as if one was going to battle.'[69] Each parish was supposed to maintain the roads within its boundaries but many were poorly repaired. Of a better standard, privately funded toll roads first appeared in the mid-seventeenth century but few were constructed until the second half of the following century.[70] Farm animals followed the same routes as people. In wet weather a road dissolved into mud while in winter a frozen surface made wheels bump and jar. Walpole and Coke travelled to Norfolk by carriage because a long journey on horseback was considered unsuitable for someone of such status, even though it was faster. A 'running footman' ran alongside his employer to pay tolls or lever out a carriage with a pole if it slipped into a deep hole in a pockmarked road. With no street lighting and towns sparsely lit, the countryside was pitch black at night. Divided into daytime travel and overnight rest, the journey from London to Norfolk took four or five days depending on the season, covering 25 miles a day at most. Attuned to natural time as well as the mechanical time of the clock, daily life was sensitive to the rhythms of the seasons, the changing weather and the shift from dusk to

69 Horace Walpole, quoted in Porter, *English Society in the Eighteenth Century*, p. 17.

70 Albert, pp. 44–55; Garry, pp. 152–166.

dawn. Arduous travel made time and distance seem long and slow, especially in the bleak depth of winter when draughty carriages and rudimentary medicines offered little protection. John Buxton, a Norfolk gentleman, writes of bad conditions more often than good in letters to his son. In November 1729, the weather could postpone even a local visit:

> I fear this has been too bad to let us now think of performing that journey. The season being also so very sickly I'm not for running any hazard of taking colds, having hitherto pretty well escaped the epidemical one, but I think London feels most of it.[71]

Disease was rife in towns and cities and a potential hazard to any journey. Having passed through Cambridge, a carriage bound for Houghton either ventured north to King's Lynn or turned towards Newmarket, following the same route as a carriage travelling to Holkham, which entered Norfolk at Swaffham.[72] In December 1731 a traveller was advised: 'You must by no means stop at Swaffam for the man's sake, but rather take warm at Hillborough if need be. The smallpox rages at Swaffam'.[73]

Draughty, poorly insulated and partially warmed by open fires, the interior of an inn or a house offered only a little more comfort and respite than a carriage. In the severe winter of 1739–1740, which initiated the coldest year since 1659 and led to a further freezing winter, Robert Marsham of Stratton Strawless in northeast Norfolk noted that water and beer turned to ice inside his home, while 'the urine in my chamber-pot froze to a cake under my bed four nights successively'.[74]

As a landowner neared his estate, church bells rang out to celebrate his arrival, alerting tenants and servants. Dominating its villages, Norfolk's grand churches reminded visitors that it had been the wealthiest county in medieval England due to the woollen trade. Norfolk's prosperity continued into the early eighteenth century. As the raw material was produced locally, agriculture and industry were bound together, unlike later in the century when textile production turned to imported cotton. Norfolk's principal ports – King's Lynn and Great Yarmouth – prospered because sea trade still focused on the North Sea and Baltic more than the Atlantic and, given the poor quality of roads, shipping was the cheapest and fastest way to transfer goods from one part of England to another. Just as political life emanated from London, new means of cultural exchange spread from the capital to the provinces. Reflecting the city's status, *The Norwich Post* was established in 1701, the first newspaper outside London. But England's second city was small and parochial in comparison to the capital, leading Evelyn's friend, Samuel Tuke, to conclude that the Norfolk gentry are 'a nation as new to mee as the Americans'.[75]

71 John Buxton to Robert Buxton, 18 November 1729, quoted in Mackley, *John Buxton Norfolk Gentleman and Architect,* p. 164.

72 James, p. 132; Mackley, 'Introduction', p. 14.

73 Roger North, 17 December 1731, quoted in Lindsay, p. 28.

74 Marsham. Refer to Lamb, p. 244.

75 Tuke, quoted in Darley, p. 183.

The foundations of the industrial revolution were being laid. Jethro Tull advertised a machine-drill in *Horse-Hoeing Husbandry*, 1731, while Thomas Newcomen constructed a rudimentary steam engine in 1712, which James Watt greatly improved in 1763. But England was not yet subject to intensive industrialisation and urbanisation. Outside of the few industrial centres, the nation remained overwhelmingly rural and sparsely populated; 90 per cent of the workforce was employed in agriculture. The principal measure of wealth, status and influence was land ownership, which Locke affirmed as one of the natural rights of man. Denis Cosgrove remarks that 'the landed estate was the economic engine of Georgian England – locus of its capital accumulation, technical innovation and social modernization'.[76]

76 Cosgrove, 'Airport/Landscape', p. 222.

Related through marriage, a few families dominated north and west Norfolk. Alongside Coke and Walpole, Charles Townshend, second Viscount Townshend, lived with his wife, Walpole's sister Dorothy, at Raynham, six miles southeast of Houghton. Less than 5 per cent of the national population had the right to vote; landowners and merchants dominated the electorate. In the 1690s, 4,000 people voted in Norfolk while 20 years later the number was still only 6,000.[77] Political power in the county was limited to very few people; first, to the Members of Parliament and, second, to the Lord Lieutenant, the monarch's representative in the county, who was responsible for the local militia and influenced the appointment of Justices of the Peace and the Sheriff.[78] In 1701 Walpole became a Member of Parliament for Castle Rising, close to Houghton, which his father had represented for over 10 years. In the following year he was elected in King's Lynn, which he continued to represent for 40 years until the end of his parliamentary career. Between 1702 and 1831 King's Lynn always had a Walpole MP except for one five-year interruption, while a Townshend represented Great Yarmouth between 1715 and 1796 except for a six-year gap. Coke entered politics with Walpole's support, becoming a Norfolk MP soon after he took control of his inheritance.

77 Lindsay, p. 152.

78 Plumb, *Sir Robert Walpole: The Making of a Statesman*, pp. 42–47.

At the time of Walpole's birth in 1676 his family were well established in Norfolk, having owned Houghton since 1307. But no previous family member had acquired such prominence and he chose to recast the estate in his image. Walpole's new garden was largely realised by 1720, when he decided to demolish the existing house and commission a new one. Construction began in 1722, soon after he became Prime Minister. In Edmund Prideaux's depiction a few years later, the new house is seen from the new garden, which is compact, formal and somewhat similar to a seventeenth-century layout in that it is ordered into a series of room-like spaces. Three sets of elegantly attired figures stroll sequentially along a broadwalk that is edged by rows of conical topiary to the north and south. Further to each side, the hedges are fully-grown and trees are maturing in two 'wilderness' gardens.[79] Houghton Hall's west elevation is partly obscured by a temporary building associated with its construction. One of James Gibbs' corner domes is complete, while another is yet to be started.[80] As the new house is slightly to the east of the old one, the diagonal paths cutting through the wilderness gardens no longer converge near the centre of the west elevation, indicating a discrepancy between house and garden and retaining the memory of the absent hall in the presence of the new one.

Celebrating Walpole's achievement in the year that construction was completed, Isaac Ware and Thomas Ripley's *The Plans, Elevations and Sections; Chimney-pieces and Ceilings of Houghton in Norfolk*, 1735, was the first architectural book dedicated to a single British house.[81] But Walpole's ostentatious display was severely criticised by those who resented his power and influence. The once close association of Walpole and Townshend became a bitter quarrel in 1730 when the Prime Minister pressurised his brother-in-law to resign from the government, primarily because he believed that the Secretary of State's policies would undermine the nation's alliance with the Austrian Hapsburgs. Townshend's

79 Williamson, *The Archaeology of the Landscape Park*, p. 35; Williamson, 'The Planting of the Park', pp. 42, 44–45.

80 Gibbs' initial design for the plans and façades was followed by Colen Campbell's contribution. Harris, 'The Architecture of the House', pp. 20–28; Moore, 'Creating a Seat in the Country', pp. 65–67; Moore, 'The Making of Houghton Hall', pp. 59–63.

81 Without mentioning Gibbs and Campbell, and attributing only chimneypieces and ceilings to Kent, Ripley is credited as the architect and Ware as the draughtsman.

Houghton Rt. Hon. Sr. Robt. Walpole. Norfolk

Edmund Prideaux, *Album of Topographical Views of England,* c.1716–1727, open at a view of Houghton Hall from the west, c.1725. Courtesy of Peter Prideaux-Brune.

distaste became so intense that he avoided Raynham whenever Walpole entertained at Houghton. According to John Hervey, second Baron Hervey, 'Lord
Townshend looked upon his own seat at Raynham as the metropolis of Norfolk,
was proud of the superiority, and considered every stone that augmented the
splendour of Houghton as a diminution of the grandeur of Raynham.'[82]

82 Hervey, quoted in Sedgwick,
pp. 46–47. Refer to Girouard, p. 4.

With his political career in London, Walpole's visits to Houghton followed a
fixed pattern from around 1725. While his wife, Catherine, preferred to stay in
London, Walpole enjoyed Houghton with his mistress, Maria Skerritt, who became
his second wife after Catherine's death.[83] His summer visits were mostly private,
lasting for about a fortnight after the close of the parliamentary session in late
May or early June. In November he entertained friends and allies at a month-long
'Norfolk Congress', which combined hare- and fox-hunting with political intrigue,
social life and cultural patronage, extending the spirit of the Kit-Cat. Walpole's
expenditure was lavish; £1,500 a year was spent on wine. In the vaulted ground
floor Arcade where hunting parties would gather, silver taps served 'Hogan', a
particularly strong beer. Hervey wrote in 1731: 'In public we drank loyal healths,
talked of the times and cultivated popularity; in private we drew plans and cultivated the country.'[84] In 1728 a thinly disguised pamphlet mocked the extravagant
'merry-making', equating Walpole to the French monarch and Houghton to his
'Palace': 'the two *most eminent Persons* of this our Day are now hunting; one of
them at *Fountainblow* and the other in *Norfolk*'.[85]

83 Morel, 'Houghton Revisited',
p. 33.

84 Hervey, 21 July 1731, quoted
in Plumb, *Sir Robert Walpole: The
King's Minister*, p. 88. Refer to
Black, *Walpole in Power*, pp. 22–24;
Cornforth, *Houghton, Norfolk*,
p. 22; Field, p. 312; Plumb, *Sir
Robert Walpole: The King's Minister*,
pp. 87–88.

85 Anonymous, pp. 4, 3.

86 Anonymous, p. 3.

> *Many plentiful Entertainments hath our Friend Hollingshead served up . . . who
> when he went to his Country Seat, took so many of the Nobility and Gentry with
> him (who were indeed all a kind of menial Attendants) that he left the Court almost
> like a Desart, and the King his master quite neglected.*[86]

Houghton Hall is not large in comparison to other grand houses but it was
designed to be a fitting setting for the Prime Minister. The plan and proportions of
the *piano nobile* were already decided when Kent was given responsibility for their
design and decoration in 1725, a wonderful commission from a prestigious client.
Three years earlier Kent, then little known, had transformed a number of rooms at
Kensington Palace for George I, alerting Walpole to his skill.

After climbing a flight of external stairs, visitors arrived at Kent's rusticated
Great Door on the first floor of Houghton's east elevation, which was then the
main entrance to the house.[87] Entering into the Stone Hall, they passed first under
sculptures of Neptune and Britannia and then under figures representing Peace
and Plenty, which emphasised Walpole's guardianship of a prosperous sea-trading

87 The stairs were later demolished.
Refer to Harris, 'The Architecture of
the House', p. 23.

William Kent, The Stone
Hall, Houghton Hall.
Courtesy of the Marquess
of Cholmondeley, Houghton
Hall.

nation that would become the dominant European naval power within 30 years.[88]
The Stone Hall was richly carpeted like Houghton's other main reception rooms
but it was sparsely furnished with just six timber benches and two side tables, as
was then typical of an entrance hall. Especially in mid-winter, the double-height
room was difficult to heat. Its volume, hard materials, sparse furniture and low
temperature suggested an external room as much as an internal one.[89]

Carved by John Michael Rysbrack, the most eminent and classical sculptor
working in early eighteenth-century Britain, the focus of the Hall is Walpole's bust
on the north wall. Combining Roman and British iconography, it depicts the Prime
Minister in a toga adorned with the Garter Star, celebrating his election as a Knight
in 1726. Increasingly after 1688, Britain's association with ancient Rome implied
a shared commitment to democracy and liberty. References to republican rather
than imperial Rome were more frequently emphasised, indicating the monarch's
diminished power, and reaffirming the nation's ancient Roman lineage offered

[88] The Stone Hall was probably
derived from Inigo Jones' Queen's
House in Greenwich, 1635. Refer to
Cornforth, *Houghton, Norfolk*, p. 17.

[89] The double-height hall fell out
of fashion in the late 1740s as the
influence of polite society became
widespread and entertaining became
less formal. Refer to Cornforth, *Early
Georgian Interiors*, p. 35.

90 Ayres, *Classical Culture*, p 10.

Britain a model to surpass as well as emulate.[90] Walpole's bust is placed slightly higher than the ancient busts that line the room, including Roman emperors such as Commodus, Marcus Aurelius and Hadrian. The Latin inscription beneath the bust translates as 'Robert Walpole, Prince of the British senate, who established, dwelt in, and made famous this house.'[91] His contemporaries would have known that the title – *princeps senatus* – was conferred on the first Roman emperor, Augustus, who 'had partly redeemed himself by giving the Empire a long peace after a century of recurring civil wars, by supporting the arts, by attempting to restore old standards of public and private morality and respect for the gods', writes Philip Ayres.[92] But contemporary accounts more often associated Walpole with the corruption, intrigue and hedonism of ancient Rome than its liberty, virtue and stoicism.[93]

91 'ROBERTUS WALPOLE /
SENATUS BRITANNICI PRINCEPS
/ QUI / HASCE AEDES / CONDIDIT
INCOLVIT ILLUSTRAVIT'. Refer to
Angelicoussis, pp. 24–30.

92 Ayres, *Classical Culture*, p. 18.

93 Ayres, *Classical Culture*,
pp. 36–41, 55–56.

Recalling ancient Rome's class structure, only aristocratic and wealthy Britons benefitted from the analogy of one empire to another. Walpole and Coke demolished existing villages, relocating them to the edges of their expanded parkland. Walpole's bust stands before a relief of *The Sacrifice of Diana*, goddess of hunting, while the carved head of a fox appears in the broken pediment above.[94] A principal theme of the early eighteenth century, the dialogue between nature and culture developed to such an extent that nature – the land, sea and air (weather) – came to represent the nation. Cultivated nature and agriculture dominated the estate but uncultivated nature and hunting were emphasised in the house's internal decoration. Unlike the manual labour and muck spreading of arable farming, hunting was a gentlemanly pursuit legally restricted to larger landowners.

94 Cornforth, 'The Genesis and
Creation of a Great Interior',
pp. 32–34; Edwards, Moore and
Archer, pp. 110–111; Wade Martins,
Coke of Norfolk, p. 51.

In Kent's *Preparatory Drawing for an Engraving of the Stone Hall Chimneypiece, Houghton Hall*, 1726, *The Sacrifice to Diana* appears as it was later constructed. Eyeing all visitors, Walpole's bust looks to his left, towards the Great Door and the park beyond, which the Prime Minister altered in 1740 to extend the view. However, in the completed chimneypiece, Walpole looks to his right, into the house and towards the doorways leading to the Saloon and Great Staircase. The reason for the change is not known but it is unlikely to have been an error or omission. A very particular patron, Walpole would have given careful attention to his own image in such an important location and it can safely be assumed that the bust faces the direction he wished. For all his extensive transformation of the estate, the direction of Walpole's gaze suggests that his principal focus must have been the representations of nature and culture within the house. The timing and duration of Walpole's visits seem to confirm that the pleasures of the landscape, apart from hunting, were not a significant concern.

William Kent, *Preparatory Drawing for an Engraving of the Stone Hall Chimneypiece, Houghton Hall*, 1726. Courtesy of the Samuel Courtauld Trust, Courtauld Gallery, London.

The Prime Minister's bust crowns the Stone Hall's only heat source, a large fireplace placed on an internal wall so that heat was retained within the house. In cooler months, the fire would have drawn visitors closer to their host's image, so that the illumination and warmth alluded to his generosity and patronage. At night, the other principal light source was the gilt chandelier with 18 candles suspended from the centre of the ceiling. In 1731, the Duke of Lorraine, the future Francis I, Holy Roman Emperor, visited Houghton. Dinner was held in the Stone Hall because the Marble Parlour was incomplete. At a cost of £15 per night, 130 candles illuminated the room, while a further 50 lit the Saloon, associating illumination with ostentation as well as enlightenment. But Houghton's candles and open fires affected the climate of the house in another way, creating a smoky haze that obscured rather than illuminated, allowing soot to land on fabrics and paintings.

Beyond the Stone Hall, the double-height Saloon is a somewhat smaller but still substantial room. The goddess of hunting reappears in the decoration, and Flora, Ceres, Bacchus and Saturn represent the seasons: spring, summer, autumn and winter. In contrast to the hard off-white Stone Hall or the dark *trompe l'oeil* Great Staircase, the Saloon was vibrant in crimson and gold and populated by paintings and furniture so that it was both physically and perceptually warmer

William Kent, The Saloon, Houghton Hall. Courtesy of the Marquess of Cholmondeley, Houghton Hall.

William Kent, View from
the Saloon towards the
Stone Hall, Houghton Hall.
Courtesy of Edwin Smith/
RIBA Library Photographs
Collection.

than either of the other rooms. While the Stone Hall was entered from the east
and illuminated by the morning sun, the Saloon faced west towards the afternoon
sun, which would have cast contrasting light conditions in early summer and mid-
winter when Walpole was usually at home. While a visit to the Stone Hall was
often brief, important guests conversed with their host in the Saloon. The Stone
Hall emphasised Walpole's political status while the adjacent room focused more

95 Painters collected by Walpole included Maratta and his pupil, Chiari, Kent's 'master'. In 1743 Horace Walpole compiled *Aedes Walpolianae*, a description of his father's painting collection, which was published in 1747, two years after Walpole's death.

96 Cornforth, *Early Georgian Interiors*, p. 138; Cornforth, *Houghton, Norfolk*, p. 34.

97 Horace Walpole, referred to in Jourdain, p. 70.

on his cultural patronage, displaying some of the grandest paintings in his lavish art collection, which was meant to mirror that of a grand Roman family, although he never visited Italy.[95]

Houghton and Holkham were key influences on a new development imported from Italy. Kent's earliest surviving designs of an interior – 1725 elevations of the north and south walls of the Saloon – were of a type that was then unusual in England, in which paintings and furniture were depicted alongside doors, windows and fireplaces so that they together formed a coherent architectural ensemble.[96] Horace Walpole suggested that his father restrained Kent by insisting that the ceilings should be painted in muted colours so that they would not draw attention away from the paintings.[97] But his claim cannot be validated and Houghton's exuberant ceilings and walls suggest otherwise, reflecting the hedonism of Kent as well as Walpole. An early patron had encouraged Kent to be *'Raphael secundus'* but his friend, Pope, concluded that 'he must expect not to imitate Raphael in

William Kent, View from the Stone Hall towards the Great Staircase, Houghton Hall. Courtesy of the Marquess of Cholmondeley, Houghton Hall.

William Kent, The Great
Staircase, Houghton Hall.
Courtesy of the Marquess
of Cholmondeley, Houghton
Hall.

anything but his untimely end'.[98] Patron and protégé since they first met in Italy in 1714, Burlington characterised Kent as 'the little rogue' while Pope also described him as 'very hot and very fat' and teasingly encouraged Burlington to 'eat a Mutton Stake in ye manner of that great Master Signor Kent'.[99]

Occupying the full height of the house, roofed in glass, and embellished with mahogany treads and balustrades, the Great Staircase connects the Stone Hall to the ground floor Arcade. Suggesting the courtyard of a Renaissance palazzo, windows line its walls, which are covered with mythological hunting scenes that seem to be murals but are instead large, interlocking, stretched canvases. Creating a further ambiguity between interior and exterior, the Doric temple at the staircase's centre is provocatively large for the space, implying that it should really be outside. Surmounting the temple, Hubert Le Sueur's *Gladiator* – a seventeenth-century copy of a classical original – aggressively mediates between the *trompe l'oeil* decoration of the Great Staircase and the muscular carving of the Stone Hall. The

98 Burrell Massingberd, draft letter to Kent, 5 July 1714, quoted in Mowl, p. 46; Pope quoted in Harris, *William Kent*, p. 2.

99 Burlington and Pope, quoted in Harris, *William Kent*, p. 2.

Saloon is very much an internal room but the Stone Hall and Great Staircase each refer to a *cortile* as much as a *piano nobile*. The Great Staircase is particularly complex because it is an internal room that mimics an external one, while its painted scenes refer to the woods beyond the garden, implying a wilderness setting for the temple rather than the expected rolling lawn. The temple's status was particularly intriguing at the time of its construction because the garden then contained no buildings, which was unusual in the early eighteenth century.[100] As garden buildings were a means to mediate between culture and nature, their absence drew further attention to the temple and the depictions of nature in the house.

Together, the Stone Hall, Saloon and Great Staircase offer a vibrant dialogue on representation and reality, power and patronage, and culture and nature. In the year following his retirement as Prime Minister, with his Downing Street paintings now displayed alongside the rest of his collection, Walpole poignantly acknowledged his isolation and that of his estate as well as Houghton's dual attractions, the park and the *piano nobile*: 'my flatterers here are all mutes, the Oaks the Beeches and the Chestnuts . . . Within doors we come a little nearer to real life and admire upon the almost speaking Canvas'.[101]

The early eighteenth century is associated with a significant transformation in the English landscape when the picturesque came to the fore with Kent as its principal exponent. Pope ascribed the picturesque to both landscape and behaviour, and Addison imagined an estate as a garden, but Horace Walpole remarked that it was Kent who 'leaped the fence, and saw that all nature was a garden'.[102] Houghton has one of Kent's most exuberant interiors and the interdependence of architecture and nature in the Great Staircase hints at his future development as a garden designer, as does the picturesque juxtaposition of Houghton's principal rooms. Kent had no involvement in Walpole's elegant but austere park and garden. But while working at Houghton for nearly 10 years he also contributed designs for the new landscape, garden buildings and house at Holkham.[103] Drawings and letters confirm Kent's lengthy involvement in the estate's transformation, which continued until his death in 1748.[104] Coke and Kent were lifelong friends who first met in 1714 on the Grand Tour, which Peter de Bolla describes as 'the education of the eye'.[105] Prosperous patrons and gifted artists spent at least three years in Italy, acquiring a cultural education, and collecting ideas, experiences and artefacts to transfer home from south to north.

Introducing a fundamental change in perception, the Italian Renaissance assumed that the drawing truthfully depicts the three-dimensional world and is a window to that world. In 1563 the painter and architect Giorgio Vasari founded the first art academy, the *Accademia del Disegno* in Florence, enabling painters, sculptors and architects to converse independently of the craft guilds, and replacing

100 Designed before 1733 by Henry Herbert, ninth Earl of Pembroke, the Water Tower is beyond the garden and not seen from the Hall. In 1728 Sir Matthew Decker mentioned 'arbours' in the two wilderness gardens but no garden buildings. Decker, quoted in Cornforth, 'The Growth of an Idea', p. 164.

101 Walpole, quoted in Kemp, p. 135.

102 Addison, in Addison and Steele, vol. 2, 25 June 1712, no. 414; Walpole, *The History of the Modern Taste in Gardening*, p. 43.

103 Kent's work at Houghton possibly extended to the completion of the stables in 1733. He may have designed the tower of St. Martin's Church, c.1727–1729, which is the only remaining building of Houghton village. But David Yaxley, the Houghton Hall archivist, notes that the only surviving drawings are by Ripley. Refer to Cornforth, *Houghton, Norfolk*, p. 47; Moore, 'Creating a Seat in the Country', pp. 59, 62; White, p. 250; Williamson, *The Archaeology of the Landscape Park*, p. 50.

104 Schmidt, 'Inventing Holkham', p. 97.

105 De Bolla, p. 166.

workshop instruction with a studio education in drawing and geometry. The term 'design' derives from *disegno*, which means drawing, and associates the drawing of a line with the drawing forth of an idea.

Classical antiquity established the principle that ideas are immaterial and that intellectual labour is superior to manual labour. In *Timaeus*, c.360 BC, Plato claims that all the things we perceive in the material world are modelled on ideal forms, which are defined by geometrical proportions.[106] Consequently, there are two distinct realms. One consists of ideal originals, which only the intellect can comprehend, the other of imperfect copies subject to decay. Plato distrusted art because it mimicked natural objects, merely adding one layer of misrepresentation onto another. Concerned to affirm their intellectual status, Italian Renaissance artists promoted a concept of beauty based on geometric ideals but undermined Plato's argument that the artwork is always inadequate. *Disegno* allowed the three visual arts – architecture, painting and sculpture – to be recognised as liberal arts concerned with ideas, a position they had rarely been accorded previously.

The command of drawing – not building – unlocked the status of the architect, emphasising the immaterial idea of architecture more than the material fabric of building. Leon Battista Alberti notably stated that 'It is quite possible to project whole forms in the mind without recourse to the material.'[107] In the new division of labour, architecture resulted not from the accumulated knowledge of a team of anonymous craftsmen working together on a construction site but the artistic creation of an individual architect in command of drawing who designed a building as a totality in a studio. Alberti emphasised that construction was to be undertaken and supervised by craftsmen who were to ensure that a design was completed exactly according to 'the author's original intentions'.[108] Asserting their intellectual status, architects made drawings with just a few delicate lines and imagined buildings that were equally immaterial. Whether in the studio or on site, they often saw not matter and mass but proportion and line. The architect associated with *disegno* was established in Italy around 1450, in France a century later and in Britain in the early 1600s with Inigo Jones.

Born in Yorkshire in 1685, the son of a joiner, Kent had little formal education but his drawing skill was soon recognised. Supported by various patrons, he left London in 1709 to study in Italy, remaining there for 10 years. At first, painting was assumed to be his principal talent. Kent travelled widely in Italy but spent most of his time in Rome, where he studied under the painter Giuseppe Chiari,[109] whom he referred to as 'my master'.[110] Chiari was a pupil of Carlo Maratta and both were indebted to the mature Raphael.[111] But Kent was no more than a capable painter; his principal commission was to complete the ceiling of San

106 Plato, *Timaeus*, p. 121.

107 Alberti, p. 7.

108 Alberti, p. 309.

109 Cereghini and Jourdain mention that Kent studied under Benedetto Luti, while Harris, Hunt, Mowl and Sicca cite Chiari and Wilson mentions both painters. Cereghini, p. 320; Harris, *William Kent*, p. 4; Hunt, *William Kent*, p. 11; Jourdain, p. 30; Mowl, pp. 29–30; Sicca, p. 136; Wilson, pp. 12, 252.

110 Kent, letter to Burrell Massingberd, 24 November 1714, quoted in Wilson, p. 252.

111 Sicca, p. 136.

William Kent, *A View at Tivoli*, c.1709–1719. Courtesy of the Victoria and Albert Museum, London.

Giuliano del Fiamminghi, a baroque church designed by Antonio Maria Borioni, one of Gian Lorenzo Bernini's assistants.

In 1714 Kent began a diary, 'Remarks by way of Painting & Archit.', which records his journeys around Italy.[112] The opening pages refer to his travels with Coke that year, the first that they undertook together.[113] Given the liveliness of his drawings and his friends' frequent references to his hedonism, the diary is at first a surprisingly sober account of buildings, paintings and gardens. Sometimes written in English, at other times in Italian, it includes small drawings and diagrams in the margins and text. Arriving in Venice on 22 July, Coke and Kent first visit Andrea Palladio's San Giorgio Maggiore, 1580. Leaving the city on 18 August, Kent separates from Coke's party at Padua and proceeds to Vicenza, where he stays just one day and which Coke visits in October later that year.[114] In Vicenza, Kent admires Palladio's Teatro Olimpico, 1585, which he illustrates with a tiny plan that identifies the elliptical seating, empty stage and perspectival

112 The diary continues into 1715 and briefly mentions 1717. Kent, ff. 1–36.

113 Listing all his master's expenses, including over 70 while they were in Venice, Edward Jarrett, Coke's treasurer and valet, provided an alternative account of their journey with a slightly different chronology. Jarrett, 'Account of Thomas Coke's Grand Tour'.

114 James, p. 189.

street scenes.[115] Elsewhere in the city he refers merely to 'several other palaces', offering no mention of Palladio's Villa Rotonda, 1569.[116] The most evocative descriptions refer to gardens. In addition to valued patrons, Italy introduced Kent to visual languages and mythological narratives that informed his later designs. At the Medici villa at Pratolino, north of Florence, he notes 'a very fine Situation & very fine Grotos adorn'd with Shells & pietrified stone work with pretty water works a Galatea coming out of her Grotto drawn by Delfini'.[117] At Guilio Romano's Palazzo Te in Mantua, c.1530, he remarks that 'in grotta at end of ye garden are very fine grottesque'.[118] Kent is also known to have admired the Renaissance gardens at the Villa Aldobrandini in Frascati and must have been a frequent visitor to the gardens of the Villa d'Este in Tivoli and the Villa Borghese in Rome.[119] Later in the diary, he turns his attention to artistic techniques: 'to paint a tempera one egg with white & yolk to-gether & tow eggs of water, after put stalk of fig leaves, or lemon pel'.[120] But the most impressive section is the final one, which contains delicate illustrations of perspective techniques in line and wash.[121] Kent refers to two guides to the subject, Giulio Troili's *Paradossi per pratticare la prospettiva*, 1683, and Pietro Accolti's *Lo inganno de gl'occi, Prospettiva pratica*, 1625, which respectively consider perspective in terms of paradox and deception. Kent copied numerous drawings and quotations from Troili, who had specialised in *quadratura*, a technique to devise and represent complex spaces on a two-dimensional surface,

[115] Kent, f. 13.

[116] Kent, f. 13.

[117] Kent, f. 3.

[118] Kent, f. 14.

[119] Hunt, *William Kent*, p. 26.

[120] Kent, f. 24.

[121] Kent, ff. 25–36.

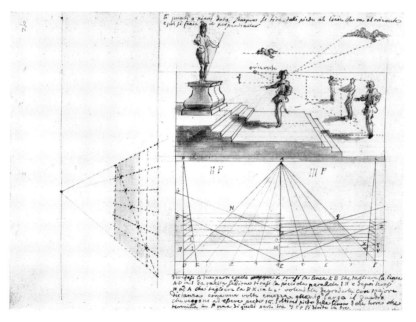

William Kent, Italian Diary ('Remarks by way of Painting and Archit.'), 1714–1717, fol. 26r. Kent's reworking of a drawing in Giulio Troili, *Paradossi per pratticare la prospettiva*, 1683. Courtesy of the Bodleian Library, Oxford.

which was used to create the illusion that painted architectural elements were part of the built architecture, and a view of painted nature was equally believable.

Equivalent to a visual and spatial diary, the process of design – from one drawing to the next iteration and from one project to another – is itself an auto-biographical 'technology of the self', formulating a design ethos for an individual or a studio. De Man concludes that the autobiography 'veils a defacement of the mind of which it is itself a cause'.[122] Having changed his name from Cant, Kent continued the tradition that Palladio had favoured, who was born Andrea di Pietro della Gondola.

A private design diary is autobiographical. An architectural drawing can also be autobiographical, as well as a means of negotiation between an architect and other individuals, and therefore subject to a more complex authorship. A building or landscape can be an autobiography of its principal author, even if many people are involved in its procurement, design, construction and use. Equally, a building or landscape may be the combined autobiographies of its many protagonists, with some getting more attention than others.

Twelve years older than his patron, Kent arranged architectural tuition for Coke, who ensured that Kent received money for his expenses and to purchase artworks and antiquities that Coke admired.[123] On one occasion their attempt to illegally export a statue of Diana threatened Coke with arrest and Kent with ban-ishment, which they fortunately avoided.[124] As Coke's parents died while he was young, his guardians were responsible for his education and inheritance until he came of age. Two figures particularly informed early eighteenth-century attitudes to educated behaviour. Believing that the mind is at first empty, Locke must have cherished his role as tutor to the future third Earl of Shaftesbury. As physician and secretary to the first Earl, Locke even attended the birth of the child, who described his tutor as my 'foster-father'.[125] Shaftesbury affirmed Locke's apprecia-tion of liberty and reason but tempered his empiricism and egalitarianism. Unlike his tutor, the pupil acknowledged an ideal order, reasserting the humanist tradition of Renaissance Italy and its respect for the 'immutable truths' of classical antiquity: 'Twas Mr. Locke that struck at all Fundamentals, threw all Order and Virtue out of the World'.[126]

Published as a three-volume collection in 1711, *Characteristicks of Men, Manners, Opinions*, *Times* established Shaftesbury as a persuasive influence on eighteenth-century thought, influencing Edmund Burke and Lord Burlington in England, Jean-Jacques Rousseau in France, and Johann Gottfried von Goethe, Johann Gottfried Herder and Immanuel Kant in Germany.[127] The first volume pro-motes the political, moral and cultural authority of an educated elite, celebrates

122 De Man, p. 81.

123 *Holkham Household Accounts*, 1717, quoted in Jourdain, p. 51.
124 Kent, letter to Burrell Massingberd, 15 June 1717, quoted in Blackett-Ord, p. 96. Refer to Brindle, pp. 102, 109, n. 141.
125 Shaftesbury, quoted in Ayres, 'Introduction', p. xiv.
126 The Cambridge Platonists such as Henry More – author of *An Antidote Against Atheism*, 1652, and *The Exploration of the Grand Mystery of Godliness*, 1660 – informed Shaftesbury's understanding of classical antiquity and spiritual appreciation of nature. Shaftesbury, *The Life*, p. 403.
127 The first two volumes had already been published separately but they were substantially revised for the 1711 three-volume edition.

their moderation and restraint, and concludes that beauty follows objective, moral and universal standards that only the most cultured intellect can appreciate.[128] Shaftesbury dismisses the baroque designs of Vanbrugh and Wren – a pivotal figure in the Royal Society who favoured scientific reason rather than immutable truth – and suggests that England needs a new architectural style.[129] Following this lead, Robert Morris' *Lectures on Architecture*, 1734–1736, denigrates Wren and Nicholas Hawksmoor's design for Kensington Palace, 1690–1705, as 'most irregular and disproption'd'.[130] Shaftesbury's implicit support for the moral and aesthetic virtues of restrained classicism as well as restrained behaviour was made explicit in Burlington's promotion of Palladio and his first British disciple, Jones. In the highly influential *Vitruvius Britannicus*, 1715–1725, Colen Campbell celebrates Palladio as heir to the classical tradition of ancient Rome and illustrates his three volumes with contemporary British examples. In the third volume, Campbell describes Burlington as 'not only a great Patron of all Arts, but the first Architect', an opinion confirmed by the subject of Campbell's sycophancy, who signed himself 'Burlington architectus'.[131] Satirising the doctrinaire Palladian revival in *Gulliver's Travels*, Swift notes 'the very melancholy Air' of Lord Munodi who felt compelled to rebuild his house according to 'the best Rules of Ancient Architecture', which the 'Grand Academy of Lagado' had imported from Laputa, a land that was assumed to be its intellectual superior.[132]

Affirmed by Shaftesbury as infinitely superior to a scholar such as Wren, the virtuoso's artistic appreciation identified him as the finest of eighteenth-century gentlemen, not just a collector but a patron and creative cultural force.[133] When he was just 14, Coke remarked to his grandfather and guardian, Sir John Newton: 'I am become since my stay in Rome, a perfect virtuoso, a great lover of pictures'.[134] For the rest of his life he remained committed to the classical revival of ancient Rome and Palladio that Shaftesbury stimulated and Burlington promoted.

The Grand Tour was an invaluable and exclusive education for architects and patrons but its pleasures were not exclusively refined, as Pope waspishly remarked: 'Led by my hand, he sauntered Europe round, / And gather'd ev'ry Vice on Christian ground'.[135] Already in 1711, Coke's tutor and mentor in Italy, Dr Thomas Hobart, had made this assessment of his pupil: 'His passions are strong and violent and should be regulated, civilised and softened.'[136] Accounts of Coke's loud and coarse behaviour continued throughout his life and were confirmed in Admiral Edward Boscawen's description of 'fat, laughing, joking' Coke, who was known for his foul temper, especially when drunk.[137] Horace Walpole recognised 'a very cunning man but not a deep one. He affected frankness and a noisy kind of buffoonery, both to disguise his art, and his superficial understanding'.[138]

128 Shaftesbury, *Characteristicks*, vol. 1, pp. 77–78, 118–119.

129 In *Ordnance des cinq espèces de colonnes selon la méthode des anciens*, 1683, which was translated into English as *A Treatise on the Five Orders of Columns in Architecture*, 1708, Claude Perrault measured ancient Roman buildings and identified no consistent proportions. Questioning the authority of the architectural orders, he stimulated a fierce debate in Britain as well as France. Shaftesbury's 'A Letter Concerning the Art, or Science of Design' was written in 1709 and widely read at that time, appearing in the second edition of the *Characteristicks* in 1714.

130 Morris, p. 72.

131 Campbell, vol. 3, p. 1.

132 Swift, pp. 165–167.

133 Shaftesbury, *Chacteristicks*, vol. 3. p. 207. Refer to Li, pp. 110–112.

134 Coke, 1714, quoted in James, p. 187.

135 Pope, *The Dunciad*, p. 41.

136 Hobart, quoted in Ford and Ingamells, p. 225.

137 Boscawen, quoted in James, p. 264.

138 Horace Walpole, 1759, in *Correspondence*, p. 43. Refer to Schmidt, 'Thomas Coke, Earl of Leicester – the Builder of Holkham', pp. 37–39.

John Villiers identified a further reason for the Grand Tour: 'Every young man should go abroad to make him feel more attached to his own country.'[139] Rather than a direct and literal translation, references to classical antiquity and Renaissance Italy were intended to cultivate principles suited to England. Pope's concern for classical antiquity led him to translate Homer – to make him 'speak good *English*'.[140] The result was a synthesis of humanism and empiricism in early eighteenth-century England.

In time for his twenty-first birthday on 17 June 1718, Coke returned to take control of his inheritance. He had extensive estates in counties closer to London and spent little of his childhood in Norfolk, but he chose to build there, gradually consolidating his landholdings at Holkham next to the North Sea. Sir Thomas Robinson described 'a large estate round an exceedingly bad old house, for his water is to [be] brought, his plantations but just begun, and a house to be built, and not fifty pounds worth of wood within two miles of the place'. Assuming that Coke 'has no other temptation than that his ancestors lived there' he concluded: 'His successors might reap an advantage, but life is too short for the first generation to receive much benefit, where there are so many disadvantages from nature, and the whole to be compassed only by art, time and expense.'[141] But what was problematic for Robinson was advantageous for Coke. Although his family had farmed there for over 100 years he recognised that his transformation could appear extreme. Coke's aim was to affirm his lineage while flattering his reputation in relation to that of

139 Villiers, 1788, quoted in Black, *The British Abroad*, p. 294.

140 Sir William Trumball, in Pope, *The Correspondence of Alexander Pope*, vol. 1, pp. 45–46.

141 Sir Thomas Robinson to Lord Carlisle, 1731, quoted in Lees-Milne, p. 246.

Sebastiano Conca, *The Vision of Aeneas in the Elysian Fields*, c.1735–40. Courtesy of Viscount Coke and the Trustees of the Holkham Estate.

his ancestors and descendants. In Sebastiano Conca's *The Vision of Aeneas in the Elysian Fields*, c.1735–1740, he is Orpheus, the charmer of trees and rivers, birds and animals, bringing culture to Holkham.[142] Years later, a stone tablet celebrating his achievement and new aristocratic title was placed above Holkham Hall's entrance, which faces north towards the sea:[143]

> THIS SEAT, on an open barren Estate,
> Was planned, planted, built, decorated,
> And inhabited the middle of the XVIIIth Century
> By THO^s COKE EARL OF LEICESTER

Alberti's advice that the architect should not oversee construction was impractical. If the designer did not fulfil this role, a supervising architect was usually appointed, such as Matthew Brettingham Sr at Holkham.[144] Kent's familiar practice was to visit a distant site infrequently.[145] Records of his journeys do not survive but given Walpole's prestige, Coke's friendship and his work at Raynham Hall between 1725 and 1731, he is likely to have visited north Norfolk more often. Travelling 10 miles as he worked concurrently at Houghton and Holkham, Kent would have passed through North Creake, a linear village along the valley of the River Burn, and then climbed the hill to the edge of the Holkham estate, where his route joined that of Coke's carriage concluding its arduous journey from London. At the crest of the ridge, the Triumphal Arch marked the start of the formal approach to the estate and established its orientation. To the south was culture – London and Rome – and to the north was nature – the dunes and sea. Although the estate's axis deviates slightly from that of the earth, two eighteenth-century maps (c.1744–1759 and 1781) depict it as exactly north–south, emphasising the estate's symbolic orientation.[146]

Kent's drawing of the Triumphal Arch, c.1732, shows pyramids on the side wings, which were built but later demolished. The rules for the selection and location of particular symbols were much discussed and a means to display learning. Kent received guidance from the 1626 Paduan edition of Vincenzo Cartari's *Imagini delli dei gl'antichi*, 1556, a popular handbook on classical mythology.[147] But he also playfully added animals to his drawings. Here a large hunting hound stands under the high central arch, or maybe it is a donkey alluding to the long, slow journey.

John Soane later described Kent as 'the father of modern gardening' and an architect of 'genius', and acquired 48 of his drawings and a number of his furniture pieces.[148] But Soane knew Norfolk well as many of his early projects were there,

[142] Hardy, pp. 138–139, 153.

[143] Coke was knighted in 1725, made Baron Lovell of Minster Lovell in 1728 and became Earl of Leicester in 1744.

[144] Alberti, p. 318.

[145] General Dormer, letter to Sir Clement Cottrell, 21 July 1741, quoted in Müller, p. 187.

[146] As the earlier map refers to Coke as Earl of Leicester, it must have been drawn between 1744 and his death in 1759.

[147] Coffin, 'The Elysian Fields of Rousham', p. 412.

[148] Soane, 'Lecture XI', 'Lecture VIII', in Watkin, *Sir John Soane*, pp. 642, 608.

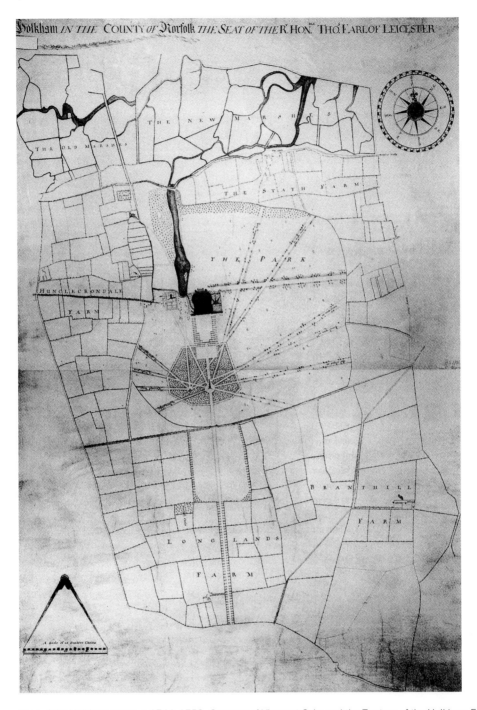

Map of the Holkham estate, c.1744–1759. Courtesy of Viscount Coke and the Trustees of the Holkham Estate.

and he questioned Kent's 'improper use of the ancient decoration', remarking that at the 'entrance into the park at Holkham, pyramids are also introduced without any better reason'.[149] However, it is likely that Kent considered the pyramid to be an appropriate symbol. Exaggerating the size of the Triumphal Arch, the side wings are dwarfed by the central block and lower than the central arch. Embedded in the wall, a local material – flint – forms a bony surface to the rustication, emphasising the association with entombment that the pyramids would have enforced. The triumphal arch is an ancient Roman tradition celebrating military heroes. Neither Coke nor his ancestors were known for their fighting prowess. But the Triumphal Arch was intended to celebrate both Coke and his most distinguished ancestor, Sir Edward Coke, once the most senior judge in Jacobean England, who began the acquisition of Holkham but did not reside there. For a family wishing to emphasise its ancestry, pyramids would have been a fitting symbol. Kent's Obelisk is a mile and a half to the north of the Triumphal Arch, so that similar allusions marked each end of the axial avenue. In other gardens, he purposively used the pyramid and other references to mortality and eternity. In Stowe's Elysian Fields, a garden named after the paradise dedicated to the heroes of classical antiquity, the Temple of British Worthies has a pyramid at its centre. At Rousham in Oxfordshire, Kent

William Kent, *Triumphal Arch, Holkham*, c.1732. Courtesy of Viscount Coke and the Trustees of the Holkham Estate.

149 Soane, 'Lecture XI', 'Lecture IV', in Watkin, *Sir John Soane,* pp. 643, 548. Refer to Dean, pp. 20, 166.

150 Kent, letter to Burlington, 28 November 1738, quoted in Tipping, p. 209.

created a garden for General James Dormer, remarking in 1738 that even though his client had severe 'Goute he is still bronzo mad'.[150] Kent had originally wanted Peter Scheemaker's sculpture, *Dying Gladiator*, to be mounted on a sarcophagus, an emphatic reference to Dormer's declining health, who died in 1741 just as the garden was completed.

A resident of the county for over 20 years, the landscape designer, Humphry Repton, remarked in 1781: 'Norfolk is by no means so flat a county as it is generally described to be, and this is chiefly owing to the hasty way in which itinerant writers view it'.[151] Gently undulating, the north Norfolk landscape offers, conceals and then reveals views to the coast. At 67 metres above sea level the Triumphal Arch is at the highest point of the Holkham estate. Framed within the high central arch, and over a mile to the north, the height of the Obelisk must have been carefully calculated because its pointed tip symbolically pierces the distant horizon of the North Sea, encapsulating the dialogue between culture and nature that defines the estate.

151 Repton, quoted in Williamson, *The Archaeology of the Landscape Park*, p. 8.

Proceeding north, the avenue is straight but the land dips slowly and evenly so that the view of the sea is lost and trees and fields are seen to each side. Norfolk is one of the driest counties in England and summer droughts are a frequent problem. In winter a cold northeast wind blows in from the sea. Air drifting over water will in time match its temperature, protecting the land from freezing conditions. But in winter the sea off the Norfolk coast is the coldest in Britain, even more than in the north of Scotland because of the diminished influence of the distant Gulf Stream.[152] Winters can be harsh, causing frost damage to young trees and less hardy species. An eighteenth-century visitor remarked: 'The country all round here is *entirely bare*, as if there were some *strict law* that *not a tree, not a shrub* should shade the *turnips*'. But due to Walpole and Coke's efforts she recognised 'a great extent of plantations enough to inform the country that trees *will grow in Norfolk*'.[153] Reversing the deforestation of previous centuries, tree planting was an aesthetic decision, as well as an attempt at local climate modification and a means to supply the nation's expanding dockyards. Coke purchased 'Forest Trees' as early as 1721 and soon began to collect specimens from neighbouring Norfolk estates.[154] Aware of Coke's passion, Walpole and his younger brother, Horatio, both donated trees.[155] Just as the Grand Tour influenced the design of buildings and gardens, a growing number of exotic trees were imported into England to stand alongside indigenous varieties. The principal tree at Holkham is *Quercus ilex*, the Holm, or Holly, Oak, a massive Mediterranean evergreen with a round head and low-hanging branches. Chosen to recall the Grand Tour and honour Sir Edward Coke, the Holm Oak is the sacred tree of Jupiter, the Roman

152 Stirling, *The Weather of Britain*, pp. 1–4.

153 Mrs Delany, 1774, quoted in James, p. 295.

154 Lees-Milne, p. 244.

155 Horatio was ennobled as first Baron Walpole of Wolterton. James, p. 267; Lees-Milne, p. 244.

god of Justice. Able to withstand strong salt winds and suited to coastal locations, it was first planted at Holkham in 1730 and soon lined the axial avenue
between the Triumphal Arch and the Obelisk, dividing the formal approach from
the fields.

Establishing Home Farm as early as 1724, Coke's ambitions for his inheritance included its prosperity. As agricultural prices did not rise during his
tenure, land enclosures and more intensive farming practices, which increased
the yield per acre, were the principal reasons for the greater profitability of his
estates.[156] The agricultural improvements at Holkham are often credited to
Coke's descendant, Thomas William Coke, who inherited the estate in 1776 and
acquired fame in farming circles as 'Coke of Norfolk', becoming the first Earl of
Leicester of the second creation after the earlier title's demise on Coke's death in
1759. But many of the agricultural advances associated with Holkham actually
occurred in Coke's tenure or even earlier. Throughout the eighteenth century,
Norfolk and East Anglia were at the forefront of innovative agriculture. In 1724
Defoe concluded:

> This part of England is remarkable for being the first where the feeding and fat-
> tening of cattle, both sheep as well as black cattle with turnips, was first practis'd
> in England, which is made a very great part of the improvement of their land to
> this day.[157]

The noted agricultural reformer, Arthur Young, remarked in 1768:

> All the country from Holkham to Houghton was a wild sheep-walk before the spirit
> of improvement seized the inhabitants; and this glorious spirit has wrought amaz-
> ing effects; for instead of boundless wilds, and uncultivated wastes, inhabited by
> scarce anything but sheep; the country is all cut into inclosures, cultivated in a
> most husband-like manner, richly manured, well peopled, and yielding an hundred
> times the produce that it did in its former state.[158]

The soil in north Norfolk is calcareous along the sea and rivers, and thus
particularly fertile and rich in nutrients, encouraging biodiversity. But in other
areas, the land is largely unsuitable for agriculture without marling, in which the
chalky alkaline subsoil is dug up and combined with the sandy topsoil to reduce
its acidity. The technique was known in medieval Norfolk when the landscape
was largely composed of open fields and heaths devoid of hedges and trees,
but it was only extensively employed in the early eighteenth century. Another

156 Parker, pp. 43–45; Wade
Martins, *Coke of Norfolk*, p. 84.

157 Defoe, *A Tour through the
Whole Island of Great Britain*, p. 58.

158 Young, pp. 21–22.

highly praised innovation was the 'Norfolk four-course', which alternated wheat, turnips, barley and clover, or other similar 'artificial grasses', in a four-year crop rotation cycle, providing nutritious winter fodder that allowed livestock numbers to increase. Turnips and cereals do not prosper in acidic soils and barley is especially badly affected. Soil bacteria also dislike acidic soils, which diminish clover's ability to act as a fertiliser fixing atmospheric nitrogen to the earth.[159] The real success of the Norfolk four-course occurred not on land that was already productive but on acidic soils in conjunction with marling. A skilful estate manager, Walpole's father utilised marling and crop rotation to transform the productivity of his estate.[160] Turnips were probably first grown at Houghton in 1673 and they were a significant crop by 1700. Farm leases on the estate soon required clover and turnips to be planted extensively. At Holkham, turnips were an important crop by 1710.[161]

Population growth was slow in the late seventeenth and early eighteenth centuries and agricultural prices were low, especially in the 1720s and 1730s when there were good summers and generous harvests, allowing prosperous estates to buy out small farms that were struggling economically.[162] Marling and crop rotation were labour intensive and suited the owner of a large farm who was in complete control of land that was not held communally, and could afford to invest and profit from economies of scale.[163] Parliamentary land enclosures benefited wealthy landowners, but they undermined the rural poor who relied on common land for at least a part of their livelihood. Heaths and pastures were ordered into regular fields before any other European nation. Beginning in the seventeenth century and increasing after 1724, over six million acres nationally were transferred from public to private use. In Norfolk 75 per cent of land enclosures occurred by 1760. The tax burden of tenant and peasant farmers was low in comparison to many other European countries, but landowners' fears of social unrest were reflected in the increasing number of crimes against property that resulted in a capital offence, including servants pilfering from their masters in 1736 and sheep stealing in 1741.[164] The increased contrast between the wealthy landowner and the diminished yeoman farmer, whose numbers dwindled throughout the eighteenth century, created a social gulf that encouraged prosperous landowners and townspeople to socialise together.[165]

According to Deist philosophy, which was influential in the early eighteenth century, God made the natural world for human benefit and offered no further intervention, leaving it in trust to humanity. In *Philosophiae Naturalis Principia Mathematica* (Mathematical Principles of Natural Philosophy), 1687, Isaac Newton concluded that material objects possess mass and are dependent on

159 Williamson, *The Archaeology of the Landscape Park*, pp. 10–12; Williamson, *The Transformation of Rural England*, pp. 67–68.

160 Plumb, *Sir Robert Walpole: The Making of a Statesman*, p. 85.

161 Plumb, 'Sir Robert Walpole and Norfolk Husbandry', pp. 87–88; Williamson, *The Transformation of Rural England*, pp. 64–65.

162 Williamson, *The Archaeology of the Landscape Park*, p. 15.

163 Williamson, *The Transformation of Rural England*, pp. 62–63, 66, 80–81.

164 Porter, *English Society in the Eighteenth Century*, pp. 135–137, 208–213.

165 Williamson, *The Archaeology of the Landscape Park*, pp. 167, 169.

forces of attraction and repulsion as in a mechanical system. As nature was conceived as a machine, mankind could have been its driver and engineer, making technical adjustments to improve performance. But in an era that associated power and status with land ownership and was yet to face the full force of industrialisation, the gentleman farmer was a model for the enlightened management of nature and society. Written in the first century BC, and derived from *georgos*, the Greek term for farmer, Virgil's four-volume *Georgics* was particularly influential in that he equated the virtuous management of the land to the benign management of Rome, underpinning Walpole's pleasure in presenting himself as a bluff Norfolk squire.[166] Coke was equally indebted to the *Georgics*; his library included several manuscripts and printed editions in Latin and in translation. Noting the attention given to parks and gardens as well as farms and fields, John Barrell concludes that the English Georgic tradition allowed 'its inhabitants a life of work and play together' and was 'concerned to soften as much as to recommend the hard moral lessons of Virgil's original *Georgics*' in which 'rewards and pleasures are always in the future'.[167] Although industriousness was a virtue for rich and poor, the prosperous were more likely to be rewarded with recreation and repose. The farm labourer's day was exhausting, extending from 6am to 6pm in summer and sunrise to sunset in winter.

In the *Eclogues*, Virgil conceived Arcadia as the setting for a blissful, bucolic life but emphasised the presence of mortality even in an idyllic location, stimulating an interpretation of Arcadia that became even more profound in the seventeenth and eighteenth centuries, when the scientific study of death gave new emphasis to the appreciation of life.[168] In an increasingly secular age, empiricism's attention to subjective experience and the natural world emphasised the seasons of a life as well as the seasons of a year, so that the pleasures of the present were acknowledged more often than the eternal joy of the afterlife.[169] In England, more than in any other European country, the garden and park became the means to contemplate the passage of time, transience of life, and delights made sweeter because they were fleeting. Dependent on the seasons and weather, gardens emphasised that life and death are necessary to one another. Kent even intended to plant dead trees in the grounds of Kensington Palace as an aid to temporal awareness.[170] In 1745, Abbé Le Blanc expressed an opinion that was widely held at the time: 'It is to the fogs with which their Island is nearly always covered that the English owe both the richness of their pastures and the melancholic spirit of their temperament.'[171] Walpole's favourite landscape artist was his contemporary John Wootton, the pre-eminent early eighteenth-century painter of hunting and sporting scenes who painted in a style reminiscent of Claude Lorrain and Gaspar Dughet. Wootton

[166] Barrell, pp. 8–9; Jankovic, pp. 16–22, 137.

[167] Barrell, pp. 36–37.

[168] Virgil's *Eclogues* were written in the first century BC. Panofsky, '*Et in Arcadia Ego*', pp. 295–320.

[169] Locke, *An Essay Concerning Human Understanding*, bk. 2, ch. 1, pp. 104–105; bk. 2, ch. 27, p. 342.

[170] Hussey, p. 130; Kames, vol. 2, p. 335; Price, *An Essay on the Picturesque*, pp. 186–187; Walpole, *The History of the Modern Taste in Gardening*, p. 59; Wilson, p. 221.

[171] Abbé (J. B.) Le Blanc, *Lettres de Monsieur Abbé Le Blanc*, rev. ed., 1751, quoted in Coffin, *The English Garden: Meditation and Memorial*, p. 3.

172 Edwards, Moore and Archer, p. 104.

173 Descartes, p. 263.

174 Hooke's essay was published in Thomas Sprat's *History of the Royal Society of London*, 1667. Weather data was collected in other European countries; for example, at the Accademia del Cimento, Florence, in the 1650s and 1660s and the Académie des Sciences after its foundation in 1666.

175 Locke, 'A Register of the Weather for the Year 1692', pp. 1919. Refer to Jankovic, pp. 35–36; Nebeker, p. 11.

depicted *Sir Robert Walpole*, c.1725, as the model of a country squire surrounded by his dogs, while the autumnal hues of Wootton's *Classical Landscape* hung in the dressing room adjacent to Walpole's bedchamber at Houghton.[172]

A concern for nature, agriculture and the seasons inevitably included a concern for the weather, which was subject to scientific investigation and farming lore as well as poetic contemplation. In *Discourse on Method, Optics, Geometry and Meteorology*, 1637, René Descartes expressed 'the hope that if I here express the nature of clouds in such a way that we will no longer have occasion to wonder at anything that descends from them, we will easily believe that it is similarly possible to find causes of everything that is admirable above the earth'.[173] In 'Method for Making a History of the Weather', 1667, Robert Hooke argued for regular and consistent weather records.[174] Locke concurred, daily recording the temperature, barometric pressure and winds for many years.[175] In 1663 Wren presented a

John Wootton and Jonathan Richardson, *Sir Robert Walpole*, c.1725. Courtesy of the Marquess of Cholmondeley, Houghton Hall.

John Wootton, *Classical Landscape*, c.1730s. Courtesy of the Marquess of Cholmondeley, Houghton Hall.

'Description of a Weather Clock' to the Royal Society and six years later Hooke constructed the mechanical 'weather wiser', the first automated weather station that recorded air pressure, humidity, temperature, rainfall, wind direction and speed.[176] A national network of meteorological observatories was first proposed in the 1680s but the idea did not receive widespread support until it was revived in the second half of the eighteenth century. Empirical investigation was not immediately and extensively applied to the weather because it was assumed to lack reason, although this was also recognised as an inviting challenge to rational explanation.

Scientific study of the atmosphere was in its infancy and an alternative method was widely supported. In classical antiquity there were two distinct attitudes to atmospheric phenomena, one a theory of airborne particles expressed in Aristotle's *Meteorologica*, c.350 BC, the other a guide to the weather exemplified by the *Georgics*. Verse not prose, and interpretation not explanation, Virgil identifies changes in nature that foretell impending weather, such as the behaviour of insects and birds, plants and skies. The *Georgics* emphasises weather's creative influence on the arts as well as daily life and even acknowledges inclement

176 Crewe, pp. 137–138.

weather as a stimulus to artistic production. A weather poem as well as a weather guide, the *Georgics* inspired both literary forms. An English translation appeared in 1697 with an introduction by Addison, inspiring Pope's *Pastorals*, 1709, and James Thomson's *The Seasons*, 1730, which was the most influential Georgic poem of the eighteenth century, presenting human activity in dialogue with an evolving natural world to a greater extent than Pope's more restrained poetry.[177] In a further poem of 1735–1736, Thomson specifically associated the English landscape garden with *Liberty*.[178] *The Seasons'* popularity was immediate and enduring, resulting in over 300 editions between 1750 and 1850. Here, Thomson describes the spring:

177 The *Georgics'* translator was John Dryden. Barrell, p. 7; Hunt, *Gardens and the Picturesque*, p. 228.

178 Thomson, *Liberty*, pp. 696–700.

William Kent, *Spring*, illustration for James Thomson, *The Seasons*, 1730. Courtesy of the British Museum.

Sound slept the Waters; no sulphureous glooms
Swell'd in the sky, and sent the lightning forth:
While sickly damps, and cold and autumnal fogs,
Sat not pernicious on the springs of life.[179]

179 Thomson, *The Seasons*, p. 20.

Sharing Thomson's sensitivity to the contrasting seasons, Kent provided four illustrations, no doubt recognising parallels between the evocative flow of Thomson's poetry and his own developing gardening concerns. Kent depicted seasonal shifts in architecture, nature and behaviour. Between 'Spring' and 'Winter', a benign sky, placid bay, relaxed figures and Palladian villa are transformed into an aggressive storm, turbulent sea, cowering figures and rustic farmhouse.

William Kent, *Winter*,
illustration for James
Thomson, *The Seasons*,
1730. Courtesy of the
British Museum.

Thomson celebrated weather's variety but recognised a fundamental order in the natural sequence of the seasons, which provided a setting for humanity to prosper. Published with *The Seasons*, in 'A Poem Sacred to the Memory of Sir Isaac Newton' nature is female, passive and subject to Newton: 'Nature herself / Stood all subdu'd by him, and open laid / Her very latent glory to his view'.[180] A drawing of Kent's pyramidal monument to Newton immediately precedes Thomson's poem to the scientist. Sculpted by Rysbrack in white and grey marble and installed in Westminster Abbey in 1731, Newton reclines on a sarcophagus, resting an arm on his most famous volumes.[181] Above, a figure representing astronomy surmounts a celestial globe. The Latin inscription praises 'a strength of mind almost divine, and mathematical principles peculiarly his own'. It is likely that, in common with his age, Kent recognised a practical and poetic appreciation of nature as well as a mechanical and secular one. But rather than a discourse on Newtonian thought, his gardens and garden drawings emphasise an engaged, lyrical and hedonistic appreciation of the natural world.

Following continental Europe, in 1752 Britain and its colonies adopted the Gregorian calendar's uniform system of measurement in place of the Julian calendar, which reflected the seasonal rhythms of farming.[182] But confidence in the weather sign persisted well into the eighteenth century. First, because it affirmed rural traditions, emphasising the social, practical and spiritual benefits that arose from co-existence with nature, which tied farming customs and celebrations to the seasonal calendar. Second, because it tempered the systematic and secular conception of nature that suited the agricultural reforms of the political establishment. However, the two conceptions of the natural world were not simply opposed in class terms; weather signs were communicated to prosperous and poor alike. Characteristic of the English Georgic tradition, attempts to resolve the two conceptions were evident in guides as well as poems.[183] One of the best-known farming guides was written by John Claridge in 1670 and republished in 1744 as *The Shepherd of Banbury's Rules to Judge of the Changes of the Weather, Grounded on Forty Years Experience*, with the subtitle 'A Rational Account . . . on the Principles of *Newtonian* Philosophy'. After an unexplained piece of weather advice, the author remarks:

> *This must be allow'd a very extraordinary Aphorism from a Country Shepherd, but at the Same Time it is very agreeable to the Observations of Dr.* Hooke, *Dr.* Derham, *Dr.* Grew, *and other able Naturalists, who with unwearied Pains and Diligence have calculated the Quality of Rain falling in one Year and compared it with what fell in another.*[184]

180 Thomson, 'A Poem Sacred to the Memory of Sir Isaac Newton', p. 243. Refer to Bate, 'Living with the Weather', pp. 433, 437.

181 Thomson, *The Seasons*, p. 240.

182 Before 1752, New Year's Day was 25 March rather than 1 January. For example, a date that would have been classified as 3 March 1715 in 1752 would have been 3 March 1714 before then.

183 Curry, p. 161; Golinski, *British Weather*, p. 72; Jankovic, pp. 153–155.

184 Claridge, p. 14.

To some extent, the two conceptions of nature were not even opposed. Characterising nature as female, as in the Biblical narrative, Bacon interpreted the 'Recovery of Eden' as mankind reaffirming its God-given dominion and thus its right to exploit and improve nature.[185] Theodor W. Adorno and Max Horkheimer identify the seeds of self-destruction in the Enlightenment's association of reason with the myth of domination: 'Men pay for the increase of their power with alienation from that over which they exercise their power. Enlightenment behaves towards things as a dictator toward men.'[186] While earlier societies conceived the world holistically, empirical science ordered natural phenomena according to distinct categories in a complete system. However, the concern for natural reason also engendered a new respect for nature, encouraging greater attention than before to both agriculture and uncultivated nature. With the development of modern scientific instruments such as the microscope and the telescope, increasingly detailed observation focused more on the properties of natural objects and less on their immediate value to humans, although this concern was never distant. Favouring the rational collection, analysis and ordering of information, the Enlightenment also concentrated attention on the relations between natural objects, which had previously been primarily measured against a human standard. Astronomers, botanists and zoologists classified planets, plants and animals, while geologists established the earth's age. In 1683 Anton van Leeuwenhoek declared 'that there were more animals in his own mouth than there were people in the United Provinces' of the Netherlands.[187] The discovery of new plants, places and creatures, and greater understanding of those already known, further stimulated appreciation of the natural world. A concern for all the earth's creatures is a characteristic of the Judaeo-Christian tradition. But it was mostly latent until the second half of the seventeenth century when scientists concluded that any natural object, however humble, could be admired if it fulfilled a purpose. Concerned to address the depletion of natural resources due to the demands of trade and industry, the Royal Society's first official publication, Evelyn's *Sylva, or A Discourse of Forest-Trees, and the Propagation of Timber in His Majesties Dominions*, 1664, marked a more sensitive attitude to the modification of nature than before.[188] Acknowledging the effects of deforestation on climate and the need for forestry science, conservation and sustainable development, Evelyn emphasised that forestry was a gentlemanly pursuit, like hunting.[189]

Cultivating a natural image alongside gridded hedgerows, the taste for formal gardens diminished and picturesque parks proliferated.[190] A mile north of the Triumphal Arch, Kent's South Lodge divided the farmland from the park beyond, which was productive as well as pleasurable, providing food and income through

185 Bacon, 'Novum Organum', pp. 52–447. Refer to Merchant, pp. 74–75.

186 Adorno and Horkheimer, p. 9; refer to p. xvi.

187 Thomas, pp. 174, 243, referring to Dobell.

188 Clarence C. Glacken mentions *Sylva* and the *French Forest Ordinance of 1669*, initiated by Jean-Baptiste Colbert, minister to Louis XIV. Brown, *French Forest Ordinance of 1669*; Evelyn, *Sylva*, pp. 112–120; Glacken, p. 485.

189 Holkham's library has a fourth, 1706, edition of *Sylva* with binding that suggests it was either acquired between 1744 and 1759 or rebound at that time.

190 Thomas, pp. 262–264.

John Evelyn, *Sylva, or
A Discourse of Forest-Trees,
and the Propagation of
Timber in His Majesties
Dominions*, 1664.
Frontispiece. Courtesy of the
British Library.

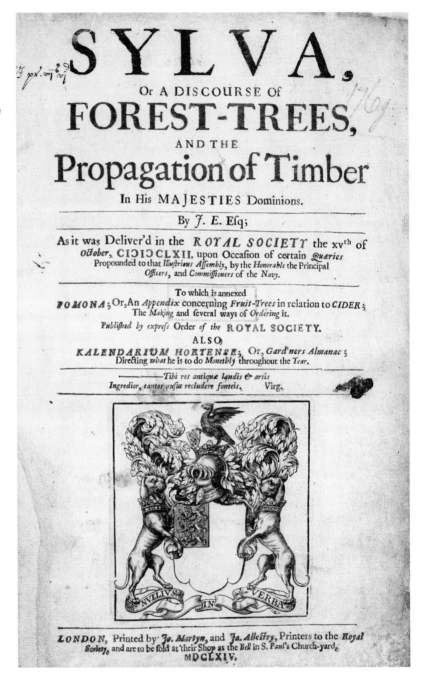

forestry and hunting. In 1723, Holkham's annual estate expenditure on stables and hounds was over three times that spent on servants.[191] Between 1730 and 1742 a pale was constructed, enclosing a park of around 360 hectares, although deer were not introduced until the nineteenth century.[192] Instead, partridges roamed on the wide lawns, where sheep and cattle grazed, finding shade under artfully scattered tree clumps. Densely planted linear copses provided protection from the bitter northeast winds and were ideally suited to pheasants and many other game birds.[193] Andrea Casali's *Thomas Coke, Earl of Leicester*, c.1744, associates the aristocrat with the hunt.[194] In front of Diana, goddess of hunting, Coke wears his peer's robe and points to the Earl's coronet on an adjacent cushion. The sporting and learned sides of Coke's character were recalled by a Norfolk neighbour after a long day's hunting at Holkham:

> I remember, when we were Fox-Hunters, and a long Day's Sport had rather tir'd than satisfied us, we often pass'd the Evening in reading the Ancient Authors: when the Beauty of their Language, the Strength, and Justness of their thoughts for ever glowing with a noble Spirit of Liberty, made us forget not only the Pains, but the Pleasures of the Day.[195]

To the north of the South Lodge, the avenue rises to the highest point within the park at 36 metres above sea level, where by 1730 Obelisk Wood was planted with Beech, Birch, Cherry, Fir, Holly, Holm Oak, Horse Chestnut, Spanish Chestnut, Sweet Chestnut, Thorn and Walnut. At the centre of the Wood, the avenue bifurcates to encircle the Obelisk before proceeding north to the edge of the trees, where the sea is visible once again, returning the vista that had been hidden since the Triumphal Arch, while expanding it into a panorama. To the west of the Obelisk and deeper among the trees, Kent's Temple – the first building commissioned by Coke – was completed for the considerable sum of £710, creating a woodland temple reminiscent of the one imagined on a smaller scale in Houghton's Great Staircase.[196] Behind a portico of four Doric columns, the high octagonal room has four semi-circular niches, which housed sculptures including Apollo, Ptolemy, Venus and a faun, a mythical forest creature. Although it was intended for occasional visits rather than continuous inhabitation, the Temple contained furniture supplied by the upholsterer who made the dining chairs for Coke's London residence.[197] A number of seats were also arranged around the Wood, including a 'great wooden seat' and 'great circular seat'.[198]

Shown in eighteenth-century estate maps, Obelisk Wood was cut by axial paths, which were soon out of fashion. In a 1736 letter to Burlington that refers to

[191] Parker, pp. 21–22.

[192] Williamson, *The Archaeology of the Landscape Park*, pp. 63–66.

[193] Coke's guardians had considered creating an enclosed deer park but did not pursue the idea. Williamson, *The Archaeology of the Landscape Park*, pp. 188–192.

[194] The portrait was painted after Coke acquired a new title in 1744.

[195] Quoted in Mortlock, p. 76. Refer to Lees-Milne, p. 242.

[196] Holkham Accounts, quoted in Williamson, *The Archaeology of the Landscape Park*, p. 63.

[197] James, p. 267.

[198] Holkham Archives, quoted in Williamson, *The Archaeology of the Landscape Park*, p. 65.

Kent's Italian nickname, Coke acknowledged as 'unpictoresk those cold & insipid strait walks' that 'make the signor sick'.[199] Reflecting Kent's opinion, this is the first recorded reference to 'picturesque' gardening. Though dismissed, the paths within the Wood had a purpose; each offered a specific tree-framed vista. A significant number looked towards the coast, connecting the cultivated wilderness of Obelisk Wood to the actual wilderness of the North Sea. Five avenues spanned from the Temple. None faced south or looked northeast to the site of the new house. The principal view from the Temple was to the north, across the lake and towards the sea. Disregarding the axial approach, eight avenues began at the Obelisk with none looking fully to the south. The principal view – the panorama – led to the sea. Even after Holkham Hall was completed in the mid-1760s, the coast was seen in the distance.

Rather than continuing on axis from Obelisk Wood toward the site of the new house, the route first turns to the northwest and then to the northeast as it arcs slowly down the slope. By early 1734, the landscape had been under way for 12 years and the Obelisk and Temple were complete. But the earliest known plans of the house were maybe eight years old and its foundations were only begun later in 1734.[200] The Obelisk and Temple were constructed of brick and stone from three sources, including Ralph Allen's Bath quarry.[201] When it became clear that there would not be a sufficient supply of Bath stone for the new house, Coke turned to brick, having purchased the nearby Burnham Brick Kiln in 1728. In *The Plans, Elevations and Sections of Holkham in Norfolk*, 1773, Matthew Brettingham Jr attempts to justify the decision by equating the brick's colour to Bath stone, and also emphasises that it was a favoured building material in ancient Rome.[202] But whatever the merit of such claims, the exterior materials of the house are less refined than those of the garden buildings and monuments, inverting the expected hierarchy.

One catastrophically poor investment is assumed to have delayed Holkham Hall.[203] Founded in 1711 to develop commerce in the Americas, the South Sea Company was initially seen as a ripe source of profit. Harvested in the Bay of Honduras, the fine carved mahogany in English houses was one consequence of the transatlantic slave trade, which was cynically justified through reference to slavery in ancient Rome. Walpole benefitted from his own administration's decision to remove export duties on mahogany, just before he began to rebuild Houghton.[204]

In the summer of 1720, shares in the South Sea Company rose 10 times but their value collapsed as sensible investors withdrew later that year, recognising that the Company had assumed too much of the national debt. Having invested over £58,000, Coke lost more than £37,000, which amounted to nearly five years

199 Coke refers to another garden, not Holkham. Coke, letter to Burlington, 20 December 1736, quoted in Tipping, p. 210. Refer to Batey, p. 107; Lees-Milne, p. 245.

200 Hiskey, p. 146.

201 Hassall, 'The Temple at Holkham, Norfolk', p. 1312.

202 His father, for whom he worked, was Matthew Brettingham Sr. Brettingham, *The Plans, Elevations and Sections of Holkham in Norfolk*, 1773, pp. ix–x.

203 Parker, pp. 12–23, 36.

204 Brown, 'Atlantic Slavery and Classical Culture', pp. 91–96; Bryant, p. 201.

of net revenues on his substantial estates. He never significantly invested in the stock market again but the damage was done, diminishing his finances for decades.[205] In 1730 he started to receive income from the most significant part of his wife's inheritance, Dungeness Lighthouse on the Sussex coast, which generated nearly £1,400 a year at first, increasing to £2,000 30 years later.[206] The profitability of his estates also continued to rise and in 1733 Coke was appointed joint Postmaster General of England at an annual salary of £1,000, which he retained until his death.[207] But even with these new sources of income he regretted his decision to start work on the house so soon.[208] In 1734 Coke still considered the garden buildings to be a more immediate priority than the house, and he later proclaimed in a poem: 'Here kent and I are planting Clumps / Not minding whom our Monarch Rumps . . . Contented I enjoy my home / Design a temple, Build a Dome, / Or raise an Obelisk . . . In time you'll come to think like me / And love your Country Seat.'[209]

Emphasising Coke and Kent's travels on the Grand Tour, historians have often underestimated the significance of the estate's coastal location and assumed that the delayed construction of Holkham Hall was merely due to Coke's financial difficulties. Instead, the initial attention given to the park may have been due to desire as well as necessity, indicating that the setting was as important as the house. Houghton Hall was fully complete in 1735, having received more attention than the park. At Holkham the priority was reversed. As he journeyed from one commission to the other, Kent may have imagined Houghtons' exuberant interior and Holkham's lavish landscape as one glorious Arcadian estate.

In the 1714 frontispiece to the second edition of *Characteristicks*, Shaftesbury poses as a Roman senator.[210] Leaning on a book-laden pedestal, he stands in front of a neo-classical arch, which frames the third, second and first natures theorised in the Renaissance and ancient Rome.[211] The sequential arrangement of regular parterres, abundant orchards and distant hills was somewhat comparable to the view from Holkham's Temple but the park was less rigidly defined and waves not hills signified the first nature. Previously, uncultivated nature was considered to be brutish and deformed and the immaterial soul, 'as a visitor in matter', could not 'be truly at home in nature', remarks Ernest Tuveson.[212] Recuperation in a wilderness was not a new theme but it acquired enhanced meaning in the early eighteenth century when nature and moral virtue were linked for the first time. Shaftesbury acknowledged an ideal order but, departing from Plato, conceived nature not as debased but as a means to contemplate the divine. Expanding ideas that he had developed in the previous decade, the second volume of *Characteristicks* praises weather and nature:[213]

205 Holkham Archives, referred to in Parker, pp. 12–20.

206 Coke's father-in-law died in 1729.

207 Parker, pp. 21–23, 36.

208 Coke, letter to Matthew Brettingham Sr, 1 April 1736, quoted in Hiskey, p. 151.

209 Coke, letter to Matthew Brettingham Sr, 1734, quoted in Hiskey, p. 148; Coke, 'An Epistle from Ld. Lovell to Lord Chesterfield at Bath, Wrote by Mr. Poulteney', written before 1742, quoted in James, pp. 230–231.

210 Although the second edition is dated 1714, it actually appeared in 1715.

211 Hunt, *Greater Perfections*, pp. 32–33.

212 Tuveson, p. 11.

213 *The Moralist, A Philosophical Rhapsody* was written in 1705 and published in 1709.

Anthony Ashley Cooper,
third Earl of Shaftesbury,
*Characteristicks of Men,
Manner, Opinions, Times*,
1711. Frontispiece to the
second edition, 1714.
Courtesy of the British
Library.

HOW comfortable is it to those who come out hence alive, to breathe a purer AIR! To see the rejoicing Light of Day! *And tread the fertile Ground! How gladly they contemplate the Surface of the Earth, their habitation heated and enliven'd by the* Sun, *and temper'd by the fresh AIR of fanning* Breezes!*[214]*

I shall no longer resist the Passion growing in me for Things of a natural kind; where neither Art, *nor the* Conceit *or Caprice of Man has spoil'd their genuine Order, by breaking in upon that primitive State. Even the* Rocks, *the mossy* Caverns, *the irregular unwrought* Grotto's, *and broken* Falls *of Waters, with all the horrid* Graces *of the* Wilderness *it-self, as representing NATURE more, will be the more engaging, and appear with a Magnificence beyond the formal Mockery of Princely Gardens.*[215]

The 1714 frontispiece suggests the formality of his own garden at Wimborne St Giles, Dorset, rather than the flowing lines of the picturesque.[216] But Shaftesbury influenced the early eighteenth-century garden whether or not he predicted it. Connecting understanding to experience, Locke emphasised humanity's right to order and improve the land, and required a degree of critical detachment from the natural world.[217] Shaftesbury's purpose was more profound, stimulating a newly spiritual engagement with nature in all its forms. Sensitivity to one's environment became as necessary as sensitivity to others.

Helping to promote Shaftesbury's ideas, as well as those of Locke, *The Spectator* published Addison's essays on 'The Pleasures of the Imagination' in 1712. Previously, nature was studied in paintings and books but Addison concluded that this appreciation was secondary to the primary pleasure of direct experience, which could cultivate a healthy body, an alert mind and a sociable manner.[218] References to the weather's influence on conversation, behaviour and health appear throughout his essays. Citing the Pantheon in Rome, he appreciates architecture's ability to evoke a single, vast idea, notably the divine.[219] Addison recognises that mountains can have a similar power but notes that wild nature is especially conducive to the imagination because it offers a multitude of ideas for association:

There is something more bold and masterly in the rough careless Strokes of Nature, than in the nice Touches and Embellishments of Art. The Beauties of the most stately Garden or Palace lie in a narrow Compass, the Imagination immediately runs them over, and requires something else to gratifie her; but, in the wide Fields of Nature, the Sight wanders up and down without Confinement, and is fed with an infinite variety of Images, without any Stint or Number.[220]

214 Shaftesbury, *Characteristicks*, vol. 2, p. 94.

215 Shaftesbury, *Characteristicks*, vol. 2, p. 101.

216 Leatherbarrow, p. 353.

217 Locke, *An Essay Concerning Human Understanding*, bk. 1, ch. 1, p. 46; bk. 2, ch. 2, pp. 119–121.

218 Addison, in Addison and Steele, vol. 2, 21, 23 and 25 June 1712, no. 411, 412, 414.

219 Addison, in Addison and Steele, vol. 2, 26 June 1712, no. 415.

220 Addison, in Addison and Steele, vol. 2, 25 June 1712, no. 414.

But rather than the natural world *per se*, he focuses on the art of making a garden appear natural, drawing a parallel with the cultivation of natural behaviour: 'The fashionable world is grown free and easy; our manners sit more loose upon us: nothing is so modish as an agreeable negligence'.[221] Concluding that the 'artificial rudeness' of a garden modelled on nature 'gives us a nobler and more exalted kind of Pleasure', Addison suggests that it can be more widely applied: 'why may not a whole Estate be thrown into a kind of Garden'.[222] His purpose was political and social as well as cultural. Unifying fields and gardens into a single landscape composition naturalised class relations, emphasising that the landowner's family and guests belonged in the garden and the farm labourers belonged in the fields.[223]

Meaning 'in the manner of painters' and suggesting a method of laying on paint in bold and irregular strokes to depict not simply a detailed copy of nature but something closer to the experience of nature, the term 'picturesque' was first applied to paintings and only later to gardens.[224] William Shenstone mentions Kent's 'picturesque gardening' in 'Unconnected Thoughts on Gardening', 1764, while Henry Home, Lord Kames, in *Elements of Criticism*, 1762, and Horace Walpole, in *The History of the Modern Taste in Gardening*, 1771, remark that Kent's gardens are composed like paintings.[225] For eighteenth-century advocates of the picturesque, garden design's status as an art depended on its relations with landscape painting. But in the opening line of *Observations on Modern Gardening, Illustrated by Descriptions*, 1770, Thomas Whately writes that 'GARDENING, in the perfection to which it has been lately brought in England, is entitled to a place of considerable rank among the liberal arts. It is as superior to landskip painting, as a reality to a representation'.[226] Later he adds that paintings 'must be only used as studies, not as models' for gardens.[227]

The picturesque is a deceptive term because it emphasises one aspect of the eighteenth-century garden to the detriment of its other qualities, such as the importance of the senses and the seasons to design, experience, understanding and the imagination. The association with painting is relevant but references to open-air theatres and other settings for human discourse and action are as important. Whether a woodland glade or a curving hillside, many of Kent's garden drawings show nature in the form of a stage, recalling the amphitheatres of classical antiquity and the close association of gardens and theatres in Renaissance Italy. The roles of actor and spectator were interchangeable in a Kent garden, as they were when actors and spectators danced together at the end of a Jones masque, which was equally indebted to Italian Renaissance gardens and a further influence on Kent. The picturesque garden extended an earlier theatrical tradition that was distinct

221 Addison, in Addison and Steele, vol. 1, 17 July 1711, no. 119.

222 Addison, in Addison and Steele, vol. 2, 25 June 1712, no. 414.

223 Cosgrove, *Geography and Vision*, p. 1; Cosgrove, *Social Formation and Symbolic Landscape*, p. 15.

224 The first French reference to the picturesque appears in Roger de Piles' codification of pictorial order, *Cours de peinture par principes*, 1708, which was translated into English as *The Principles of Painting*, 1743.

225 Shenstone, quoted in Hunt, *The Picturesque Garden in Europe*, p. 26; Kames, vol. 2, p. 327; Walpole, *The History of the Modern Taste in Gardening*, pp.43–44.

226 Whately, p. 1.

227 Whately, p. 147.

from the development of eighteenth-century theatre, and bourgeois art in general, in which the separation of actors and audiences, and artworks and viewers, became increasingly common.

The picturesque garden is more than a painting or a play in that it is experienced not in a concentrated time period but in motion and over days and seasons, linking appreciation of the changing natural world to journeys in self-understanding. In classicism, the gaze and the body follow the same path. But in the picturesque, they diverge. The eye is drawn to a distant object but the path is not direct or singular. Immersion within a garden stimulates a questioning attitude to vision in which self-reflective viewers perceive themselves viewing, and observe others doing the same, so that their experiences are both personal and social, and equivalent to 'the phenomenology of the eye', as de Bolla concludes.[228] The picturesque draws attention to the problems as well as the pleasures of vision, which is no more than 'intelligent guesswork' 'from limited sensory evidence', writes Richard Gregory.[229] Consequently, informed by memory, 'perceptions are hypotheses. This is suggested by the fact that retinal images are open to an infinity of interpretations'.[230] What we see is affected by what we touch, feel, taste, smell and hear. Even when the garden visitor is static, physical and perceptual movement is implicit because any past or future journey is understood in relation to other potential journeys and is but one part of a complex and changeable whole.

Incorporating farming, hunting and forestry as well as discourse and leisure, the picturesque landscape was firmly within the English Georgic tradition. Like Virgil's volumes, the picturesque drew attention to the weather. But the enhanced fascination for the human subject and the natural world, and the relations between them, meant that the weather acquired further significance. In 'Of the Seasons', the final chapter in *Observations on Modern Gardening*, Whately argues that gardens must be designed for the weather's 'transitory effects' and those that are more predictable: 'The seasons thus become subjects of consideration in gardening . . . Different parts may thus be adapted to different seasons; and each in its turn will be in perfection.'[231] One of the picturesque garden's principal themes – the cycles of life and death – was tangible in plants and trees and represented in monuments and buildings, which were also seen to age and decay. Just as the daily weather was part of a larger weather pattern, the eighteenth-century garden was a means to engage the social as well as the self. History, politics, love and death were all represented and discussed among garden glades and monuments. A member of a leading Whig family and once a general in the Duke of Marlborough's army, Cobham conceived Stowe – the grandest early eighteenth-century English

228 De Bolla, pp. 25, 220.

229 Gregory, p. 5. Refer to Harrison, p. 215.

230 Gregory, p. 10.

231 Whately, pp. 245, 242–243.

William Kent, *The Vale of Venus, Rousham*, 1737–1741. Courtesy of C. Cottrell-Dormer.

232 Kames, vol. 2, p. 331.

garden, alongside Holkham – as a political and cultural statement, while erotic love and mortal decay are themes of Rousham, a more intimate garden.

The picturesque was also understood as an expression of national identity. Associating the axial geometry of a French garden with an absolutist Catholic monarchy, Kames disparagingly concluded: 'The gardens of Versailles, executed with infinite expense by men at that time of high repute, are a lasting monument of a taste the most vicious and depraved.'[232] The picturesque came to fruition in England. But given its precedents in Renaissance gardens, Chinese landscape drawings and seventeenth-century Italian paintings, compatibility with French and German rococo, and varied development internationally, it cannot be described as exclusively English. Indeed, its diverse origins were valued in the eighteenth century. Accommodating multiple journeys, abundant allegories and imported trees, the picturesque was associated with the choices and opportunities available to the fortunate and prosperous in English society, and came to personify the liberty and liberalism they professed.

The influence of Addison, Pope and Thomson on the early eighteenth-century landscape is recognised. But the novel's relationship to the picturesque garden has not been widely acknowledged, even though they were each a response to empiricism and informed each other. Emphasising a fascination for landscape and its relationship to dwelling that was to become a principal theme of English literature, Robinson Crusoe even had 'my Country-House, and my Sea-Coast-House' on his shipwreck island.[233] Kent and his patrons probably read the first novels because the authors, such as Defoe and Swift, were well known to them. Kent prepared a sketch of the 'Exorcism of Don Quixote's Library', c.1725, and contributed an illustration to a 1738 Spanish edition of Miguel de Cervantes' Don Quixote, 1605–1615, which is often described as the first European novel.[234] Self-reflection stimulated questions of identity, fractured narratives and digressions in the garden as well as the novel, although the landscape designer emphasised classical mythologies alongside current events. Conveying new ideas and values, as well as the contemporary meaning of classical antiquity, the picturesque garden was both a novel and a romance, two genres that sometimes merged in eighteenth-century fiction.[235] Reinforcing its literary aspirations, the picturesque was conceived according to *ut pictura poesis* – as with painting, so also with poetry – a concept that originated in classical antiquity and acquired further resonance due to Locke's concern for the association of ideas. At Stowe, Kent designed a pyramidal monument to celebrate a regular visitor, Congreve, who was best known as a poet and playwright of human folly. On the edge of the lake, a monkey looks into a mirror, culminating the monument. The carved inscription attests that 'Comedy is the imitation of life and the mirror of society'.

Equally, the picturesque garden was equivalent to a history, formulating an interpretation of the past in the present through classical reconstructions, antique sculptures and Mediterranean trees. As ancient Rome was a model for Georgian Britain, classical forms were of contemporary relevance, and simultaneously ancient and modern, especially when seen in a newly picturesque setting. In Kent's Elysian Fields at Stowe, busts of Whig heroes such as the Black Prince, King Alfred and John Locke appear in the Temple of British Worthies, which is reminiscent of a semi-circular Roman shrine. But villains also featured in the Elysian Fields. As a counterpoint to the pristine Temple of Ancient Virtue, c.1736–1737, which was one of the first attempts to precisely recreate an ancient building in Britain, the Temple of Modern Virtue was built as a gothic ruin and housed a headless sculpture of Walpole, who Cobham opposed when he was a government minister, implying Britain's moral decline under the Prime Minister.

In drawing attention to the conditions that inform self-understanding to a greater extent than in the Renaissance and baroque, the eighteenth century fundamentally transformed the visual arts, its objects, authors and viewers. In Britain, the title of architect associated with *disegno* was in its infancy when another

233 Defoe, *Robinson Crusoe*, p. 87. Refer to Forty, 'Architectural Description: Fact or Fiction?', pp 197–198; Vidler, *The Writing of the Walls*, pp. 12–14.

234 Richietti, pp. 15–18; Savage, pp. 430, 436.

235 Black, 'Romance Redivivus', p. 247.

61

appeared alongside it, exemplifying a new type of design and a new way of designing that valued the ideas and emotions evoked through experience. This new design practice focused first on gardens not buildings because they were more clearly subject to time and the changing natural world. Although the pleasures and liberties of the picturesque were limited to the educated and prosperous, notable principles were established. Rather than refer to universal ideas, forms and proportions, design could draw forth ideas that were provisional, changeable and dependent on experience at conception, production and reception. Rather than follow an inflexible vision, the garden was designed in detailed response to site conditions, and creative adjustments were made during construction. Valuing the individuality of the designer and the occupant, the picturesque acknowledged that beauty is subjective and encouraged varied allegories and diverse interpretations. Rather than being conceived according to the rules of geometry in a distant studio, the garden was designed the way it was experienced, by a figure moving across a landscape and imagining future movements, while special attention was given to drawings that explored the relations between site and experience. Kent represented his garden designs – and often his garden buildings too – in perspectives, but he depicted his building designs in orthogonal drawings. In his letter to Pope Leo X, c.1519, Raphael associated the picture with the painter and the plan with the architect, confirming an opinion earlier expressed by Alberti.[236] However, the value given to experience in the eighteenth century made this distinction less convincing. Indebted to *ut pictura poesis* but surpassing it, the picturesque landscape was conceived as a spatial poem dependent on all the senses not just vision. Interdependent with literary developments, it was equivalent to a novel as well as a history.

In a significant design innovation, the picturesque gave new emphasis to an evolving environment, exploring human activity in dialogue with the natural world. Rather than a complete and timeless object, a garden building was understood as an incident in an environment with which it conversed, establishing an architectural environmentalism that profoundly influenced subsequent centuries. At first this new environmentalism was specific to the garden and park. But with romanticism it led to a much wider engagement with the natural world.

Ancient and modern, this new design practice combined a more intense passion for nature with a fascination for the gardens of classical antiquity. Like other advocates of the British Enlightenment, Coke's purpose was to translate and surpass Renaissance Italy and ancient Rome, referring both to sixteenth- and seventeenth-century gardens and the classical models that inspired them. Alongside the Holm Oak, he imported numerous exotic trees, plants and seeds that recalled

236 Raphael, p. 188; Alberti, p. 34. Refer to Carpo, pp. 17–19.

the luxuriant gardens and landscapes he had observed on the Grand Tour.[237] In 1727 he commissioned the kitchen gardens to the west of the proposed house.[238] High walls provided protection from the harsh sea winds. In the coldest months, 'firewalls' – air warmed in brickwork cavity walls – resisted the frost. The diversity of species was prodigious. Alongside a pineapple house there were six varieties of apricot, 10 of cherry, 12 of grape, five of fig, nine of nectarine, 24 of peach, 13 of pear, 21 of plum and dozens of apple varieties.[239] Cultivating exotic plants behind glass and brick, Coke aimed to transfer the Mediterranean to the North Sea and the Italian landscape to England.

Allusions to classical antiquity relied on garden descriptions rather than gardens themselves, of which there was little evidence. Coke's library contained three copies of Pliny the Younger's letter to his friend Gallus in the first century AD, in which he mentions frescoes, fountains, fruit trees, terraces and vistas, extolling the pleasures of a relaxed rural retreat. The term 'villa' is derived from the Latin for farm. But Pliny's account, like that of Virgil, is an urbanite's impression of the countryside, inspiring others to follow his model. One of his villas occupied a rolling site in the Tuscan Apennines while another was located on the coast near Rome:

> You wonder I am so much delighted with Laurentinum, or, if you had rather, Laurens, my Country-Seat: But you will cease to do so, when you are acquainted with the Beauty of the Villa, the Conveniency of the Place, and the Spaciousness of the Coast . . . The Country on both Sides affords a great Variety of Views; in some Places the Prospect is confin'd by Woods, in others it is extended over large and Spacious Meadows . . . The Shore is adorn'd with a grateful Variety . . . Which sometimes is soften'd by a long Calm, but is more often harden'd by the contending Waves.[240]

Funded by Burlington, Pliny's gardens received renewed attention with the publication of *The Villas of the Ancients Illustrated*, 1728, in which Robert Castell provided an English translation alongside Pliny's original Latin account. Castell's commentary identifies a formal garden, a natural garden, and one that combines the two:

> whose Beauty consisted in a close Imitation of Nature; where, tho' the parts are disposed with the greatest Art, the Irregularity is still preserved; so that their Manner may not improperly be said to be an artful Confusion, where there is no Appearance of that Skill which is made use of, their Rocks, Cascades, and Trees, bearing their natural Forms.[241]

[237] Klausmeier, pp. 72–75.

[238] Adding a serpentine twist to the southern end of the lake, Thomas William Coke demolished Thomas Coke's walled kitchen gardens in the 1770s, and built new ones further to the west.

[239] Klausmeier, pp. 72–75; Soissons, p. 33.

[240] Pliny, 'Letter to Gallus', translated in Castell, pp. 1–15.

[241] Castell, p. 116–117.

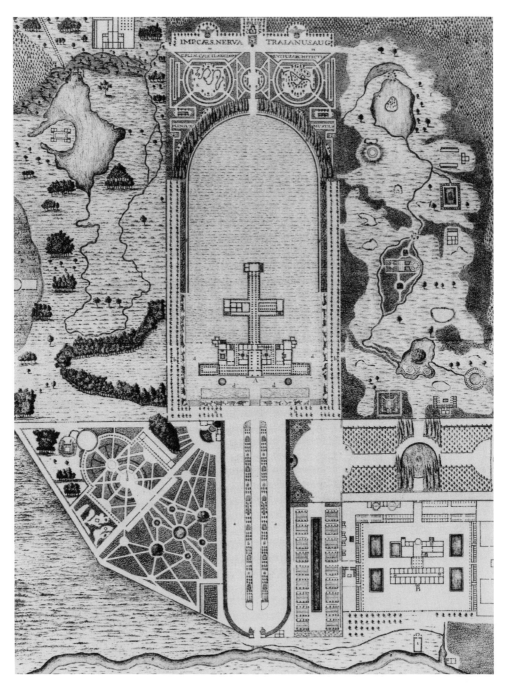

Robert Castell, *The Villas of the Ancients Illustrated*, 1728. Reconstructed plan of the gardens and buildings at Pliny the Younger's Tuscan villa. Courtesy of the British Library.

Supporting Castell's interpretation, the accompanying plans give greater emphasis to 'wild' nature than was familiar in the Renaissance and suggest a classical precedent for the irregular garden.[242]

Early eighteenth-century north Norfolk was not reminiscent of the Tuscan hills but it was comparable to the setting of Pliny's other villa. Coke must have recognised that Holkham's coastal site would allow his magnificent collection and civilising command of nature to be seen against the contrasting natural drama of the turbulent seas and vast skies. In 1721, Coke's cousin, Michael Newton, remarked that Holkham 'is as beautiful as other places, it stands in a very clear Air, & no Fenns within Twenty miles of it . . . Mr Coke likes this place so well now that I believe if ever he builds it will be here'.[243] Newton's words recall Hippocrates' attention to air quality, Virgil's designation of his coastal villa under 'Health', and Evelyn's advice that a city resident would be 'restored to their former habit; so soon as they are retired to their Homes and they enjoy fresh *Aer* again'.[244] Equally, they herald the new engagement with the natural world that Shaftesbury inspired, which led to a fascination for uncultivated nature and an appreciation of the North Sea on its own terms, not just as a surrogate Mediterranean.

The influence of climate on character had been professed since classical antiquity, which concluded that beyond the temperate Greco-Roman world lay sequential zones that were either occupied by people of dubious character or largely unfit for inhabitation. Recognising the value of his Italian experience to his English reputation, Kent scattered Italian terms and phrases throughout his letters and was happily known as 'Signor', 'Giuglielmo', 'Kentino'. In January 1720, barely a month after returning to England, he complained that his 'Italian constitution' could not endure the winter weather of 'this Gothick country'.[245] But his remark was partly in jest, given his enthusiasm for gothic and its association with English history, the north not the south, and nature more than culture. Teasingly, Pope called the Yorkshireman a 'wild goth'.[246]

Kent's enthusiasm for gothic was expressed in his long-held admiration for Edmund Spenser's *The Faerie Queene*, 1595, an Elizabethan poem that recalled the epic narratives of classical antiquity but featured chivalrous medieval knights rather than ancient Greek heroes. Most likely introduced to the poem by Pope, Kent reportedly acquired 'his taste in Gardening from reading the picturesque descriptions of Spenser'.[247] Depicting scenes from *The Faerie Queene*, Francesco Sleter's murals decorated the interiors of two of Kent's pavilions at Stowe – the Temple of Venus and the Hermitage – and Kent's 32 illustrations for a new edition of Spenser's poem also emphasised his fascination for the gothic alongside the classical.[248]

242 Coke did not acquire Castell's book but the Holkham library includes at least two printed versions and one manuscript of Pliny's letter Castell, pp. 116–117. Refer to Giles Worsley, 'Taking the Ancients Literally: Archaeological Neoclassicism in Mid Eighteenth-Century Britain', 1988, unpublished conference paper, quoted to Ayres, *Classical Culture*, p. 126.

243 Sir John Newton offered the opposite opinion, concluding that the coastal site was unhealthy. Michael Newton, quoted in Schmidt, 'Inventing Holkham', pp. 88–89; refer to Soissons, p. 25. Sir John Newton, quoted in Garry, p. 16, refer to p. 128.

244 Evelyn, *Fumifugium*, p. 24.

245 Kent, 30 January 1720, quoted in Hunt, *William Kent*, p. 51.

246 Pope, quoted in Batey, p. 103.

247 William Mason, *The English Garden*, 1811, quoted in Batey, p. 103.

248 Thomas Birch's 1751 edition of Spenser's poem was published three years after Kent's death.

William Kent, *Redcross Knight & Una invited by Subtle Archimago to his Cell*, illustration for Edmund Spenser, *The Faerie Queene,* 1751 edition. Kent's design for a hermitage is seen to the left. Courtesy of the Victoria and Albert Museum, London.

William Kent, *The Temple of the Mill and the Triumphal Arch beyond the Gardens, Rousham,* 1737–1741. Courtesy of C. Cottrell-Dormer.

249 Coffin also mentions the gothic profile of the Triumphal Arch on a distant ridge. His thesis is feasible only if the major section of the garden is considered, as well as fields to the north, and the rest is ignored. Kent gave the house a gothic profile, which is to the south, as is the Gothic Seat. Coffin, 'The Elysian Fields of Rousham', p. 419.

Analysing the Temple of the Mill in the fields beyond Rousham and the Pyramid Building and Praeneste Terrace within the garden, David Coffin suggests that 'The architecture of these garden buildings seems to be determined by their geographical orientation: Gothic toward the north, Egyptian at the east, and ancient Roman at the south.'[249] Pope developed a similar theme in his allegorical poem *The Temple of Fame*, 1715, in which he associated the orientation of façades with different geographical regions.

At Holkham the ancient Roman grandeur of the Triumphal Arch is to the south but faced in local flint, while the pyramids on its side wings referred to ancient Egypt. To the north is another Egyptian structure, the Obelisk, and to its west is the Temple, which was identified with Palladio's Veneto.[250] To the north of Obelisk Wood, the Seat on the Mount resembled the Praeneste Terrace, which was named after an ancient Roman town. Kent is identified with the second Palladian revival in England, just as Jones is associated with the first. Like the Temple, his design for the Hall is indebted to Palladio. But Rome was as significant an influence. Inspired by Raphael and Guilio Romano, he conceived the wall as a three-dimensional sculpted surface and contrasted finely chiselled and roughly hewn stone to emphasise the dialogue between artifice and nature, as in the refined pediment and raw flint of the Triumphal Arch.[251] However, Coke's commitment to Palladio restrained Kent's debt to contemporary Rome and denied the Gothic, ensuring that no stylistic, geographical pattern is evident in the garden structures despite the estate's north-south orientation.[252]

Kent and Coke conceived according to the *genius loci*, a principle that originated in classical antiquity. At Holkham, the genius of the place was made as much as found, the fusion of new ideas, forms and spaces with those already in place, which were sometimes the results of earlier migrations. The hybridisation of historical and geographical references was characteristic of the picturesque. For an early-eighteenth century architect or patron, classical buildings in an Arcadian setting would have conjured associations with the architecture and landscape of ancient Rome and Renaissance Italy, translated and improved for a new environment. But for many visitors an estate that now seems quintessentially English would also have seemed shockingly new.

Given Coke's education on the Grand Tour, it is likely that a new estate was in his imagination long before he returned to England. Influencing the garden and the house, he accumulated paintings, sculptures and antiquities in two principal phases; first, in his youth in Italy and then around 30 years later when Holkham Hall was under construction. Kent's design incorporates a central building with a substantial 'pavilion' at each of its four corners.[253] The first part of the Hall to be occupied was the southwest pavilion in 1740 – the Family Wing – which includes 'a fine library' that Coke described as 'certainly one of the greatest ornaments to a Gentleman or his family'.[254] Only in the 1720s was a library first included among the principal rooms of a country house and Kent's design for Houghton is the earliest surviving example in England.[255] While Walpole's Library was a private

[250] Coke, letter to Matthew Brettingham Sr, 1734, quoted in Hiskey, p. 148; Hassall, 'The Temple at Holkham, Norfolk', p. 1310; Lees-Milne, p. 246.

[251] Sicca, pp. 134, 146.

[252] Coke, letter to Matthew Brettingham Sr, 1734, quoted in Hiskey, p. 147.

[253] Salmon, pp. 63–96.

[254] Coke, quoted in Mortlock, p. 36.

[255] Cornforth, *Early Georgian Interiors*, p. 68–70.

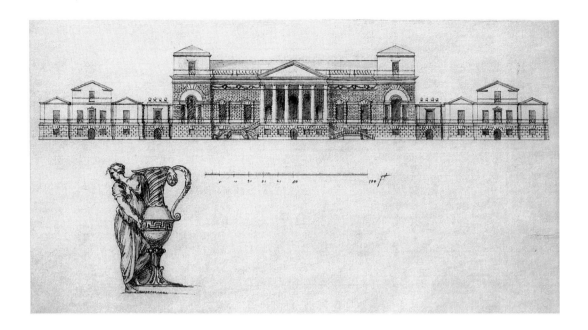

William Kent, *Design for South Front, Holkham Hall*, c.1731–1734. Courtesy of Viscount Coke and the Trustees of the Holkham Estate.

study, Coke's Library was the focus of family life.[256] In addition to commissioning a volume on Houghton, Walpole subscribed to several of the best-known architectural books of the time, as did Coke.

The history of the architectural book is interdependent with that of the architect, and has been crucial to the architect's status since the Renaissance. In the new division of labour, architects acquired complementary means to practice architecture – drawing and writing – that were as important as building, creating an interdependent and multi-directional web of influences that together stimulated architects' creative development. To affirm their newly acquired status, architects began increasingly to theorise architecture both for themselves and for their patrons, ensuring that the authored book became more valuable to architects than to painters and sculptors, whose status as liberal artists was more secure and means to acquire commissions less demanding. In contrast to the architectural drawing, which is seen in relation to other drawings and a building, the painting and sculpture are unique and need not refer to an external object, thus appearing further removed from the material world and closer to that of ideas. The purpose of the architectural drawing is complex because it depends on two related but distinct concepts, which both depend on the architect's ability to precisely conceive and represent a building. One indicates that drawing is an intellectual, artistic activity distant from the grubby materiality of construction. The other emphasises

256 Edwards, Moore and Archer, p. 97; Plumb, *Sir Robert Walpole: The Making of a Statesman*, p. 82.

drawing's essential role in the architect's mastery of the complex and collaborative building process. Creativity as well as confusion has arisen from this contradiction.

In the early fifteenth century, searching through the monastic library at St. Gallen for Latin manuscripts that would support his humanist beliefs, the Florentine scholar Poggio Bracciolini came upon a manuscript copy of Vitruvius' treatise *De architectura libri decem*. The discovery of the only architectural text to survive from classical antiquity was to be hugely influential. Modelled on Vitruvius' example, Alberti's *De re aedificatoria* (Ten Books on Architecture) was the first thorough investigation of the Renaissance architect as artist and intellectual. Alberti's concern that manuscript copies of his text were completely accurate mirrored his demand that a design was completed according to 'the author's original intentions'.[257] Written in around 1450, *De re aedificatoria* was first published in 1485, over a decade after Alberti's death.

Francesco Colonna's *Hypnerotomachia Poliphili,* 1499, was the second architectural book by a Renaissance author and the first to be printed with illustrations,

257 Alberti, p. 309. Refer to Carpo, pp. 20–26.

fine di quella floribonda copertura peruenì,&riguardando una innume rofa turba di iuuentude promifcua celebremente feftigiante mi apparue, Cum fonore uoce,&cum melodie di uarii foni,Cum uenufti & ludibon di tripudii & plaufi,Et cum molta &iocundiffima lætitia, In una amplif fima planitie agminatamente folatiantife. Dique per quefta tale & grata nouitate in uafo fopra fedendo admiratiuo,di piu oltra procedere,tra pen fofo io fteti.

Et ecco una come infigne & feftiua Nympha dindi cum la fua arden¬

Francesco Colonna, *Hypnerotomachia Poliphili,* 1499. Engraving, study for a garden. Courtesy of the British Library.

258 The first part of Colonna's title – *Hypnerotomachia* – derives from three Greek words, *hypnos*, *eros* and *mache*, which respectively mean sleep, love and strife, so that they roughly translate as the 'strife of love in a dream'. The second part – *Poliphili* – refers to the principal character, Poliphilo, who has a restless night after being rejected by his love, Polia.

259 Colonna, p. 24.

260 Palladio, pp. 1–10. For an alternative categorisation of architectural books, refer to Forty, 'Architectural Description: Fact or Fiction?', pp. 200–201.

261 Mortlock, pp. 8, 60.

262 It first appeared in installments between 1716 and 1720 in a dual English and French edition, with Nicholas Dubois providing the French translation.

263 Brindle, p. 109, n. 145.

establishing the multimedia interdependence of text and image that has been essential to architectural books ever since.[258] One model for the architectural book, *Hypnerotomachia Poliphili* is a fictional narrative illustrated with pictorial drawings, in which love is lost and won in a sylvan landscape among monuments and ruins that are themselves erotic, not just locations for lust and desire. Although Colonna's tale is a romance, it has been an enduring influence on novelistic architectural books. Some of Colonna's designs may have been invented while others were taken from ancient and Renaissance sites in Italy, Greece and Asia Minor. The most impressive structures are composites. The largest consists of varied forms mounted one on top of the other: a plinth, a pyramid, a stone cube, an obelisk and, finally, a winged statue 'revolving easily at every breath of wind, making such a noise, from the friction of the hollow metal device, as was never heard from the Roman treasury'.[259]

A second model is the analytical manifesto justified through principles and examples and illustrated with orthogonal drawings, such as Palladio's *I quattro libri dell'architettura* (The Four Books of Architecture), 1570. The relationship between history and design was central to Colonna and Palladio, although they did not aim to be rigorous and objective in the manner of later historians. Historical references appear in both books but for different purposes. In one they enrich a specific story, in the other they legitimise generic solutions. A further literary model, the manual conveys practical knowledge and is illustrated with diagrams and calculations. But these models are not hermetic and many architectural books refer to more than one, as is the case with Palladio's attention to practical matters.[260]

Featuring revered ancient buildings and his own designs, *The Four Books* was the principal reason for Palladio's extensive influence on English architecture in the seventeenth and eighteenth centuries. Coke's library contained a first edition that may have been acquired by his ancestor Sir Edward Coke, who had an extensive library praised by Evelyn, and Coke added two further early editions.[261] The first complete English translation appeared in 1721 when a Venetian architect, Giacomo (James) Leoni replaced the original woodcut illustrations with his own versions engraved in copper.[262] Dismissive of Leoni's publication, Burlington commissioned his own translation by Isaac Ware, which was published in 1738 with more precise copper engravings of the original woodcuts.

Kent owned copies of Vitruvius' text in Latin and in Italian, and acquired Palladio's *Four Books* in Italian as well as Ware's English translation, to which he had contributed additional illustrations. Kent also owned several copies of *Hypnerotomachia Poliphili*.[263] Although Colonna and Palladio influenced his designs, Kent adopted Palladio as his principal literary model. Rather than

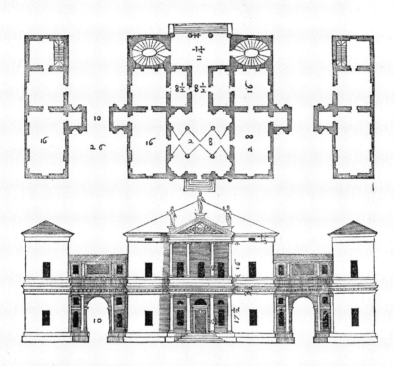

LA FABRICA

Andrea Palladio, *I quattro libri dell' archittetura, Venice,* 1570, bk. II, p. 52. Plan and elevation of Villa Pisani, Montagnana. Courtesy of the RIBA Library Photographs Collection.

directly refer to the Venetian architect, Kent published *The Designs of Inigo Jones, Consisting of Plans and Elevations for Publick and Private Buildings*, 1727, and his assistant, John Vardy, gathered together *Some Designs of Mr. Inigo Jones and Mr. William Kent,* 1744. However, the scope and ambition of each book is much less than Palladio's treatise in that they only focus on contemporary designs and have a minimal text.

Since the Italian Renaissance, it is evident that researching, testing and transforming the limits of architecture have occurred through drawing and writing as well as building. Consequently, influential architects tend to draw, write and publish as well as build. Palladio and Kent are notable early exponents of this tradition. The relations between the drawing, text and building are multi-directional. For example, drawing may lead to building, writing may lead to drawing, or building may lead to writing and drawing. If everyone reading this book listed all the architectural works that influence them, some would be drawings, some would be texts, and others would be buildings either visited or described in drawings and texts.

The Four Books' influence on British architecture exemplifies these complex interdependent relations. Classical antiquity associated the immaterial with timeless order and the material with temporal decay. Emphasising the immaterial idea of architecture not the material fabric of building, *disegno* restricted the architectural imagination to the universal geometries of ideal forms. But in built architecture, the relations between the immaterial and the material were sometimes considered with great subtlety. In most cases modestly scaled working farms, Palladio's villas recall the rural life evoked in classical antiquity by Virgil and Pliny, while their elegant but inexact proportions refer to the immaterial and its uncertain presence in the material world. Emphasising this distinction, the buildings drawn in *The Four Books* are each an ideal, not those actually built, while Palladio also included advice on construction, climate and the means to combine domestic and agricultural programmes in one composition.[264] Palladio's conjunction of rational humanism, agrarian purpose and pastoral idyll appealed to British architects and patrons, and his attention to climate was transferred to a northern setting. Windows were larger than in Palladio's model, reflecting the need for light rather than shade, while fireplaces were placed on internal walls, retaining heat with a house. But other subtle distinctions were ignored as few British architects and patrons visited the rural villas, which were less accessible than the urban centres of Venice and Vicenza. Often, the designs studied were not the buildings themselves but those illustrated in *The Four Books*, which were combined and expanded to suit the grandiose ambitions of British landowners. The Holkham

264 Palladio, pp. 46–53.

THE

DESIGNS

OF

INIGO JONES,

Confifting of

PLANS and ELEVATIONS

FOR

Publick and *Private* Buildings.

Publifh'd by WILLIAM KENT,
With fome Additional Defigns.

The FIRST VOLUME.

M. DCC. XXVII.

Andrea Palladio, Villa Emo,
Fanzolo di Vedelago, 1565.
Photograph, Jonathan Hill.

estate accommodated modestly scaled buildings among its gardens, forests and fields, but none combined domestic and agricultural activities. Less sensitive still, the isolated and expansive Hall is too large for the setting, with each of its pavilions the size of one of Palladio's villas.

Kent was the major design influence on Holkham's staterooms although he died before they were completed in the 1750s. The Statue Gallery displays ancient Roman sculptures from the first and third centuries AD. Political sym-

William Kent, The Statue
Gallery, Holkham Hall.
Courtesy of the Collection
of the Earl of Leicester,
Holkham Hall, Norfolk/
Bridgeman Images.

bolism was not one of Coke's principal concerns, unlike Walpole's display of
Roman emperors at Houghton. However, representations of nature appear in both
houses. Referring to nature tamed and cultivated, the Gallery's northern apse
includes Ceres, the goddess of the harvest, and Minerva, the discoverer of olives
and their oil. The southern apse includes two fauns and refers to nature wild
and uncultivated.[265] Along the east wall, the figures include Diana, goddess of
the hunt, Faunus, god of the forest, and Neptune, god of the sea, closest to
the southern apse. The distinction between tamed and untamed nature is evident in the house as well as the estate.[266] But the location of the figures in the
Gallery does not match the orientation of the site unless the room's purpose
was either to emphasise the fabricated wilderness to the south, Obelisk Wood,
not the actual wilderness to the north, the North Sea, or to reflect the site as
in a mirror.

The orientation of another stateroom is particularly intriguing. The Landscape
Room faces south, seemingly associating its contents with the Mediterranean.
Displaying primarily seventeenth-century artists who influenced the early
eighteenth-century English garden, the 22 paintings include seven by Claude
Lorrain, who spent much of his career in Italy, and one by Salvator Rosa. In
the seventeenth century, historical, literary and biblical themes were held in the

265 Hardy, 'The Interiors', p. 169.

266 Hardy, 'The Interiors', p. 169.

William Kent, The
Landscape Room, Holkham
Hall. Courtesy of the
Collection of the Earl of
Leicester, Holkham Hall,
Norfolk/Bridgeman Images.

highest esteem and nature was most often presented as a setting for mythological and human figures. Composed into fore-, middle- and background, Claude's
paintings present a pastoral Arcadia of classical temples, rolling landscapes and
relaxed rural life. Rosa depicted a wilder, more dramatic landscape that fuelled
the growing concern for the natural sublime. Set in gold frames, the paintings
were hung on the north, east and west walls. Left free of pictures, the south wall
contained the only window, which framed Holkham's principal contribution to the

Claude Lorrain, *Classical River Scene with a View of a Town*. Courtesy of the Collection of the Earl of Leicester, Holkham Hall, Norfolk/Bridgeman Images.

Salvator Rosa, *A Rocky Landscape*, c.1640. Courtesy of the Collection of the Earl of Leicester, Holkham Hall, Norfolk/ Photograph, Mark Fiennes/ Bridgeman Images.

Arcadian landscape tradition as if it too was a painting: *The South Lawn*. A golden light illuminated the scene; a burnisher was permanently employed to maintain the gilding on the glazing bars of the Hall's sash windows.[267]

Coke created the 'picture' before the 'frame'. In 1724 work began on the rising slope from the site of the new house up to Obelisk Wood. Three years later, two formal tree lines were planted to the east and west, framing the slope. At the base of the rising ground, a geometric basin was completed in 1734 and two small pavilions – the 'porches' – were constructed at its southern edge by 1736, each terminating a tree line. In the second half of that decade Kent began to influence the design of the garden as well as its buildings.[268] The basin became irregular and the area around it was transformed as in Kent's drawing, c.1739. An artificial hillock at the western end of the basin, the New Mount, was created in 1742, flanked by a casually planted wood. The Seat on the Mount was completed in the following year. Scheemaker's sculptured figures adorned its four pilasters, each representing a season.[269] Beneath a pediment, an arched opening led to a small room, which faced the morning sun and had two small side windows to the north and south. The basin was connected to the lake by a meandering river, over which crossed a stone bridge and the main route to the house. Indicating that the view from the Hall was secondary to direct experience, the sloping trees and billowing clouds reflect the

267 Lees-Milne, p. 252.

268 Hassall, 'Views from the Holkham Windows', p. 310; Williamson, *The Archaeology of the Landscape Park*, p. 66.

269 Brettingham, *The Plans, Elevations and Sections of Holkham in Norfolk*, 1773, p. 7.

prevailing wind, a lady fishes in a boat as a pony and trap passes by, a dog watches as a couple chat and wild animals scamper around in the background of Kent's drawing. When Friedrich Carl von Hardenberg, the Hanoverian court director of buildings and gardens, visited Holkham in 1744, Coke remarked that the gardens were 'all by Kent'.[270] Sadly, little of them now remain. Contemporaneous with Rousham and also arranged along sloping ground, the South Lawn, irregular basin and Seat on the Mount would have been somewhat reminiscent of the luxuriant delights of General Dormer's garden, which Coke visited in 1741 as it was nearing completion.[271]

A window can be like a painting and a painting can be like a window. Claude's *Queen Esther Approaching the Palace of Ahasuerus*, c.1658, occupies the centre of the Landscape Room's north wall because 'it corresponds to the view through the window' opposite, suggests John Hardy.[272] If correct, this analysis supports the assumption that the disposition of figures in the Statue Gallery is a mirror image of the site. The Landscape Room includes coastal paintings alongside country scenes, drawing associations with the north as well as the south. The depicted coastlines tend to be rocky rather than sandy but the reference to the North Sea is implicit in their selection and arrangement. In 1773 Matthew Brettingham

270 Coke, quoted in Schmidt, Keller and Feversham, 'Building Holkham', p. 110.

271 Garry, p. 164.

272 Landscape is the focus of the painting as the section depicting the palace was destroyed in a fire at Fonthill, Wiltshire, in around 1755. Hardy, 'The Interiors', p. 154.

William Kent, *Seat on the Mount with Irregular Basin, Holkham*, c.1739. Courtesy of Viscount Coke and the Trustees of the Holkham Estate.

273 The painting is sometimes called *Coast View with Perseus and the Origin of Coral*. Brettingham, *The Plans, Elevations and Sections of Holkham in Norfolk*, 1773, p. 7; Hardy, 'The Interiors', p. 155.

274 The painter is Claude-Joseph Vernet. England's ties to the Netherlands reinforced this message. Late seventeenth-century Dutch marine paintings were some of the earliest to depict storm-battered ships at sea, influencing English painters. Alpers, pp. 100–102, 109; Schama, pp. 38, 47–49.

275 Coke, quoted in Porter, *English Society in the Eighteenth Century*, p. 60.

Jr acknowledged the 'romantic Air' depicted in Claude's *The Origin of Coral or Perseus with the Head of Medusa*, 1674, while Hardy concludes that the room is arranged so that the paintings higher up the walls move 'landscape painting into a more romantic domain' in which ruins and seas predominate.[273] One painting depicts a shipwreck, which is a type of ruin, indicating the turbulent sea is the author of ruination here.[274]

Whether found or fabricated, ruined buildings were a feature of many eighteenth-century estates. For example, Stowe's Temple of Modern Virtue was intended as a cutting political statement while Rousham's Temple of the Mill was based on an earlier building, which Kent's additions gave the impression of a partially ruined medieval church. Completed in 1731, Kent's Richmond Hermitage was faced in roughly hewn stone and had a ruined pediment and just one turret. A contemporary observer described it as 'a heap of stones thrown into a very artful disorder, and curiously embellished with moss and shrubs' (quoted in Hunt, 'Landscape Architecture', p. 374). No such ruins were built at Holkham but to transform his estate Coke demolished the earlier manor house, farms and village. The Hall is the ruin of the manor. The dammed lake is the ruin of the river. The seventeenth-century icehouse and St Withburga's church – the only surviving buildings – are the ruin of the village. While Coke gained a magnificent coastal estate, he lost people as well as places: 'It is a melancholy thing to stand alone in one's own country', he remarked. 'I look around, not a house to be seen but for my own. I am Giant, of Giant's Castle, and have ate up all my neighbours.'[275]

Claude Lorrain, *The Origin of Coral or Perseus with the Head of Medusa*, 1674. Courtesy of the Collection of the Earl of Leicester, Holkham Hall, Norfolk/ Bridgeman Images.

The concern for ruination was known in ancient Rome and furthered in the Renaissance in terms of the humanist conception of cyclical historical development in which art matures, ages and dies like a human body. In his letter to Pope Leo X, Raphael argued that 'by preserving the example of the ancients, may your Holiness seek to equal and better them'.[276] Ruins were a regular feature of the English landscape because, beginning in 1536, the Dissolution of the Monasteries had disbanded religious houses and transferred their assets to the monarch, which led to the destruction of many abbeys, including one of the most revered pilgrimage sites, Walsingham, close to Holkham. At the end of the sixteenth century, English 'painters began to introduce ruins into the backgrounds of their society portraits. They were metaphors of the inevitability of the subject's death', remarks Christopher Woodward.[277]

But the ruin meant more in the eighteenth century than in the sixteenth century. The concern for ruination came to fruition due to empiricism's detailed observation of life and death in plants and creatures, the attention to subjective experience and fractured identity in an increasingly secular society, the heightened historical awareness in the Enlightenment's concern for origins and archaeology, and the value given to nature, time and the imagination in the picturesque and romanticism.

In 1709, anticipating picturesque theory later in the century, Vanbrugh argued unsuccessfully that the medieval remains of 'ancient Woodstock' manor should be retained for their historical association and visual effect when seen from Blenheim Palace, then being constructed for John Churchill, first Duke of Marlborough.[278] Together, the ruins and their setting 'wou'd make One of the Most Agreeable Objects that the best of Landskip Painters can invent'.[279] Clearly unappreciative, the Duchess of Marlborough dismissed Vanbrugh's request as 'ridiculous'.[280]

Many of Kent's pyramidal buildings were based on illustrations in *Hypnerotomachia Poliphili*, which was an early stimulus to the fascination for ruins.[281] In Italy, he admired the collapsing columns in the frescoes at the Palazzo Te and met Giovanni Paolo Panini, who focused on ruins more than any painter before him. Panini had studied *quadratura* under Ferdinando Galli Bibiena, Troili's pupil and the author of *L'Architettura Civile* (Civil Architecture), 1711, learning to combine multiple oblique perspectives in a single composition.[282] The ruin and the multiple perspective came to dominate the picturesque because they both referred to temporal experience, the choices open to individuals and the effects of nature and chance upon art and life.

Archaeological investigations focused attention on the ruins of classical antiquity, adding further encouragement to a classical resurgence in opposition to the

[276] Raphael, p. 181.

[277] Woodward, *In Ruins*, p. 95.

[278] Vanbrugh, p. 231.

[279] Vanbrugh, p. 232.
[280] Sarah, Duchess of Marlborough, quoted in Vanbrugh, p. 232.

[281] An English translation of *Hypnerotomachia Poliphili* appeared as *The Strife of Love in a Dreame*, 1592, but its influence was limited due to a mediocre translation and poor image quality. Lefaivre, p. 23; Macaulay, pp. 15–16; Watkin, 'Built Ruins', p. 5.

[282] Cereghini, p. 320; Rykwert, p. 110.

baroque. Exposing what was once concealed within a structure to indicate its construction, ruination was a means to reveal temporal layers not simply destroy them. Antoine Desgodtez' *Les Édifices antiques de Rome, dessinés et mesurés trés exactement*, 1682, was one of the most influential early publications, providing some details for the interior at Holkham, notably in the Marble Hall.[283] Excavations began at Herculaneum in 1711 and at Pompeii in 1733. The Society of Dilettanti, which Coke joined in 1740, financed Robert Wood's visit to Syria that led to *The Ruins of Palmyra*, 1753. Represented respectively by Panini and Wood, the merits of two attitudes to ruins – poetic evocations and analytical depictions – were keenly debated but not mutually exclusive.

In the Renaissance, the effects of time, nature and weather on buildings were understood to be negative. In contrast, the picturesque adopted the ruin as its emblem – a hybrid of architecture and landscape, nature and culture – which was understood to represent growth as well as decay, potential as well as loss, the future as well as the past. Rather than a finite object, the ruin acknowledged the effects of time and place, emphasising its symbiotic relations with its ever-changing immediate and wider contexts, and celebrating the creative influence of natural as well as cultural forces. Rather than only associate the immaterial with timeless geometries, the eighteenth century increasingly conceived the immaterial as temporal and experiential, not only in the actual absence of matter, but also in the perceived absence of matter seen through mists and storms, establishing a dialogue between the immaterial and material that associated self-understanding with the experience of objects subject to nature and weather.

Depicting architecture in multiple states, whether occupied, ruined or under construction, eighteenth-century architects concluded that a monumental ruin exemplified the majesty and emotive power of architecture more eloquently even than a complete building because it not only indicated the destructive power of nature but also heroic resistance to decay. Though diminishing objects physically, ruination was understood to expand architecture's metaphorical potential: 'for imperfection and obscurity are their properties; and to carry the imagination to something greater than is seen, their effect', concluded Whately in 1770.[284]

Ruination is often a precursor to change. Relating the present to a particular past – imagined or real – the ruin can evoke a lost idyll that will never be repeated, transfer gravitas and authority from one era to another, or imply that the successes of the present will surpass those of the past. In revealing not only what is lost but also what is incomplete, the ruin can indicate that the present situation is not inevitable and imply an alternative future. Equally, conceiving a future ruin is a further means to imagine what is yet to come.

283 Lees-Milne, pp. 256–257; Ayres, *Classical Culture*, pp. 106–108.

284 Whately, p. 131. Refer to Benjamin, *The Origin of German Tragic Drama*, p. 178; Simmel, 'The Ruin', p. 259–266.

Eighteenth-century Britain became so associated with its landscape that the ruin provided a means to negotiate between culture and nature and was synonymous with the fluctuating fate of the nation, establishing an eloquent and meaningful tradition that continued in later centuries. Evoking life and death in a single object, the ruin of a building was linked to the ruin of a person or a place, as well as their potential for renewal. For an individual or an island nation, self-understanding was associated with the experience of landscape in all its forms: the air and the sea as well as the land.[285]

A journey from the Triumphal Arch to the North Sea, the Holkham estate is a dialogue between culture and nature, and between differing conceptions of nature. The Hall looks both ways, south to the Grand Tour and north to the North Sea. Its entrance portico surveys the park, marshes, dunes and sea, so that even when Coke travelled to London he looked north before turning south. Kent's drawing of the North Lawn, c.1740, is quite different to his design for the South Lawn. Emphasising the attention that Kent paid to the landscape and garden buildings, the Hall appears in none of his perspectives of the Holkham estate, except as a partial plan in this drawing. In the distance, the North Lodge continues the north-south axis but no avenue connects it to the Hall. Between the two buildings, tree clumps are loosely mirrored to each side of the central axis so as to exaggerate

[285] Baridon, pp. 93–94; Janowitz, p. 5.

William Kent, *North Lawn, Holkham,* c.1740. Courtesy of Viscount Coke and the Trustees of the Holkham Estate.

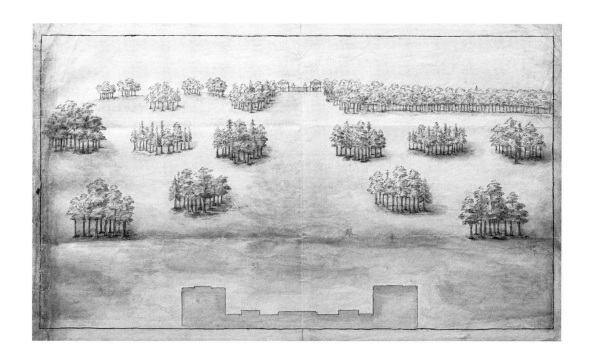

the perspective and suggest humanity's modification of nature in a less emphatic manner than elsewhere on the estate.

In gardens as well as novels, emblems were effective if their meanings were widely understood. In contrast to the emblematic garden of the South Lawn, the North Lawn can be understood as an expressive garden, which came to prominence in the second half of the eighteenth century when patrons were less concerned to display their learning due to the increased emphasis on subjective ideas and emotions. Rather than erudite analysis of the emblematic garden's numerous architectural and topographical incidents, the expressive garden's open and empty vistas were assumed to leave more space for the imagination, as Whately concluded in 1770:

> The power of such characters is not confined to the ideas which the objects immediately suggest; for these are connected with others, which insensibly lead to subjects, far distant perhaps from the original thought, and related to it only by a similitude in the sensations they excite.[286]

In practice, a simple opposition between garden types was not evident in the early and mid-eighteenth century. Holkham and Rousham are both emblematic and expressive.[287]

In Matthew Brettingham Jr, *The Plans, Elevations and Sections of Holkham in Norfolk*, 1761, the north and south elevations of the North Lodge's side pavilions each have an arched central window flanked by two smaller windows. Apart from the Temple, the North Lodge is the only garden building shown in section and Brettingham also includes a ceiling plan of the high dome in each pavilion. Even the much larger Triumphal Arch is not shown in section. In Kent's drawing it is windowless, while Brettingham shows very small windows to the north and south, which were built.[288] The Triumphal Arch was primarily conceived as an object in the landscape but the Temple and North Lodge were intended for short visits, which the careful furnishing of the Temple confirms.[289] The Temple faces the coast while the North Lodge offered a more immediate experience of the turbulent sea, implying that a deeper engagement with nature was developing within the English Georgic tradition, heralding a burgeoning romanticism.[290]

Just beyond the North Lodge, the coast road marked the transition from undulating hills to a flatter landscape. The creeks and inlets winding through the mud flats and salt marshes along the north Norfolk coast were perfect for smugglers, offering numerous alternative routes between the sea and the land. Smuggling was widespread and faced little deterrence because revenue officers were poorly paid

286 Whately, p. 154.

287 Hunt, *Gardens and the Picturesque*, p. 98; Hunt, 'Verbal Versus Visual Meanings in Garden History', p. 178.

288 Brettingham, *The Plans, Elevations and Sections of Holkham in Norfolk*, 1761, p. 27.

289 There is no such record for the North Lodge. Brettingham, *The Plans, Elevations and Sections of Holkham in Norfolk*, 1773, p. viii; James, p. 267.

290 Repton's Holkham 'Red Book', 1789, includes a proposal for 'a Room … reserved for a sea view', probably Kent's North Lodge. Repton, quoted in Williamson, 'The Development of Holkham Park', p. 68.

and few in number.[291] By the start of the eighteenth century, import smuggling had surpassed export smuggling and the volume was so significant that farm workers were hired to transport goods to and from the coast. Fulfilling his public duty and private desire without moral conflict, Walpole increased the punishment for smuggling but tried to evade the customs officers many times.[292] Involving a cargo of wine from the Netherlands, one smuggling enterprise early in his parliamentary career was even undertaken with Josiah Burchett, the Secretary of the Admiralty. He also frequently traded with Swanton, the smuggler from Wells, the port just to the east of Holkham. One supply of fine Dutch linen cost £25.[293]

The Holkham salt marshes were once tidal mud flats like those to the east, where few plants grow due to the unstable ground. Algae and eel grass provide winter food for ducks and geese, while other grasses and samphire appear on the higher mud flats. If sufficient roots begin to stabilise the mud, silt builds up among the plant cover, the ground level rises and the salt marsh gradually forms. Lower areas, which are more regularly flooded and less suitable for plant growth, are made deeper by the actions of the tides, creating the pattern of creeks that meander across the marshes.[294] Different plant types are zoned vertically according to the tides. Saltwater-tolerant plants such as Sea Meadow Grass and Sea Aster are at the lowest level. Sea Arrow Grass and Sea Lavender appear a little higher, while Red Fescue, Sea Pink and Sea Spurrey are higher still, all within a landscape that appears flat at first sight. Coke reclaimed 400 acres of salt marshes in around 1719, continuing the practice of his seventeenth-century ancestors. Among the reclaimed salt marshes, small saltwater lakes are the broken remains of once tidal creeks that previously led to the sea, encouraging plants that flourish in these conditions.[295]

Animals and birds inhabit specific habitats. Marine creatures in the sand and mud include the Acorn Barnacle, Bristle Worm, Sand Hopper and Shore Crab. Among the fish in the tidal pools are the Common Goby, Lesser Sand-eel and Stickleback. Seals are found along the coast. Rabbits are most common in the dunes and hares dominate the reclaimed marshes to the south. The coastline is well known for over 150 species of migratory birds, including numerous varieties of geese. Other creatures include the Common Lizard, Field Mouse, Natterjack Toad and Pigmy Shrew. Among the butterflies and other insects are the Common Blue, Meadow Brown, Painted Lady, Red Admiral, Cinnabar Moth, Ladybird and Yellow Meadow Ant.

Between the salt marshes and the sea, the sand dunes – the Holkham Meals – develop in stages.[296] First, winds, waves and tides encourage the formation of shingle banks offshore, where plants will not grow if they are regularly submerged.

291 Hipper, pp. 109, 132.

292 Plumb, *Sir Robert Walpole: The Making of a Statesman*, pp. 121, 237–238.

293 Wells-on-Sea was renamed Wells-next-the-Sea in the early nineteenth century. Plumb, *Sir Robert Walpole: The Making of a Statesman*, p. 121.

294 *Holkham National Nature Reserve*, unpaginated.

295 *Holkham National Nature Reserve*, unpaginated.

296 *Holkham National Nature Reserve*, unpaginated; Soissons, p. 60; Wade Martins, *A Great Estate at Work*, p. 83.

But once the banks rise above normal tides, plants that can survive occasional flooding – such as Sea Rocket, Sea Sandwort, Saltwort and Sand Couch Grass – establish dense roots within the shingle, drawing moisture from the dew and nutrients from the sea. As the plants collect wind-blown sand, the dunes start to form and stabilise. Less resistant to seawater, Marram Grass dominates the highest of the young dunes. Other plants that appear at this stage include Common Ragwort, Creeping Thistle, Red Fescue, Hound's Tongue, Rose-bay Willow Herb, Sea Bindweed and Sea Lyme Grass. Later still, plant diversity increases and shrubs – such as Brambles, Dog Rose, Elder, Hawthorn, Sea Buckthorn, Spindle and Wild Privet – appear alongside flowers and grasses.

The seas and winds have the potential to expand as well as disperse the dunes, which are subject to both steady change and violent alteration. Waves from the northeast have the greatest effect because the open sea allows a considerable swell to accumulate, and the incoming tide travels quickly over the beach. The Meals are broken only at Holkham Gap, which the sea fills during spring and storm tides.[297] Depicting a tidal channel leading from Holkham Staithe – a Norse term for wharf – to Wells, eighteenth-century maps indicate that the sea and dunes were moving inland in Coke's lifetime. Maybe he did not need ruined buildings on his estate because the ruinous threat of the sea was so close. Barely a mile from the North Lodge, the North Sea represented not nature tamed but the raw threat of the sublime.

Written in the first century AD, Dionysius Longinus' *Peri Hupsos* (*On the Sublime*) refers to oratory. Sublime nature did not receive extensive praise until the late seventeenth and early eighteenth centuries.[298] To reach Italy many Grand Tourists experienced both a sea voyage and a journey through the Alps. In addition to Rosa's paintings, early evocations of sublime nature include Thomas Burnet's *Telluris Theoria Sacra* (The Sacred Theory of the Earth), 1681–1689; John Dennis' account of his 1688 journey across the Alps, published in *Miscellanies in Verse and Prose*, 1693; Defoe's *An Historical Narrative of the Great and Tremendous Storm Which Happened on Nov. 26th, 1703*, 1704; and Addison's 'The Pleasures of the Imagination', 1712, all of which were in Coke's library.

The Great Storm caused havoc on land and at sea, sinking hundreds of vessels and killing thousands of people. But amidst the devastation, Defoe ascribes its 'wonderful effects' to divine intervention and acknowledges 'that pleasure may be mixed with terror, and astonishment!'[299] Just 15 years after his account of the Great Storm, Defoe tied Crusoe's fate to the sea, emphasising its overriding importance in the psyche of an island nation engaged in trade across seas and oceans that cover seven-tenths of the Earth. In a similar vein, Addison remarked that

297 Reclaiming the marshes gradually caused silting and disconnected Holkham Staithe from the sea. Holkham Archives, quoted in Parker, p. 13; *Holkham National Nature Reserve*, unpaginated; Soissons, p. 19; Stirling, *Coke of Norfolk and his Friends*, vol. 1, p. 16; Steers, 'The Physical Features of Scolt Head Island and Blakeney Point', p. 14; Steers, 'Physiography and Evolution', p. 52; Wade Martins, *Coke of Norfolk*, pp. 93–94.

298 Nicolson, pp. 38–43.

299 Defoe, *An Historical Narrative of the Great and Tremendous Storm*, pp. 49–50. Refer to Wheeler, pp. 419–427.

of all the Objects that I have ever seen, there is none which affects my Imagination so much as the Sea or Ocean. I cannot see the Heavings of this prodigious Bulk of Waters, even in a Calm, without a pleasing Astonishment; but when it is worked up in a Tempest, so that the Horizon on every side is nothing but foaming Billows and floating Mountains, it is impossible to describe the agreeable Horror that rises from such a Prospect. [300]

Detailing the weather in 1703, the year of the Great Storm, the unpublished diary of an anonymous Oxford graduate was once owned by Henry Bland, Walpole's friend and the Rector at Great Bircham, near Houghton. [301] The 1703 diarist was interested in the natural causes of weather but was not reasonable, moderate and impersonal in the manner of contemporary medical diarists who aspired to establish connections between the weather and the transmission of disease, extending the Hippocratic tradition. [302] Instead, experiencing the weather and writing a weather diary were means of self-expression and self-understanding. The 1703 diarist profusely refers to himself and his relations with the weather, describing his diary as 'the grand history & picture of my own life'. [303] Rather than quantify the daily weather, he describes it poetically, emphasising its effects on his thoughts and moods. [304] Depending upon his state of mind, differing weathers encourage varied thoughts and perceptions, whether sublime, sexual, divine, heroic or melancholic. A lightning flash is 'so superlative & extraordinary enormous a fright I never was sensible of in all my life'. [305] Rain is 'spermatic irrigation'. [306] A heavily overcast October day is a 'temper of weather [that] exactly corresponds to my saturnine & quiet melancholy Genius'. [307] Misty August drizzle is 'a distillation of divine juice'. [308]

The 1703 diarist's description of the weather as an agent of spiritual transcendence paralleled Shaftesbury's conception of nature as a means to contemplate the divine. [309] But his effusive language was in contrast to the Earl's comparative restraint. The 1703 diarist's psychological and emotional engagement with the weather was romantic, as was his assumption that an individual can be immersed in nature and subject to its influence but also capable of a higher understanding and union. [310] Rather than a lone original, the 1703 weather diarist was just one indication of a developing romanticism.

The sublime was an established concept well before Edmund Burke's *Philosophical Enquiry into the Origin of our Ideas of the Sublime and Beautiful*, 1757, but his achievement was to compile a system that provided a coherent argument for the sublime. Undermining the classical tradition that prioritises harmonious, formal beauty, Burke equates the sublime with darkness, vastness and

300 Addison, in Addison and Steele, vol. 3, 20 September 2012, p. 489.

301 As was then common practice, Bland rarely attended Great Bircham and was committed to other more prestigious roles such as Headmaster of Eton. Jan Golinski suggests that the author may have been Thomas Appletree, a graduate of Balliol College living in Worcestershire. 1703 Weather Diary, Lancing College Archives, discussed in Golinski, 'Exquisite Atmography', pp. 149–171.

302 Many of these doctors were either educated under Herman Boerhaave at the University of Leiden or were influenced by the importance he attached to accurate records. James Jurin – Boerhaave's pupil and Secretary of the Royal Society – appealed for a uniform method of observation and measurement in the Society's journal, *Philosophical Transactions*, in 1723. Brimblecombe, 'Interest in Air Pollution Among the Early Fellows of the Royal Society', p. 125; Manley, pp. 300-307.

303 1703 Weather Diary, quoted in Golinski, 'Exquisite Atmography', p. 166.

304 Golinski, 'Exquisite Atmography', p. 155.

305 1703 Weather Diary, quoted in Golinski, 'Exquisite Atmography', p. 167.

306 1703 Weather Diary, quoted in Golinski, 'Exquisite Atmography', p. 168.

307 1703 Weather Diary, quoted in Golinski, 'Exquisite Atmography', p. 167.

308 1703 Weather Diary, quoted in Golinski, 'Exquisite Atmography', p. 167.

309 Golinski, 'Exquisite Atmography', p. 171; Shaftesbury, *Characteristicks*, vol. 2, p. 101.

310 Golinski, 'Exquisite Atmography', p. 151.

311 Burke, pp. 39–40, 72–73, 102–104, 144–147, 124. Refer to Perry, pp. 110–112.

312 Burke, p. 39–40.

313 Burke, p. 76.

314 Kant, part 1, pp. 94–117. Refer to Crowther, p. 52; Wiedmann, pp. 25–26.

315 Mortlock, p. 82.

316 Coke, 'An Account of a Meteor Seen near Holkam in Norfolk, Aug 1741', pp. 183–184.

317 Bacon, *Sylva Sylvarum*, pp. 107–110, 171–175, 187.

318 Newton, pp. 379–380. Refer to Jankovic, p. 28.

even deformity. While the beautiful is merely pleasant, the sublime is magnificent.[311] Its pleasure derives from initial terror and subsequent reassurance: 'When danger or pain presses too nearly, they are incapable of giving any delight, and are simply terrible; but at certain distances, and certain modifications, they may be, and they are delightful, as we everyday experience.'[312] Furthering the fascination for uncultivated nature, Burke identifies the sublime with desolate and expansive landscapes that are subject to the drama of natural forces. But he also attributes it to human constructions, stimulating artistic and architectural speculations on the sublime. He concludes: 'Designs that are vast only by their dimensions, are always the sign of a common and low imagination. No work of art can be great, but as it deceives; to be otherwise is the prerogative of nature only.'[313] In response to Burke's recognition of the imagination's sublime potential, Immanuel Kant concluded in *Critique of Judgement*, 1790, that humanity's ability to remain rational in the presence of terrifying phenomena is itself sublime.[314]

Soon after Kent depicted the North Lawn, Coke submitted 'An Account of a Meteor Seen near Holkam in Norfolk, Aug 1741' to *Philosophical Transactions*, the Royal Society's journal, which he avidly collected:[315]

> It passed through the Field where they were at Plough, tore up the Stubble in the ploughed Ground, and also the Grass besides the same, for Two Miles in Length, and Thirty Yards in Breadth . . . And, what is most remarkable, that every-where else but in this Place, the Weather was clear and fine, and no Sign of any Storm or Disturbance whatsoever.[316]

A Fellow of the Royal Society since 1735 and thus an advocate of scientific investigation, Coke echoed Bacon's assumption that extraordinary weather events could be even more revealing than everyday occurrences.[317] A falling meteor was a particularly valuable sighting because Aristotle's *Meteorologica* was still the acknowledged authority on atmospheric phenomena, referred to in the 1723 third edition of Newton's *Opticks* and only gradually questioned by the new science.[318] Given the many contemporary descriptions of the sublime, Coke's account was most likely a tale of wonder as well as reason, exemplifying a response to terrifying natural phenomena that Defoe and Addison had earlier described and Burke and Kant later theorised.

Empiricism's influence on Britain has been profound and enduring, establishing measured and modest behaviour as a model. But in drawing attention to the ambiguities of identity and limits of objectivity, its success could only be relative. Increasingly in the eighteenth century, the recognition that we make our own reality was exploited for its creative potential, contradicting Locke's grounded reasonableness of a mechanistic mind and Shaftesbury's defence of educated opinion. Individuality was lauded and affirmed while it was recognised to be uncertain. Undoubtedly this was part of its attraction. The elusive quarry stimulated the hunt, establishing principles that have influenced the arts ever since. On the one hand the value given to subjectivity focused attention on the viewer, on the other hand it celebrated the transformative power of the artist.

The end of the Enlightenment and beginning of romanticism are often associated with the violent aftermath of the French Revolution in 1789, which undermined faith in reason and reasonableness. But the limits of reason were debated throughout the eighteenth century. The industrial revolution in the second half of the eighteenth century is cited as a further catalyst for the romantic appreciation of nature. But the nation's citizens had experienced London's 'Hellish Cloud' at least 100 years earlier and wild landscapes were appreciated many years before the focus of production shifted from agriculture to industry.

Rather than distinct and sequential, the Enlightenment and romanticism were evolving and interdependent philosophical traditions present throughout the eighteenth century and evident in the landscape garden. This was especially the case at Holkham because, alongside the influence of the Grand Tour and empiricism, Coke chose a turbulent coastal setting and commissioned a landscape before a house. The Enlightenment and romanticism both conceived the world as a dynamic whole, praised nature and primitive origins, cherished a mythical past, denied immutable standards, questioned the authority of the classical canon, and promoted personal liberty and the potential of the imagination. But they favoured a different land, sea and air. One reasoned with nature and remained detached, staring south towards the placid Mediterranean and its piercing light. The other did not discard reason but eulogised nature as the means of spiritual self-revelation, travelling north into the stormy sea and overcast sky. As Charles Baudelaire concluded: 'Romanticism is a child of the North . . . dreams and fairy tales are children of the mist.'[319]

319 Baudelaire, 'What is Romanticism?', p. 53.

2

architecture in ruins

J.M.W. Turner, *Snow Storm – Steam-Boat off a Harbour's Mouth Making Signals in Shallow Water, and Going by the Lead. The Author Was in this Storm on the Night the Ariel Left Harwich*, 1842. Courtesy of the Tate, London.

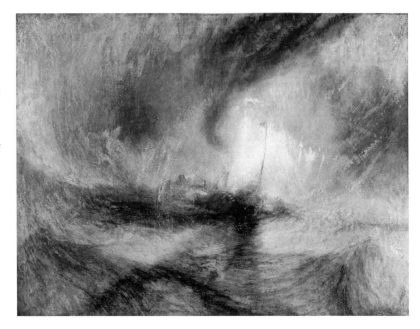

I did not paint it to be understood, but I wished to show what such a scene was like: I got the sailors to lash me to the mast to observe it; I was lashed for four hours, and I did not expect to escape, but I felt bound to record it if I did. But no one has any business to like the picture.[1]

1 Turner, in a conversation recorded by the Rev. William Kingsley, published in Ruskin, *Modern Painters*, vol. 5, p. 445. Refer to Brown, *Romanticism*, p. 21.

A hundred years after Coke observed a meteor at Holkham, Britain's most famous romantic painter, Joseph Mallord William Turner, was on a paddle steamer as it powered into a turbulent night-time snow storm off the East Anglian coast. The painting's lengthy title adds drama and detail, confirming that Turner wanted to convey the full experience at sea, not the view from safe distance on solid land: *Snow Storm – Steam-Boat off a Harbour's Mouth Making Signals in Shallow Water, and Going by the Lead. The Author Was in this Storm on the Night the Ariel Left Harwich*, 1842. The painter was at the centre of the storm and is at the centre of the painting; the ship's vertical mast represents his bound body. No previous painter had made himself the focus of visual experience in such a heroic manner and with such determination to convey the scene, or indicated such disregard for the painting's reception.

2 Andrews, p. 177; Butlin and Joll, pp. 246–247; Riding, p. 247; Venning, pp. 123–124; Wilton, *Turner and the Sublime*, pp. 17–19; Wilton, *Turner as Draughtsman*, p. 103.

Turner's account has been disputed because he was then in his late fifties and unlikely to have endured hours lashed to a mast.[2] But he was an avid traveller who had experienced storms on land and at sea, and the painting is most likely a composite of past experiences. Turner's sketchbooks show that he fastidiously returned to a pictorial subject, recording it at different times, in different weathers and from different points of view as a means to fully appreciate the genius of a place and a person. Recognising the particular advantages that the British climate offers the landscape painter, many of his paintings focus on changes in the weather and human response to those changes:

> In our variable climate the seasons are recognizable in one day . . . how happily is the landscape painter situated, how roused by every change in nature in every moment, that allows no languor even in her effects which she places before him, and demands most peremptorily every moment his admiration and investigation, to store his mind with every change of time and place.[3]

Romanticism gendered nature as female, as did the Enlightenment. But rather than conceive nature as passive and subject to enlightened management, romanticism characterised it as active and independent.[4] Romantic art was understood as a self-organising creative force alongside the natural world – a second nature – and also a means to establish a deeper understanding of the union of the human and the natural. In 'On German Architecture', 1772, Goethe states that art is the expression of creative spirit and is endowed with that spirit. Eulogising the 'genius' of Erwin von Steinbach, he conceives Strasbourg's gothic cathedral as a representation of national character: 'you have the same destiny as that Architect who piled up his mountains to the clouds'.[5] In the Renaissance, an artist was rarely described as divine and only in the eighteenth century was the term regularly applied to an artist as well as to God.

Herder added further emphasis to the national sense of *genius loci* in *Ideen zu einer Philosophie der Geschichte der Menschheit*, 1784–1791, which was translated into English as *Outlines of a Philosophy of the History of Man*, 1799. Combining nationalism and romanticism in opposition to French influence, he argued that nations have different identities due to the influence of climate and language on character, conceiving a creative interaction between a people and an environment.[6]

The two great exponents of German and British romantic painting – Caspar David Friedrich and J.M.W. Turner respectively – shared a concern for the union of nature and humanity but depicted a different nature and a different humanity. A devout Lutheran, Friedrich concluded that the path to God is personal: 'The painter should not paint merely what he sees in front of him, but also what he sees within himself.'[7] In *Monk by the Sea*, 1809, transcendent nature is still

[3] Turner, quoted in Wilton, *The Life and Work of J.M.W. Turner*, p. 107.

[4] Merchant, p. 133.

[5] Goethe, 'On German Architecture (1772)', pp. 104–108.

[6] Herder was a pupil of Kant and contemporary of Goethe. Herder, pp. 172–177, 561.

[7] Friedrich, quoted in Koerner, p. 74.

Caspar David Friedrich, *Monk by the Sea*, 1809. Courtesy of the Bildagentur für Kunst, Kultur und Geschichte, Berlin.

and distant, and the painter is contemplative and on land. Standing on the jagged coastline at its furthest point, the small, single figure stares out towards the horizon, willing the sky closer, searching for the supernatural in the natural.[8] Rather than the sequential arrangement of fore-, middle- and background that is characteristic of the picturesque, the foreground and background are emphasised.

Idealism's influence led German romanticism to assert the mind's ability to construct reality, placing less emphasis on the direct experience of wilder nature, which fascinated British romanticism. In *Snow Storm – Steam-Boat off a Harbour's Mouth*, the horizon is absent and the foreground alone remains; dynamic nature is energetic and immediate. Not known to be religious, and informed by empiricism's influence on British society, Turner placed the painter at sea, within the painting, not at its edge. No other European nation has so eulogised such scenes. The British have traversed mountains and seas in search of nature and their own identity. In British romanticism and the environmentalism it inspired, the environment is active not passive and, as Turner's paintings so vividly depict, the human is part of that environment.

8 X-rays have revealed that Friedrich painted over several boats, which he had originally intended to include. Rosenblum, p. 13.

Turner's visual and verbal account of the *Ariel* seems to confirm the stereotype of the solitary romantic artist immersed in nature and distant from industry and society. But noting his friendship with Mary Somerville and Michael Faraday, James Hamilton suggests an alternative interpretation that refers to their research:

> In Snow Storm – Steam-Boat off a Harbour's Mouth *Turner is giving graphic expression to the very real lines of force that his scientist friends had showed were being emitted from all points of the earth's surface at all times . . . Turner subtly links the imagery of iron filings on paper in an invisible magnetic field with energised sea water surrounding and acting upon a magnetic iron ship.*[9]

The painting depicts the complex interweaving of intense natural energy with the era's most formidable machine, the steam engine, which is vulnerable to the force of the sea. Air, fire and water are drawn into a single, elemental vortex so powerful and sublime that Turner 'did not expect to escape', evoking a parallel, romantic passion for life and death.

Like the picturesque, the term 'romanticism' has sometimes been applied pejoratively, suggesting a disengagement from contemporary concerns and retreat to the natural world. Claiming to heal the rupture of culture from nature, the romantic imagination may instead conflate the inner journey into the mind with the outer journey into the world and thus misrepresent nature, further its commodification, and prevent critical engagement with the natural world. But this was not the case in early nineteenth-century London, when collaborations and conversations between painters, poets, scientists and architects indicated their mutual respect and overlapping concerns. Rather than discard reason, the search for understanding led the romantic mind to cultivate a dialogue between the rational and irrational. Valuing intellect as well as emotion, invention as well as history, time as well as place, industry as well as nature, romanticism was promoted in science as well as art, which were not then opposed in the way they have sometimes subsequently been. Acknowledging the union of nature and culture, romanticism recognised a responsibility to them both. Rather than the myth of objective expertise too often promoted by the Enlightenment, the romantic scientist was not external to nature, and neither was the romantic painter.

Humphry Davy climbed the Lake District with William Wordsworth in 1805, while three years later, as Professor of Chemistry, he invited Samuel Taylor Coleridge to lecture on 'Poetry and the Imagination' at the Royal Institution, which was founded in 1799 to complement the more theoretical concerns of the Royal Society. Identifying the seeds of romanticism within Georgic England,

9 Hamilton, *Turner and the Scientists*, p. 128. Refer to Hamilton, *Faraday*, pp. 240, 359–361, 375–377; Hamilton, 'Earth's Humid Bubbles', pp. 52–64; Jones, vol. 1, p. 378; Pepper, pp. 188–205; Rodner, pp. 80–83; Wiedmann, p. 8.

Davy admired Thomson's *The Seasons*, which inspired his own poems on natural energy, drawing parallels between the scientific and artistic minds:

> *The perception of truth is almost as simple a feeling as the perception of beauty; and the genius of Newton, of Shakespeare, of Michel Angelo, and of Handel, are not very remote in character from each other. Imagination, as well as reason, is necessary to perfection in the philosophical mind.* A rapidity of combination, a power of perceiving analogies, and of comparing them by facts, is the creative source of discovery. *Discrimination and delicacy of sensation, so important in physical research, are other words for taste; and love of nature is the same passion, as is the love of the magnificent, the sublime and the beautiful.*[10]

In his preface to the 1802 edition of *Lyrical Ballads*, which Coleridge and he had first published in 1798, Wordsworth considers the convergence of poetry and science, with Davy as the likely model:

> *If the labours of Men of Science should ever create any material revolution, direct or indirect, in our condition, and in the impressions which we habitually receive, the Poet will sleep no more than at present, but he will be ready to follow the steps of the Man of Science, not only in those general indirect effects, but he will be at his side, carrying sensation into the midst of the objects of Science itself. The remotest discoveries of the Chemist, the Botanist, or Mineralogist, will be as proper objects of the Poet's art as any upon which it can be employed*[11]

Laying the foundations of a new science in the spirit of this romanticism, Luke Howard's *On the Modification of Clouds*, 1803, provided the first systematic and widely accepted investigation of atmospheric formations.[12] Recognising that clouds are formed when water vapour cools and condenses, he employed Latin terminology in line with other classificatory systems of the natural world and illustrated his research with evocative watercolours. Howard ordered clouds according to their visual resemblance to wisps of hair (Cirrus), a bulbous heap (Cumulus), sheets layered together (Stratus), or sub-categories that were combinations of these basic cloud types. Turner praised Howard, as did Goethe, who admired his schema because it relied on observation, indicating the union of art and science and the interconnectedness of the human and natural worlds. Goethe even composed a poem to Howard's research, which was included in a later edition of *On the Modification of Clouds*. In the following decade, Howard focused on the ways in which the city creates its own clouds, extending the implications of Evelyn's earlier

10 Davy, quoted in Holmes, p. 276. Refer to Hamilton, *Turner and the Scientists*, p. 12; Holmes, pp. 243, 295–300.

11 Wordsworth, p. xxxviii. Refer to Bate, *Romantic Ecology*, p. 40.

12 Jean-Baptiste Lamarck categorised cloud types in *Annuaire méteorologique*, 1802, but resistance to the French regime and language limited his influence. More systematic, *On the Modification of Clouds* was serialised in the July, September and October editions of the *Philosophical Magazine* in 1803, and was published as a single volume in the following year.

research.[13] *The Climate of London* appeared in two volumes in 1818 and 1820 and as an expanded edition in 1833 with *On the Modification of Clouds* as the introduction. Howard did not dismiss the weather signs tradition of the farming guide but considered the new science to be a superior alternative, which borrowed Aristotle's term even though its focus was quite different, leading to the formation of the Meteorological Society of London in 1823.[14] But in the first volume of *The Climate of London*, Howard acknowledged that the climate and weather continued to defy prediction: 'Meteorology . . . is yet far from having acquired the regular and consistent form of a science.'[15]

In the eighteenth century, alongside science and morality/ethics, art emerged as one of three independent value systems within European society, each with its own specific concerns so that one did not interfere with the other, but in practice this transition was neither immediate nor universal.[16] The Royal Society and the Royal Academy were then based in William Chambers' Somerset House, London, remaining there until 1837. On leaving the Strand, the visitor passed into the high entrance portico, which framed the expansive central courtyard beyond. To the left was the entrance to the Royal Society, which promoted the sciences. To the right was the entrance to the Royal Academy, which promoted the arts. Their proximity encouraged the members of one institution to attend the meetings of the other, so that new scientific theories informed artistic practices, and vice versa. It was not unusual for a Royal Academician to also be a Fellow of the Royal Society, as in the case of the architect Sir John Soane and sculptor Sir Francis Chantrey.

Turner was most likely a visitor to the Royal Society and conversed with a number of eminent scientists there and elsewhere. In addition to Davy, Faraday and Somerville, his acquaintances included Charles Babbage, creator of the Difference Engine, and David Brewster, the inventor of the kaleidoscope in 1815, who in 1839 published 'Statistics and Philosophy of Storms' in the *Edinburgh Review*, a journal that Turner regularly consulted. He had a first edition of Somerville's *Mechanism of the Heavens*, 1831, and admired her experiment on the magnetising properties of certain colours of light, notably violet and indigo.[17] She, in turn, admired his paintings. It is likely that Faraday and Turner first became acquainted due to their mutual friendship with the physician James Carrick Moore and his eldest daughter, Harriet, who gave the painter a nickname he enjoyed: 'Mr Avalanche Jenkinson'. A member of a sect that adhered strictly to the Bible, Faraday considered nature to be divine.[18] Sharing Turner's concern for the detailed observation of nature, he describes a sublime natural event, an avalanche:

[13] Howard, vol. 2, pp. 288–289.

[14] The Meteorological Society of London became the British Meteorological Society in 1850 and Royal Meteorological Society in 1883.

[15] Howard, vol. 1, p. iii. Refer to Boia, pp. 85–88; Fleming, p. 37; Golinski, *British Weather,* pp. 74–75; Hamblyn, pp. 184–203; Jankovic, pp. 154–156.

[16] Kant provided the first detailed codification of the three systems in *Critique of Pure Reason*, *Critique of Practical Reason* and *Critique of Judgement*, published respectively in 1781, 1788 and 1790.

[17] *Mechanism of the Heavens* was a translation and interpretation of Pierre Simon Laplace's *Traité de mécanique céleste*, 1798–1827. Refer to Gage, *Colour in Turner*, p. 107; Hamilton, *Faraday*, p. 277.

[18] The sect was named after Robert Sandeman.

Rarely is it seen in the commencement, but the ear tells first of something strange happening, and then looking, the eye sees a falling cloud of snow, or else what was a moment before a cataract of water changed into a tumultuous and heavily waving rush of snow, ice, and fluid, which, as it descends through the air, looks like water thickened, but as it runs over the inclined surfaces of the heaps below, moves heavily like paste, stopping and going as the mass behind accumulates or is dispersed.[19]

19 Faraday, 5 August 1841, quoted in Hamilton, *Faraday*, pp. 301–302; refer to pp. 241–242.

Faraday offered Turner advice on colour formation and admired the painter's depictions of sea storms, hanging one – most likely an engraving or a copy – in his study as Davy's successor at the Royal Institution. Faraday's research on electricity was probably his principal influence on Turner. In 1831 he submitted his seminal paper on electromagnetic induction to the Royal Society, the first of a series of over 30 papers that he produced during the following decades with the collective title 'Experimental Researches in Electricity'. Indicating that magnetism in motion can guarantee a consistent current, Faraday's discovery heralded the demise of steam power and the rise of the electrical age. Aware of the earth's magnetic force, in 1842 he conducted an experiment into terrestrial electromagnetic induction in the Thames at Waterloo Bridge, stimulating romantic fascination for scientific understanding of the earth's forces.

A Londoner throughout his life, Turner had painted the very same site in the previous decade, which was close to the Royal Academy and less than a mile from his birthplace near Covent Garden Market in 1775. Transforming Britain, industrialisation intensified in the final third of the eighteenth century. Improved credit systems facilitated extensive investment in industrial production and a national distribution network, while agriculture expanded to cater for a booming population, which doubled in Turner's lifetime. The transformation to an industrial economy displaced many of the rural poor, creating even worse working conditions and social unrest.[20] In the capital city, nearly every industry was found.

20 Helsinger, pp. 107, 118–119.

Annual coal consumption increased by a million tons in just 40 years, reaching 2,500,000 tons in 1790, when its population was 10 times that of any other English city. Severe smogs were increasingly common and the city acquired the nickname the 'Big Smoke'. Charles Dickens opens *Bleak House*, 1852–1853, with an atmospheric account of 'Smoke lowering down from chimney-pots, making a soft blank drizzle, with flakes of soot in it as big as full-grown snow-flakes – gone into mourning, one might imagine, for the death of the sun.'[21] Natural as well as human life was affected. A new strain of the moth *Biston betularia* evolved in just a few decades as its habitat was transformed. Renamed *Biston*

21 Dickens, p. 11.

J.M.W. Turner, *The Thames above Waterloo Bridge*, c.1830–1835. Courtesy of the Tate, London.

carbonaria, its pale wings had turned black, offering camouflage against predators in soot-clad cities.

Turner's reaction to the polluted air of the world's largest industrial city was fascination rather than repulsion. Its light and colour effects especially intrigued him, extending to the city the romantic concern for colour's emotive impact. Noting the smog's predominantly yellow tinge, Peter Brimblecombe concludes 'that fine smoke particles in the atmosphere could absorb the blue wavelengths from the sunlight above the fog in such a way that the fog at ground level was illuminated by a yellow light . . . It is also possible that the colour might have been the result of tarry compounds present in fog droplets'.[22] Representing a myriad of colours alongside dominant yellows, *The Thames above Waterloo Bridge*, c. 1830–1835, depicts the city as a heady haze.[23] Buildings, barges, figures and fumes are all absorbed into a single atmosphere in which divisions between the natural and man-made are indistinct. Here, the city is the smog. Immersed in the hybridised atmospheres and energies that defined early nineteenth-century London, which nature and industry had together created, Turner offered an early image of anthropogenic climate change.

Personifying romanticism's faith in the genius – which continued in modernism – the artist was understood to be both outside familiar society and able to redirect it through the appreciation of truths that only the imagination can

22 Brimblecombe, *The Big Smoke*, p. 125.

23 The painting was not exhibited during Turner's lifetime. Butlin and Joll, p. 306.

24 Benjamin, 'The Author as
Producer', p. 230; Benjamin, 'The
Work of Art', p. 240–241; Crary,
p. 143, n. 15.

25 Wilton, Turner as Draughtsman,
pp. 117–118.

26 Kant, part 1, pp. 94–117. Refer
to Wiedmann, pp. 25–26.

27 Turner occasionally referred to
the sublime. There is no indication
that he read Burke's account of the
sublime but he may have done so
and must have known of it through
conversations. Burke, pp. 73–74.

28 Gage, Colour in Turner,
pp. 54–55; Gage, J.M.W. Turner,
p. 108; Nicholson, pp. 56–71;
Wilton, Turner as Draughtsman,
p. 103.

29 Turner, letter to the painter and
collector James Holworthy, who was
then building a house at Hathersage,
Derbyshire, 7 January 1826, quoted
in Gage, Collected Correspondence of
J.M.W. Turner, p. 96.

30 Turner, quoted in Solkin,
'Education and Emulation', p. 99.

discover.[24] Due to the value given to the creative imagination, and in response to the expanded market of professional and mercantile art collectors, the authority of the patron was reduced and that of the artist increased, who more often selected the subject and site of an artwork. Turner's growing reputation was influential in raising the status of landscape painting. He was also effective in expanding the meaning of 'landscape' and the types of scenes depicted, which included the most mundane of tasks, whether agricultural or industrial. *Ploughing Up Turnips near Slough*, c.1809, is far removed from a pastoral Arcadia, while *Interior of an Iron Foundry*, c.1797, is equally direct.

The wars with France had curtailed foreign travel, encouraging an appreciation of British settings that continued after Napoleon's final defeat at the Battle of Waterloo in 1815. The Treaty of Amiens in 1802 initiated a temporary peace, which allowed Turner to visit France and Switzerland but he did not see Italy until 1819. In peacetime the expanding bourgeois market increasingly favoured comforting domestic dramas and the sublime was less considered.[25] But Turner's interest in the sublime continued throughout his life, and he particularly associated British national identity with sea power both in terms of military struggle and global trade. Especially since the industrial revolution, a terrifying and thrilling presence on land or sea could be man-made or natural. Later in his life in particular, Turner depicted distinct objects dissolving into formless energies, combining two aspects of the sublime identified by Kant: the mathematical and the dynamic.[26] One is a result of magnitude, the other of might. But, in addressing a range of emotions not just pleasure and terror, Turner's romanticism was more subtle and complex than Burke's original thesis and not exclusive to the sublime.[27]

As well as painting contemporary scenes, Turner was indebted to the art of the past, which was an important feature of the education he received at the Royal Academy. Some of his paintings of contemporary as well as historical themes refer to seventeenth-century painters who inspired the picturesque and the association of ideas, notably Claude and Nicolas Poussin. Turner painted his own versions of paintings he admired, both to acknowledge his respect and to suggest his even greater skill, depicting grand narratives with a new lively intensity.[28]

Turner is best known as a painter but he was also a keen architect, remarking in a letter: 'you talk of mountains high as the moon . . . but consider the pleasure of being your own architect day by day, its growing honours hour by hour, increasing strata by strata'.[29] Turner first worked in the offices of the architect Thomas Hardwick and the architectural draughtsman Thomas Malton, who he later described as his 'real master'.[30] After entering the Royal Academy Schools in 1789, when he was just 14, Turner initially continued his career as an architectural draughtsman alongside his work as an artist. As an architect, his largest completed building was Sandycombe Lodge, 1813, a compact villa for his own use at Twickenham, then a fashionable country town associated with Pope's villa, which Turner fondly recalled, and close to New Brentford, where he had spent part of his childhood living with his uncle. Sharing a fascination for history, landscape, weather and the picturesque, it is likely that Soane – Turner's great friend – influenced his design.[31] The early eighteenth century had emphasised ancient Rome, but later continental journeys and archaeological investigations drew increasing praise to ancient Greece. Soane remarked in 1809: 'The Greeks were the fathers of science and of art', concluding that their architecture 'now claims our attention'.[32] Acknowledging the influence of classical antiquity on British architecture, Grecian brick corbels and deep Italianate eaves surmount the Lodge's restrained, symmetrical elevations, while the entrance hall is reminiscent of Pitzhanger Manor, Ealing, which Soane began to rebuild as his country residence in 1800. Later in his life, Turner even remarked that if he had the chance to start again, he would want to be an architect.[33]

Throughout this time, Turner maintained a London home and studio. Artistic convention favoured oil paintings rather than drawings and watercolours, which Turner painted for a decade before he completed his first oil painting in 1796. Drawing in situ was an important feature of his artistic practice, both as an end in itself and as an aid to studio painting. But only a small number of his watercolours and even fewer oil paintings were made outdoors. *House beside the River, with Trees and Sheep*, c.1806–1812, is splattered with raindrops. More often Turner painted in his studio. *Snow Storm – Steam-Boat off a Harbour's Mouth* and *The Thames above Waterloo Bridge* were both painted there, while he sometimes completed a painting on Varnishing Day at the Royal Academy, indicating his virtuosity. In 1799 Turner moved to 64 Harley Street. Combining his vocations as a painter and an architect, in 1802 he bought a lease on the property and designed a first floor gallery for the display of his paintings, which was completed two years later. In 1810 Turner moved to 47 Queen Anne Street West close by, where in 1822 he designed a second gallery painted Pompeiian red as Soane favoured.[34] An early visitor admired the most elegant house and best lit gallery he had ever seen.[35] From the adjacent studio, Turner could remain unseen, observing his visitors through a peephole in the dividing wall.[36] His transformation of 47 Queen Anne Street West occurred by use as much as by design. Twenty years later, another visitor described a quite different scene:

> *The house had a desolate look. The door was shabby, and nearly destitute of paint, and the windows were obscured by dirt . . . When I entered the gallery and looked*

31 Originally called Solus Lodge, Turner sold the house in 1826. Refer to Dean, p. 183; Dorey, *John Soane and J.M.W. Turner*, p. 26; Parry-Wingfield, pp. 23–30.

32 Soane, 'Lecture I', in Watkin, *Sir John Soane*, p. 497.

33 Wilton, 'Forward', p. 4.

34 Dorey, *John Soane and J.M.W. Turner*, p. 13. Refer to Finberg, pp. 267–269; Gage, *Colour in Turner*, p. 134; Gage, *J.M.W. Turner*, p. 68; Townsend, *Turner's Painting Techniques*, p. 58.

35 Rev. William Kingsley, quoted in Gage, *Colour in Turner*, p. 162.

36 Hamilton, *Turner*, p. 213.

at the pictures I was astonished, and the state in which they were shocked me. The skylights on the roof were excessively dirty, many of the panes of glass were broken, and some were awanting altogether. It was a cold wet day in autumn, and the rain was coming through the broken glass, on to the middle of the floor, and all the time I was there – fully an hour – I had to keep my umbrella up over my head.[37]

37 A. MacGeorge, quoted in Gage, *J.M.W. Turner*, pp. 152–153. Walter Thornbury, Turner's first biographer, describes a similar scene. Thornbury, p. 362.

Decay must have begun much earlier for the house, gallery and studio to reach such a level of decrepitude by the early 1840s, when Turner painted *Snow Storm – Steam-Boat off a Harbour's Mouth*. His father's death in 1829 may have been a contributing factor as he undertook many everyday chores for his son. Historians and curators cite Turner's old age and curmudgeonly character to explain the decay. David Blayney Brown describes Turner as 'a profound pessimist' and 'depressive whose resolve, in old age, has so far flagged that he could not be bothered to look after the works he intended for posterity'.[38] Painting conservationists identify a number of reasons for the poor condition of Turner's paintings today, all significantly due to his working practices including the dilapidated state of his studio:

38 Brown, *Romanticism*, p. 161. Refer to Gage, *Colour in Turner*, p. 171.

Turner's tendency to keep his unfinished and unsold works in a damp studio which had rain leaking in, and was possibly poorly heated when he worked there (since his indifference to extreme and unpleasant weather was remarked on in his lifetime) promoted such damaging mould growth, perhaps before the paint dried.[39]

39 Townsend, 'Turner's Use of Materials', p. 6.

As unfinished paintings were left in the studio they acquired a layer of dirt and grease, which Turner should have cleaned away before adding further paint. But he did not. The layer of dirt became part of the painting, decreasing adhesion between the old and new layers and causing flaking.[40]

40 Hackney, pp. 53–54.

The finished paintings . . . frequently suffer from moisture sensitivity, disfiguring mould growth, flaking of priming from canvas, flaking of paint from paint, wrinkled and cracked paint, discoloured glazes and shadows, loss of texture as a result of early lining treatments, extreme temperature sensitivity and extreme solvent sensibility.[41]

41 Townsend, 'Turner's Use of Materials', p. 5.

42 Turner considered doing so in 1844. Refer to Finberg, p. 397; Gage, *Colour in Turner*, p. 171.

A successful and wealthy artist, Turner could have had his studio repaired if he had wished.[42] But instead of indicating pessimism and disinterest, it is likely that his treatment of the paintings was deliberate and necessary.

Turner's principal advocate, John Ruskin, remarks in *The Stones of Venice*, 1851–1853, that 'art is valuable or otherwise, only as it expresses the personality, activity and living perception of a good and great human soul', indicating his debt to Goethe's 'On German Architecture'.[43] Emphasising the social value of this theme in *The Seven Lamps of Architecture*, 1849, Ruskin extends the eighteenth-century theory of association to the politics of human labour, valuing 'not only what men have thought and felt, but what their hands have handled, and their strength wrought'.[44] Celebrating architecture's communion with nature, he praises the variations formed by craft, use and weather: 'For, indeed, the greatest glory of a building is not in its stones, or its gold. Its glory is in its Age . . . it is in that golden stain of time, that we are to look for the real light, and colour, and preciousness of architecture.'[45]

Admiring Howard's *On the Modification of Clouds*, Ruskin cites '*cloudiness*' as 'characteristic' of 'modern landscape' painting and eulogises Turner's skill in this regard.[46] But Ruskin distinguishes between the clouds of nature and industry. Unlike Turner, he regrets industrialisation, which he characterises as dehumanising and associates with 'the storm-cloud of the nineteenth century', a sign of the spiritual abstinence of the modern world.[47] In the first volume of *Modern Painters*, 1843, Ruskin states that Turner's genius depends on his ability to represent nature, which he associates with moral truth.[48] In the fourth volume, 1856, Ruskin refines his argument, recognising discrepancies between actual places and Turner's depictions, and famously concludes: 'First, he receives a true impression from the place itself . . . and then he sets himself as far as possible to reproduce that impression on the mind of the spectator'.[49] It is likely that Turner identified the progressive decay and gradual ruination of his studio as a means to paint the impression of a place in relation to time and weather.

Whether at sea or in the city, Turner painted what he experienced. In London, his deliberately dilapidated studio enabled him to paint *in situ* and perceive the sublime at home. Turner's subject literally entered his work in pigments and pollution. The dirt and rain that landed on unfinished canvases were incorporated into his paintings, and combined with composites of natural and industrial pigments, which he used before any contemporary.[50] His subject, site and painting practice were perfectly aligned. Rather than a retreat to an idealised nature, Turner's romanticism acknowledged the complexity of his time, its industry, landscape and weather.

Turner's lengthy transformation of 47 Queen Anne Street mirrored Soane's reimagining of 12–14 Lincoln's Inn Fields, just a mile to the east. Indicating the depth of their friendship, they regularly dined together, attended each other's

43 Ruskin, *The Stones of Venice*, vol. 1, pp. 35–45; Goethe, 'On German Architecture', pp. 106–108.

44 Ruskin, *The Seven Lamps of Architecture*, p. 169.

45 Ruskin, *The Seven Lamps of Architecture*, p. 177.

46 Ruskin, *Modern Painters*, vol. 3, p. 254; Ruskin, *Modern Painters*, vol. 1, pp. 233–234.

47 Ruskin, *The Storm-Cloud of the Nineteenth Century*, pp. 55–63.

48 Ruskin, *Modern Painters*, vol. 1, p. 180.

49 Ruskin, *Modern Painters*, vol. 4, pp. 21–22.

50 Townsend, 'Turner's Use of Materials', p. 5.

lectures, went fishing on the Thames, and spent Christmas Eve together after the death of Soane's wife, Eliza, in November 1815. Self-made men who prospered at the Royal Academy, first as students and later as professors, their personal histories affirmed their friendship. Turner's father was a barber and wigmaker. On his election as a full Royal Academician in 1802, he no longer signed his paintings 'William Turner', selecting instead the more formal 'J.M.W. Turner'. The child of a bricklayer and a poor and uneducated family that he never mentioned, Soan created Soane in 1783, even correcting all his earlier signatures to match his chosen name.[51]

51 Du Prey, p. 4.

Soane enrolled to study architecture at the Royal Academy in 1771, just three years after its foundation by eminent practitioners including the architect Sir William Chambers and painters Sir Joshua Reynolds and Angelica Kauffman, a rare example of a woman achieving such status in the eighteenth century. In 1777 Soane was awarded the King's Travelling Scholarship, which funded a tour of Italy: 'This was the most fortunate event of my life, for it was the means by which I formed those connexions to which I owe all the advantages I have since enjoyed.'[52] Offering guidance, Chambers gave him a copy of a letter he had earlier prepared for another pupil: 'Seek for those who have most reputation, young or old, amongst which forget not Piranesi, whom you may see in my name; he is full of matter, extravagant it is true, often absurd, but from his overflowings you may gather much information.'[53] Chambers failed to fully understand Piranesi but Soane was much more appreciative and met him shortly before his death. Donating four engraved views of the ancient monuments and ruins of the city, the 'tutor' indicated his respect for the 'pupil'.

52 Soane, *Memoirs*, p. 12.

53 Chambers, letter to a pupil,

5 August 1774, quoted in Soane,

Memoirs, p. 12.

In 1806, by then a successful practitioner, Soane became the Professor of Architecture at the Royal Academy and soon argued that a new Professor of Perspective should be appointed. Of particular relevance to the education of architects the post was less prestigious than that of the Professor of Painting. Reynolds recounted Chambers' opinion 'that any one qualified, in all points, to be an Academician, would never condescend to teach an inferior and mechanick branch of the art'.[54] But Turner, the only candidate, was appointed in the following year.

54 Reynolds, p. 107.

During his lifetime, Soane witnessed not only an industrial revolution but also a transformation in the status and practice of many disciplines. The right to be a Royal Academician was limited to visual artists. Since the Renaissance, architects' status had been less assured than that of painters and sculptors, but the eighteenth and nineteenth centuries brought further uncertainty. The reclassification of the arts into fine arts opposed to utility – notably poetry, music, painting, sculpture and architecture – was problematic for architects and Kant concluded that architecture's aesthetic potential was even less than that of a garden.[55] Associated with utility, the design disciplines that proliferated due to industrialisation were categorised as applied arts at best. In the Renaissance a form was synonymous with an idea. But painters and sculptors discarded design once it became associated with collective authorship, industrial production and forms made without an idea in mind. Among the three original visual arts, only in architecture was the term 'design' still in regular use. In public discourse, design was increasingly associated with the newer design disciplines, which affected how architectural design was understood. But in the discourse and practice of architects, the older and the newer meanings of design were both in evidence, stimulating an openness to new technologies as well as new ideas.

Influencing the humanities and social sciences as well as industrial production, the nineteenth century is associated with the sub-division of existing practices and the proliferation of new ones, in which the technocrat was the model practitioner. Increasingly during the course of the century, history was assumed to be a science capable of objective statements, which led to an emphasis on archival research as well as the precise study of artefacts, and established the art and architectural historian as an independent specialist distinct from art and design practice. Science is supported in its claim to objectivity by the presence of its objects of study in front of the scientist, while history is an understanding of the past written in the present. Any artefact or archive, however complete, cannot return the historian to the past and no analysis is more than an interpretation. Any history expresses a particular ideology, as does any scientific statement. Selectively focusing on certain pieces of information while ignoring others, neither can be neutral. Whether implicit or explicit, a critique of the present and a prospect of the future are evident in both historical and scientific statements.

Despite the emergence of the specialist historian, the interdependence of design and history remained essential to the buildings and treatises of nineteenth-century architects. Rather than pseudo-scientific, Soane's appreciation of history referred to an earlier novelistic model. One of the residential squares that developed around the City of London, and close to the Inns of Court, Lincoln's Inn Fields was run by a trust that maintained the square and the garden at its centre. In the rapidly expanding city, the trustees struggled to protect the square from beggars, vagrants and litter, which led an observer to remark in 1790: 'The spot has the most uncouth and dismal appearance of any square in or about the metropolis.'[56] Appointed architect to the Bank of England in 1788 and inheriting a fortune from his wife's uncle two years later, Soane bought 12 Lincoln's Inn Fields in 1792 and

[55] The Abbé Batteux provided the first detailed categorisation of the fine arts in *Les beaux arts reduits à un même principe*, 1746; Kant, part 2, p. 210.

[56] Anonymous letter, 1 November 1790, quoted in Palmer, p. 19.

soon rebuilt it, moving there in 1794. In the early nineteenth century he acquired and rebuilt two further houses, transforming 12–14 Lincoln's Inn Fields into his house, office and museum. Soane's ambition to establish an architectural dynasty was frustrated by the limited ability of his sons, George and John.[57] Instead, he established a dynasty of influence, offering 12–14 Lincoln's Inn Fields as a model for prospective architects. Four years before his death, the Soane Museum Act of Parliament, 1833, established future public access. In the discussions that preceded the Act, Sir Robert Peel proposed that the collection should be absorbed within the British Museum, which had been established in 1753 as a national museum typical of the Enlightenment. But Peel failed to recognise that the building fabric was part of Soane's collection, and essential to his 'union of the arts'.[58] Britain's first museum of architecture, 12–14 Lincoln's Inn Fields reflects the Enlightenment's attention to ancient artefacts and concern for categorisation by discipline. Reflecting the expansion of worldwide trade and Britain's imperial reach, Soane's collection includes objects from Egypt, China and South America as well as Europe. But they are not ordered by subject, type and chronology. Instead, objects and settings are composed according to mood and effect. In March 1825 Soane held three candle-lit evening receptions for nearly 900 guests to view a recent acquisition, the thirteenth-century BC Sarcophagus of Pharoah Seti I, which had been recently discovered.[59] Lamps illuminated the façade to the square, while the interior flickered with candlelight and the sarcophagus was discovered in the crypt, alluding to its burial site. Turner and Coleridge were among the guests.[60] Soane's friend, Barbara Hofland, recalled the scene:

> Had any one of that gay company been placed alone in the sepulchral chamber, at the 'witching hour of night,' when 'Churchyards yawn, and graves give up their dead,' when the flickering lights became self-extinguished, and the last murmuring sounds from without ceased to speak of the living world, – it is probable that even the healthiest pulse would have been affected with the darker train of emotions which a situation so unallied to common life is calculated to produce.[61]

Due to its eclectic collection, emotive atmosphere, poetic appreciation of history and identification with an individual, 12–14 Lincoln's Inn Fields is more a museum of the romantic self than the Enlightenment one.[62] Soane admired *The Confessions of Jean-Jacques Rousseau*, 1781, a seminal and uncompromising manifestation of modern consciousness in which Rousseau created Rousseau, and he aimed for a comparable level of self-expression.[63] Equally, 12–14 Lincoln's Inn Fields is indebted to the English novel's origins in the fictional autobiography,

57 Soane had four children but only two, George and John, survived childhood. John died quite young in 1823.

58 Soane, quoted in Watkin, *Sir John Soane*, p. 81.

59 Discovered by Giovanni Belzoni in 1817.

60 Benjamin Robert Haydon, in a letter to Mary Russell Mitford, referred to in Summerson and Dorey, p. 47.

61 Hofland, quoted in Soane, *Description of the House and Museum*, 1835, p. 39.

62 Millenson, pp. 134–146.

63 In 1770 Rousseau began private readings of his autobiographical *Confessions*, which was published posthumously in 1781. Soane refers to Rousseau twice in his memoirs. Soane, *Memoirs*, pp. 19, 59. Refer to Watkin, *Sir John Soane*, pp. 7–8.

Joseph Michael Gandy,
*The Dome Area at Night,
Looking East*, 1811,
12–14 Lincoln's Inn Fields.
Courtesy of the Trustees of
Sir John Soane's Museum,
London.

acknowledges the interdependence of the picturesque and the novel and celebrates their influence on architecture.

Published in nine volumes between 1759 and 1767, Laurence Sterne's *The Life and Opinions of Tristram Shandy, Gentleman* exploits a picturesque fascination for fragmentation, incompletion and ruination as a means to engage the reader. With storytelling now part of the story, Sterne's highly self-conscious and meandering narration profoundly influenced the course of literature. The narrator sets out to tell the story of his life but rarely gets beyond his conception, birth and early childhood. As a person is a fluid accumulation of ideas, emotions and experiences and a life is not necessarily remembered, or even experienced, as a progressive sequence, the story does not develop chronologically but moves back, forward, around and sideways. Sterne remarks: 'Digressions, incontestably, are the sun-shine; – they are the life, the soul of reading; – take them out of this book for instance, – you might as well take the book along with them'.[64] Through *Tristram Shandy*'s fractured narrative we actually acquire a more honest, detailed, nuanced and convincing portrait of a person than in a linear narrative. Digressions occur in life as well as literature. Even the attention given to Tristram's formative years is an accurate representation of his concerns. As a metaphor for life itself, the final line of the book mocks the purposeless but pleasurable journey the reader has followed: 'A COCK and a BULL, said Yorick – And one of the best of its kind, I ever heard.'[65]

The novel is surprisingly accepting of life's many accidents and failures, given that Sterne wrote *Tristram Shandy* late in his life, when his health was poor and after all but one of his children had died within days of birth. Indicating a teasing affection for Locke, Sterne attributes the novel's fractured narrative and playful misassociation of ideas to the effect of climate on character: 'that this strange irregularity in our climate, producing so strange an irregularity in our characters, – doth thereby, in some sort, make us amends, by giving us somewhat to make us merry with when the weather will not suffer us to go out of doors'.[66]

An amateur painter, Sterne precisely controlled the visual quality of the printed page. Typographical devices indicate specific actions and images appear in place of words. A cross means that someone crosses himself and two small dots indicate that Colonel Trim snaps his fingers. Sterne's complex visual and typographical devices – 'tripping us up as we read' – are the narrator's means to check that the reader is alert.[67] Communicating in a manner that words cannot, images call attention to the possibilities and limitations of both means of communication. For example, two black pages follow a reference to Yorick's grave.[68] Elsewhere, enticing the reader into action and leaving the following page blank, Sterne asks the reader to imagine Widow Wadman: 'To conceive this right, – call for pen and

64 Sterne, vol. 1, ch. 28, p. 64.

65 Sterne, vol. 9, ch. 33, p. 588.

66 Sterne, vol. 1, ch. 21, p. 57; refer to Sterne, vol. 1, ch. 4, p. 9.

67 Holtz, p. 88. Refer to Voogd, p. 386.

68 Sterne, vol. 1, ch. 12, pp. 31–32.

ink – here's paper ready to your hand. – Sit down, Sir, paint her to your own mind – as like your mistress as you can – as unlike your wife as your conscience will let you – 'tis all one to me – please but your fancy in it.'[69]

12–14 Lincoln's Inn Fields is an architectural equivalent to *Tristram Shandy*. Having carefully prepared two series of professorial lectures at the Royal Academy – the first beginning in 1809, the second in 1815 Soane mentioned Sterne early in his first lecture and again in his two final lectures.[70] A further reference

69 Sterne, vol. 6, ch. 38, p. 422.

70 Soane, 'Lecture I', 'Lecture XI' and 'Lecture XII', in Watkin, *Sir John Soane*, pp. 491, 647, 653.

Sir John Soane, Exterior, 12–14 Lincoln's Inn Fields. Photograph, Martin Charles. Courtesy of the Trustees of Sir John Soane's Museum, London.

71 Soane, 'Crude Hints', p. 63. Refer

to Dorey, 'Crude Hints', p. 76, n. 16.

72 Soane, *Memoirs*, pp. 65–66.

73 Soane, 'Lecture X', in Watkin,

Sir John Soane, pp. 624–626.

74 Porter, *Flesh in the Age of*

Reason, p. 304.

75 Soane referring to Pitzhanger

Manor, quoted in Watkin, 'John

Soane', p. 82.

76 George Soane, *The Champion*,

September 1815, quoted in Watkin,

Sir John Soane, p. 419.

77 The bust was carved in 1828.

78 The Soane Museum Act of

Parliament, quoted in Summerson

and Dorey, p. 126.

79 Soane, 'Crude Hints', pp. 61, 65.

80 In *The Union of Architecture,*

Sculpture and Painting; Exemplified

by a Series of Illustrations, with

Descriptive Accounts of the House

and Galleries of John Soane, 1827,

John Britton repeatedly refers to

the picturesque. John Summerson

describes 1806–1821 as Soane's

picturesque period but this

chronology is unlikely as Soane's

concern for the picturesque was

longstanding. Summerson, 'Soane:

The Man and the Style', pp. 10, 14.

81 Gordon, pp. 71–72.

82 Soane, *Description of the House*

and Museum, 1832, p. 17.

83 Soane refers to Piranesi's

etchings of imaginary prisons, the

Carceri, 1750. Soane, 'Crude Hints',

p. 63.

appears in 'Crude Hints towards an History of my House in L(incoln's) I(nn) Fields', 1812, Soane's novelistic history of his home.[71] Soane's narrative descriptions echo *Tristram Shandy* with architectural characters introduced alongside human ones. In his *Memoirs*, 1835, he refers to 'Padre Giovanni', a monk living among the ruins of 12–14 Lincoln's Inn Fields, who is of course Soane himself.[72] Picturesque, self-conscious, fragmented and meandering narration was Soane's method as a designer as well as a writer.

As in *Tristram Shandy*, a concern for the association of ideas runs through Soane's lectures, including a lengthy discussion of its relationship to gardens and ruins in the tenth lecture, in which he describes a built ruin as a history, an interpretation of the past in the present.[73] Sterne made the Lockean self appear complex, comical and sympathetic as well as sad.[74] But Soane took himself more seriously, intensely describing his home 'as a sort of portrait'.[75] In two anonymous articles, which Soane blamed for the death of his wife, George Soane mocked his father and 12–14 Lincoln's Inn Fields:

> *The exterior, from its exceeding heaviness and monumental gloom, seems as*
> *if it were intended to convey a satire upon himself; it looks like a record of the*
> *departed, and can only mean that considering himself as deficient in that part of*
> *humanity – the mind and its affections – he has reared this mausoleum for the*
> *enshrinement of his body.*[76]

Inserted after the 1833 Act, Chantrey's white marble bust of Soane is the focus of the Dome Area at the museum's centre.[77] At his request, the Act required that the house, office and museum should remain 'as nearly as possible in the state in which Sir John Soane shall leave it'.[78] Wanting to preserve 12–14 Lincoln's Inn Fields as his monument, Soane protected it from ruination but the ruin is a recurring theme of his architecture,[79] indebted to Colonna, Panini, Piranesi and the picturesque.[80] Like Kent, Soane owned several copies of *Hypnerotomachia Poliphili*.[81] Piranesi's ink and wash drawings of Paestum hang on the hinged walls of Soane's Picture Room, close to 'two Drawings of Ruins' by Panini and two watercolour sketches of scenes from Sterne's *A Sentimental Journey Through France and Italy*, 1768.[82] Some of Piranesi's images refer to known places while others are fictive, but all are works of the imagination. Acknowledging his debt, Soane described part of 12–14 Lincoln's Inn Fields as like 'one of those Carcerian dark Staircases represented in some of Piranesi's ingenious dreams for prisons'.[83]

Including thirteenth-century stonework from the Old Palace of Westminster, the fabricated ruins in the Monk's Yard are gothic, which Soane associated with

Giovanni Battista Piranesi, *An Architectural Fantasy*, 1755. Courtesy of the Trustees of Sir John Soane's Museum, London.

Joseph Michael Gandy, *The Monk's Yard Looking East*, 1825, 12–14 Lincoln's Inn Fields. Courtesy of the Trustees of Sir John Soane's Museum, London.

84 Soane, 'Lecture X', in Watkin, *Sir John Soane*, p. 626. Refer to Dorey, 'Sir John Soane's Courtyard Gardens at Lincoln's Inn Fields', pp. 18–21.

85 Soane, 'Lecture X', in Watkin, *Sir John Soane*, p. 626.

86 Soane, 'Crude Hints', p. 73.

87 Soane entered the office of George Dance the younger in 1768 at the age of 15. Soane, *Memoirs*, p. 29.

88 Soane, *Memoirs*, p. 60.

English history as had others before him.[84] Rather than recently built, he imagined that the ruins had been recently discovered: 'to produce pleasing sensations there must be an appearance of truth and they must recall to the mind the idea of real objects and not be considered as mere pictures'.[85]

In 'Crude Hints' Soane is obsessed by his future reputation and concerned that it will fall into ruin. He imagines that his home is first occupied and then left to decay. On finding it empty and assumed to be haunted, a future visitor attempts to decipher its earlier purpose and character.[86] In 1802 Soane acquired the eight paintings of William Hogarth's *A Rake's Progress*, 1733–1734, a painter who Sterne also admired. In Tom Rakewell's decline from prosperity to Bedlam, Soane may have seen the moral inverse to his own social rise. But in his *Memoirs* he recalls his unsuccessful application to be Surveyor to St Paul's Cathedral: 'I was represented as a man unqualified for the situation – ignorant of the principles of Architecture – brought up as a hack in Mr. Dance's office.'[87] Cataloguing a lifetime of criticism, he continues: 'I have been charged with suffering my nearest relatives to exist in a state of "pauperism" whilst I am squandering my money by hundreds and thousands in the ostentatious gratification of pride and vanity'.[88] Fearful of his fate, Soane may have feared *An Architect's Progress*, like that of his contemporary

William Hogarth, *A Rake's Progress, Scene VIII. The Madhouse*, 1733–1734. Courtesy of the Trustees of Sir John Soane's Museum, London.

John Matthews, which he recounts in his *Description of the House and Museum on the North Side of Lincoln's Inn Fields*, 1832:

> This ingenious and indefatigable Artist, having failed in an attempt to gain the gold medal given in the Royal Academy in 1771, for the best Design of a Nobleman's Villa, felt the disappointment so poignantly, that he neglected his studies and passion for Architecture, became dissolute and sottish, and finally ended his days in a prison.[89]

Introspective speculation on impending ruination is debilitating, as Soane acknowledged: 'At home all day a prey to melancholy and gloomy reflections'.[90] For such a depressive character, the ruin of a building was linked to the ruin of a life. But ruins represent potential as well as loss, and Soane's concern for ruination was inseparable from his fascination for construction. At his request, in 1798 Joseph Gandy painted *The Bank of England, London: View of the Rotunda Imagined as a Ruin* in a manner reminiscent of Piranesi, depicting workers picking over the debris in a dark and foreboding light, while some 30 years later the painting was exhibited at the Royal Academy as *Architectural Ruins – A Vision*. Depicting

Joseph Michael Gandy, *The Bank of England, London: View of the Rotunda Imagined as a Ruin*, 1798, exhibited at the Royal Academy in 1832 as *Architectural Ruins – A Vision*. Courtesy of the Trustees of Sir John Soane's Museum, London.

89 Soane, *Description of the House and Museum*, 1832, p. 25.
A slightly different version appears in Soane, *Description of the House and Museum*, 1830, p. 24.

90 Soane, 'Soane's Note Books', vol. 11, 1820–1822, p. 29.

the bank as an enduring ruin implies that Soane's architecture is equal to that of classic antiquity. Ruins represent potential as well as loss, and Soane's concern for ruination was inseparable from his fascination for construction. Demolition is essential to construction and building sites often appear ruinous.[91] Intrigued by a building's unfinished state, Soane required his pupils to further their education by drawing his buildings under construction, and he purchased three engravings of Piranesi's 1794 rendering of Robert Mylne's Blackfriars Bridge, maybe the most famous eighteenth-century depiction of the construction process.[92]

12–14 Lincoln's Inn Fields is an appropriate memorial to an era that emphasised temporal disjunctions, fractured narratives and multiple meanings, and lauded subjectivity but recognised it to be complex and uncertain. Soane continued to alter his house, office and museum between the 1833 Act and his death four years later at the age of 84. If he had lived longer he would no doubt have made further changes, despite his failing eyesight. Aware that no art form can fully describe a person and a life, Soane turned an impossible task to creative advantage. 12–14 Lincoln's Inn Fields is an intensely personal, highly self-conscious and decisively meandering fictional autobiography in which the author edited and reinvented his life as he reflected upon it. A construction site for over 40 years, Soane conceived his home as a ruin as well as a monument and ruined as much as he built. As he remained on site while the three adjacent buildings were constructed, demolished and rebuilt, it was then a living ruin unlike the preserved ruin it became after his death.

Soane's concern for the ruin was inseparable from the picturesque, which continued to fascinate him even though it was less in fashion later in his life. Describing the architecture of classical antiquity as an invaluable model, he criticised the literal transfer of architecture from one place to another and emphasised the influence of local conditions such as culture, climate and site.[93] In his tenth lecture in 1815, Soane identifies gardening as an exception to the general superiority of 'the ancients over the moderns'. Discussing a building and its setting, he remarks: 'Architecture being thus identified with gardening, it becomes a necessary part of the education of the architect that he shall be well acquainted with the principles of modern decorative landscape gardening.'[94] As well as picturesque novels such as *Tristram Shandy*, Soane was indebted to early eighteenth-century gardens – notably those of Kent – and to late eighteenth-century theories of William Gilpin, Uvedale Price and Richard Payne Knight, when opinions on the picturesque were vividly opposed.

The industrial revolution would not have been possible without an equivalent 'agricultural revolution'.[95] Greater efficiency and productivity ensured that far

91 Robert Smithson describes this as *'ruins in reverse'*. Smithson, 'A Tour of the Monuments of Passaic, New Jersey', p. 72.

92 Richardson, *Building in Progress*, pp. 2, 7; Thornton and Dorey, p. 39.

93 Soane, 'Lecture I', 'Lecture VIII', in Watkin, *Sir John Soane*, pp. 492, 595. Refer to Lukacher, pp. 38–41.

94 Soane, 'Lecture X', in Watkin, *Sir John Soane*, pp. 627–628, 624. Refer to Le Camus de Mézières, p. 88; Soane, quoted in Watkin, *Sir John Soane*, p. 228; Watkin, 'John Soane', p. 82.

95 Williamson, *An Environmental History of Wildlife in England*, pp. 91–113.

fewer people were employed as farmworkers than in previous centuries, stimulating changing attitudes to landscape. Gilpin's first travel guide was published in 1782, extending the picturesque aesthetic to the tourist economy and encouraging the expanding middle class to appreciate wilder, uncultivated landscapes that contrasted with the newly developed regions in which they prospered.[96] Gilpin's appreciation of decay extended to buildings:

> A piece of Palladian architecture may be elegant in the last degree . . . Should we wish to give it picturesque beauty, we must use the mallet, instead of the chisel: we must beat down one half of it, deface the other, and throw the mutilated members around in heaps. In short, from a smooth *building*, we must turn it into a rough *ruin*.[97]

Such descriptions led Ruskin to characterise the 'lower picturesque' as 'heartless' because it focuses on surface effects to the detriment of deeper social concerns.[98] In contrast, he praises the 'nobler', *'Turnerian Picturesque'*, concluding 'that the dignity of the picturesque increases from lower to higher, in exact proportion to the sympathy of the artist with his subject'.[99]

Soane only owned one of Gilpin's books and paid him little attention. Also in his Library were first and second editions of Price's *An Essay on the Picturesque*, 1794, which he acquired the year it was published, influencing his sixth and ninth lectures. Extending Burke's classificatory system to include the picturesque, Price concludes that each aesthetic category is distinct but the picturesque sits between the beautiful and the sublime and 'is more frequently and more happily blended with them both than they are with each other'.[100] Emphasising time as a means to identify the differences between aesthetic categories, Price equates beauty with youth and the picturesque with age. He associates decay with the effects of weather, which 'loosen the stones themselves; they tumble in irregular masses upon what was perhaps smooth turf or pavement, or nicely trimmed walks and shrubberies, now mixed and overgrown with wild plants and creepers, that crawl and shoot among the fallen ruins'.[101] Price's conception of the picturesque evokes English landscapes and its muted colours are English too, emphasising 'the mosses, lichens, and incrustations on bark and on wood, on stones, old walls, and buildings of every kind'.[102]

Praised by both Whately and Horace Walpole, Lancelot 'Capability' Brown was the pre-eminent English landscape designer in the second half of the eighteenth century.[103] But Price criticises the monotonous artificiality of Brown's softly rolling landscapes, and concludes that they deny nature's liberty and are thus not

96 Defined in the late eighteenth century, the term 'tourist' soon developed negative connotations. Gilpin, *Observations*, vol. 1, p. 197. Refer to Copley, p. 54; Copley and Garside, 'Introduction', p. 7.

97 Gilpin, *Three Essays*, pp. 7–8.

98 Ruskin, *Modern Painters*, vol. 4, p. 19.

99 Ruskin, *Modern Painters*, vol. 4, pp. 24–26, 23.

100 Price, *An Essay on the Picturesque*, p. 76.

101 Price, *An Essay on the Picturesque*, p. 49.

102 Price, *Essays on the Picturesque*, vol. 1, pp. 169–170.

103 Walpole, *The History of the Modern Taste in Gardening*, p. 57; Whately, pp. 213–227.

104 Price, *An Essay on the Picturesque*, pp. 9–16, 184–190.

105 Price, *Essays on the Picturesque*, vol. 1, pp. 32–33.

106 Knight, *The Landscape, A Didactic Poem*, p. 18.

107 The illustrator is Thomas Hearne.

108 Knight, *The Landscape, A Didactic Poem*, pp. 93–97. Refer to Whale, pp. 188–189.

109 Knight, *The Landscape, A Didactic Poem*, p. 34.

110 Repton commissioned William Coombe to write 'A Letter to Uvedale Price, Esq.'.

111 Knight, *The Landscape, A Didactic Poem*, p. 43n; Repton, p. 101. Refer to Ballantyne, pp. 217–218; Hipple, p. 249.

picturesque.[104] For similar reasons he also decides that Kent's gardens are not picturesque even though they differ significantly from those of Brown. Referring to two characters in *Tristram Shandy* – 'Uncle Toby, under the direction of Corporal Trim, for they had converted this varied bank into a perfect glacis' – Price dismisses the 'military style' of gardening that succeeds in 'spoiling a picturesque spot'.[105]

Excluding Kent from his criticism, Knight directs his attention at gardens that do not deserve to be called picturesque.[106] In *The Landscape, A Didactic Poem*, 1794, two illustrations contrast a neo-classical villa in a barren Brownian setting with an asymmetrical house in a verdant, irregular and overgrown landscape, which Knight assumes to be more conducive to the association of ideas.[107]

Landowners and Whig Members of Parliament, Knight and Price's criticisms were social as well as cultural. Still the dominant political party, the Whigs' liberal agenda sponsored the abolition of slavery, Catholic emancipation and parliamentary reform in the first half of the nineteenth century. Price's criticism of the Brownian landscape concerned its lack of social diversity as well as its repetitive aesthetic. He interpreted the picturesque broadly and cited the variety of his Herefordshire estate – from fields to farm cottages to woodland walks – as a means to establish social cohesion between landowner, tenant farmer and agricultural labourer, maintaining the existing hierarchy and affirming the Georgic tradition. In an extensive footnote at the end of *The Landscape, A Didactic Poem*, Knight recoils from the turmoil of the 1789 French Revolution.[108] A reference such as 'Walls, mellow'd into harmony by time' is a metaphor for the social benefits of continuity and compromise as well as a building description.[109]

Knight and Price had an extensive knowledge of paintings and treatises, but they were less certain of their status than the aristocrats, generals and major landowners who commissioned early eighteenth-century gardens, and they resented professionals such as Brown and Repton who earned a living from garden design. Indebted to Brown, Repton's slowly winding paths and softly rolling lawns have few architectural and topographical incidents and neither the intimacy of the early eighteenth-century picturesque nor the savagery of the later picturesque advocated by Gilpin, Price and Knight. As Brown was dead, Repton responded to the criticisms, concluding that Brown's inadequate imitators were to blame, not Brown.[110] Questioning Knight's assertion that Brown was 'ignorant of painting' and had a formulaic disregard for nature's variety, Repton returned the criticism. Dismissing the 'wild neglect' of Knight's illustration of a picturesque landscape, he concluded that Knight saw 'no delight but in the scenes of Salvator Rosa'.[111]

Richard Payne Knight,
The Landscape,
A Didactic Poem,
1794, two comparative
illustrations by Thomas
Hearne. Courtesy of the
British Library.

Humphry Repton,
Illustration from *Sketches
and Hints on Landscape
Gardening*, 1794. Courtesy
of Private Collection/
Photograph, Christie's
images/Bridgeman Images.

Marc-Antoine Laugier, *Essai sur l'architecture*, 1753.
Frontispiece to the second edition, 1755. Courtesy of
the British Library.

Soane praised Kent's influence on garden design, and did not significantly criticise Brown; while a student he had worked in the partnership that Brown shared with the architect Henry Holland.[112] But he acknowledged Price's influence and his debt to Knight was deeper still. Purchased the year it was published, Knight's *An Analytical Inquiry into the Principles of Taste*, 1805, states that richly varied picturesque effects stimulate the association of ideas, inspiring extensive notes during Soane's preparation for his second lecture series.[113]

Soane's concern for architecture's relations with nature relied on Enlightenment architecture as well as the picturesque landscape, which shared a substantial debt to the writings of Locke, Shaftesbury and Burke. Enlightenment architects argued that architecture is superior to the other arts because it follows nature's principles not merely its image, an opinion that Soane proudly affirmed.[114] In the frontispiece to the second, 1755 edition of Marc-Antoine's Laugier's *Essai sur l'architecture*, 1753, the primitive hut – four tree-trunks supporting a pediment of branches – is deemed to be perfect because it follows the reason inherent in nature and humanity alike. Extending the analogy and praising the picturesque, Laugier writes: 'One must look at a town as a forest . . . Let us carry out this idea and use the design of our parks as plan for our towns.'[115] Laugier's proposal was practical as well as aesthetic. Writing before the industrial revolution, he advocated physiocracy, an economic theory popular in the mid-eighteenth century in which a nation's wealth and city's wellbeing depended on their relations with agricultural development.[116]

Soane admired Laugier, owning many copies of the various editions of *Essai sur l'architecture*, which was first published in English as *An Essay on Architecture*, 1755. In common with other architects who were inspired by Laugier's example, Soane's confidence in architecture's natural origins was sincere if unsubstantiated. He made little attempt to understand and investigate nature even though it was increasingly a subject of scientific research. Nature was but a useful concept, first to justify reason as natural, then to justify feelings as natural, and ultimately to make any human intervention appear natural, whether a building, garden or city. Soane's concern for reason and nature was stimulated rather than undermined by the ambiguity of these terms with regard to architecture because his ultimate concern was the architectural imagination.

Responding to Laugier and also to Nicolas Le Camus de Mézières' claim in *Le génie de l'architecture; ou, l'analogie de cet art avec nos sensations*, 1780, (*The Genius of Architecture; or, The Analogy of that Art With Our Sensations*) that a house and a garden can be designed according to similar principles, Soane conceived 12–14 Lincoln's Inn Fields as a garden of architecture.[117] Drawings,

112 Soane, 'Lecture XI', 'Lecture VIII', in Watkin, *Sir John Soane*, p. 642.

113 Knight, *An Analytical Inquiry*, pp. 139–140.

114 Soane, 'Lecture III', in Watkin, *Sir John Soane*, p. 532.

115 Soane's reference to first garden design and then urban design in his tenth lecture is indebted to Laugier. Laugier, pp. 128–129; Soane, 'Lecture X', in Watkin, *Sir John Soane*, p. 628.

116 Cosgrove, *Social Formation and Symbolic Landscape*, p. 220.

117 Le Camus de Mézières, p. 74. Refer to Middleton, 'Introduction', pp. 51–54; Pelletier, 131–137.

Sir John Soane, The Dome
Area with Soane's bust,
12–14 Lincoln's Inn Fields.
Photograph: Martin Charles.
Courtesy of the Trustees of
Sir John Soane's Museum,
London.

118 Identifying two devices available in the eighteenth century, Deborah Jane Warner and Arnaud Maillet distinguish between the Claude Mirror, a tinted convex mirror, and the Claude Glass, a flat coloured glass, sometimes presented as an array of separately tinted sheets. But I refer to the tinted convex mirror as the Claude Glass, which, as Maillet acknowledges, is an English convention. Warner, pp. 158–159; Maillet, pp. 31–32.

119 Soane regularly visited Oxford and Blenheim, and also travelled on the road between Oxford and Banbury, which passes close to Rousham, only 30 miles from his birthplace. Soane, 'Soane's Note Books', vol. 5, 1803–1804, p. 5; vol. 10, 1817–1819, p. 22; vol. 12, 1823–1828, p. 106.

paintings and windows offer vistas and routes punctuated by ruins and monuments. To disperse light and views, mirrors are positioned in every direction. Many are flat and tinted or convex and round, collectively recalling the Claude Glass, a device named after Claude but never used by him, which alters a landscape according to picturesque conventions of composition and colour.[118] 12–14 Lincoln's Inn Fields is so excessively emblematic that it is expressive. Even for a frequent visitor, learned interpretation of all the artefacts on view is impossible. Sculptures and antiquities cover every surface like architectural foliage, recalling the shaggy aesthetic of the late eighteenth-century picturesque, while alternative routes and intricately interconnecting spaces are reminiscent of the early picturesque.[119]

Avid for acquisition and adjustment, Soane's inquisitive imagination guaranteed seasonal and yearly transformations. Concerned to engender ideas and emotions, wonder as well as discourse, Soane eulogised 'the poetry of Architecture', noting the creative influence of climate on architecture and emphasising the lyrical effects of weather on architectural experience.[120] Beyond the city he enjoyed the shifting modulations of mist and light. But in London his sensory appreciation extended no further than the boundaries of his home, concluding that retreat was the appropriate response to the city's heavy pollution.

With rudimentary drainage, open fires and candle lighting, the eighteenth-century house was no more successful a climate modifier than those of previous centuries. But the emergence of new technologies, such as central heating and water closets, ensured that the nineteenth-century house provided a more comfortable internal environment. At 12–14 Lincoln's Inn Fields, Soane designed a climate as well as a garden. He displayed eleven instruments to measure time and atmosphere, including a late seventeenth-century barometer, and experimented with new heating and lighting technologies. Soane dedicated a lengthy passage to heating systems in his eighth lecture, and particularly appreciated modern ones that could be justified by reference to ancient Roman steam and hot water systems.[121] Modulating light and temperature, he employed an invention of the industrial era, central heating, to render his garden habitable and counter a by-product of industrialisation, intense pollution. To bathe his garden in a golden light he inserted coloured glass skylights and limited visits to sunnier days. Distinguishing between a benign internal climate and a malign external climate, Soane created an architectural garden to exclude London. He fabricated a climate just as he fabricated a ruin. Only he determined his garden's growth and decay. Conceiving 12–14 Lincoln's Inn Fields as a means of self-expression and morbidly concerned for his reputation and ruin, Soane displayed some of the characteristics of a romantic artist. But in attempting to deny the weather, he ignored a crucial aspect of the picturesque and isolated himself from the direct and unmediated engagement with nature and atmospheric phenomena that characterised romanticism.

Undermining Soane's intentions, the internal climate was susceptible to unexpected weather conditions. In 1812 the Gas Light and Coke Company received a Royal Charter to illuminate the cities of London and Westminster, as well as the borough of Southwark.[122] Soane experimented with domestic gas lamps before they were widely adopted but blackened internal surfaces were a consequence, even more so than with earlier lighting technologies such as oil lamps and wax candles. A contemporary observer remarked: 'When you needed your ceiling

120 Soane, *Description of the House and Museum*, 1835, p. 54; Soane, 'Lecture I', in Watkin, *Sir John Soane*, p. 497. Refer to Saisselin, pp. 247–248.

121 Soane, 'Lecture VIII', in Watkin, *Sir John Soane*, pp. 595–598; Richardson, *A Popular Treatise*, p. 52, quoted in Willmert, pp. 47–48.

122 Dillon, p. 229.

123 Edis, p. 143.

124 Bailey, quoted in Harris, 'Sir John Soane's Library', p. 246.

whitewashed once a year, now you have to have it done three or four times. The filth from the impurities of the gas is something extraordinary.'[123] In 1837 George Bailey, the first curator of Sir John Soane's Museum, noted the damage caused by the glass-fronted bookcases, which Soane no doubt appreciated for their reflective qualities: 'Many of the Books were found to have suffered from mildew; in many instances evidently from having being closed immediately after being bound up.'[124]

12–14 Lincoln's Inn Fields is an evocative architectural expression of the interdependence of landscape, history and fiction, but Soane achieved so much by looking inwards. Soane and Turner lived barely a mile apart. But their attitudes to London's atmosphere were distant. Soane created a clear division between a benign internal climate and a malign external one, while Turner acknowledged a creative interaction between the domestic and urban scales. Soane recognised the poetic potential of an internal climate, while Turner celebrated London's fog and smog in his dilapidated studio. Soane wished to control ruination while Turner accepted decay. To some extent, their differing professions determined their differing attitudes. Creating a consistent and comfortable environment, the architect has a responsibility to everyday use that need not concern the painter. But Soane and Turner also represent differing responses to architectural authorship. There is a fundamental difference between an isolated interior in which the designer aims for complete control and a complex and inter-related environment in which the designer accepts a myriad of contributing influences and acknowledges the weather as a significant authorial voice.

3

the history man

1 Clark, quoted in Woodward,

In Ruins, p. 212.

'Bomb damage is itself picturesque', responded Kenneth Clark – director of the National Gallery and chairman of the War Artists Advisory Committee – following the aerial bombardment of London during the Blitz.[1] Clark's stoic embrace of disorder and ruin was in line with a burgeoning romanticism in 1940s Britain, which celebrated national identity and affirmed the association of a people with a place, bolstering the nation against military aggression. The tenets of this romanticism soon found support among other figures of Britain's intelligentsia, with Clark joined by T. S. Eliot and John Maynard Keynes in writing a letter to *The Times* in 1944 in which they state that a ruined church would be an evocative monument to wartime sacrifices.[2] Their letter was reprinted in a subsequent

2 Clark et al., in Casson, Colvin and

Groag, p. 4.

publication, *Bombed Churches as War Memorials*, 1945, in which the landscape architect Brenda Colvin complements this recognition of the cultural value of a damaged ruin with a corresponding call for an enveloping and unkempt nature. Her landscape proposal for Christopher Wren's Christ Church, Newgate Street, would 'emphasise the passing seasons' in relation to the 'charred and battered' church and 'the crisp polished facades of the surrounding buildings', reintroducing 'the self-sown flowers' that had flourished during the sustained German bombing raids of 1940 and 1941.[3] Returning to this theme in the sec-

3 Colvin, 'A Planting Plan',

pp. 26, 28, 30.

ond edition of *Land and Landscape,* 1947, she writes: 'With a little imagination one might visualise a London left to nature's healing hand after all mankind was doomed, and see, in the mind's eye, a lost and broken city hidden under a great forest of sycamore'.[4] As before, the ruin was adopted as an image of hope as well as loss.

4 Colvin, *Land and Landscape*,

1970, p. 222.

Colvin's purpose was metaphysical and spiritual as well as practical and social, two attitudes to nature that developed alongside each other during the seventeenth and eighteenth centuries. She acknowledged the influence on the English landscape of Addison, Pope and Kent, but gave particular attention to Evelyn, who had emphasised forestry science and sustainable development in *Sylva, or A Discourse of Forest-Trees*, 1664, of which she owned a copy.[5] Colvin was a member of the Institute of Landscape Architects' wartime

5 Colvin, *Land and Landscape*,

1970, pp. 34–35, 59, 61; Evelyn,

Sylva, pp. 112–120.

Forestry Committee, which reported its conclusions in the October 1944 issue of *Wartime Journal*: 'just as the scenery in lowland Britain owes so much to the landscape planting of the eighteenth century, so we of this generation . . . have the power to create a new and hitherto undreamt of scenery'.[6] Proposing

6 Colvin et al., *Wartime Journal*,

October 1944, quoted in Gibson,

p. 108.

a vocabulary for postwar reforestation in *Trees for Town and Country*, 1947, she notes that just 23 of the 60 trees in her book originated in Britain and invokes an allegory of liberalism: 'Although introduced to Britain by human agency, the Spanish chestnut grows well on light soils and suits our landscape. It has become so well integrated that the eye accepts it as a native tree.'[7]

Nikolaus Pevsner, the most sustained advocate of the twentieth-century picturesque, and himself something of a non-native transplant, offered a human equivalent to Colvin's sylvan allegory: 'England has indeed profited just as much from the un-Englishness of the immigrants as they have profited from the Englishing they underwent'.[8] The diverse origins of the picturesque and its openness to new influences were important in the eighteenth century and again two centuries later, when at the height of the war Pevsner recalled the traditional two-way cultural dialogue between England and continental Europe, describing the picturesque as England's principal contribution to European architecture.[9] For Pevsner, the picturesque was 'tied up with English outdoor life and ultimately even the general British philosophy of liberalism and liberty'.[10] His promotion of the picturesque culminated in 'The Englishness of English Art', the 1955 BBC Reith Lectures, which soon appeared in book form. The first chapter emphasises the prevalence of climate in the nation's art and literature and suggests that a phlegmatic pleasure in unreliable weather is particularly English.[11] While recognising that national character is far from permanent and that a fascination for the atmosphere is European as well as English, Pevsner attributes two traits of English liberalism – moderation and imagination – to a mild and misty climate: 'That moisture steams out of Turner's canvases . . . and lays a haze over man and building, dissolving their bodily solidity.'[12]

Eight years earlier, and in conjunction with his colleagues at *The Architectural Review* – Hubert de Cronin Hastings, Osbert Lancaster and J. M. Richards – Pevsner had published an editorial in the celebratory fiftieth anniversary issue titled 'The Second Half Century'. Calling for a 'new humanism' alongside a new environmentalism, this text, which implied a reassessment of modernism as well as the magazine itself, promoted 'a new richness and differentiation of character, the pursuit of difference rather than sameness, the re-emergence of monumentality, the cultivation of idiosyncrasy and the development of those regional dissimilarities that people have always taken pride in'.[13]

In contrast to early modernism's concern for lightness and impermanence, the new attention to monumentality was a reaction to modernism's failure to articulate societal values and gain widespread respect. Stimulated by Sigfried Giedion's lecture at the Royal Institute of British Architects (RIBA) in September 1946, *The Architectural Review* arranged a symposium entitled 'In Search of a New Monumentality', which was attended by Giedion, Walter Gropius and Henry-Russell Hitchcock among others, and published in 1948.[14] Reflecting on the symposium, the editors continued in a similar vein, praising the successful

7 Colvin, *Land and Landscape*, 1970, p. 220.

8 Pevsner, *The Englishness of English Art*, p. 185.

9 Pevsner, 'The Genesis of the Picturesque', p. 139.

10 Pevsner, 'The Genius of the Place', p. 232.

11 Pevsner, *The Englishness of English Art*, p. 14.

12 Pevsner, *The Englishness of English Art*, pp. 18–19, 185–187, 163–164.

13 Hastings et al., 'The Second Half Century', p. 36.

14 In 1943, Giedion, Fernand Léger and José Luis Sert prepared a joint essay, 'Nine Points on Monumentality', commissioned by the association of American Abstract Artists (AAA). When the AAA publication failed to appear in print, Giedion arranged for his essay, 'The Need for a New Monumentality', to open the section entitled 'The Problem of a New Monumentality' in Paul Zucker's symposium 'New Architecture and City Planning' at Columbia University in 1944, which also appeared as an edited book. Giedion, Léger and Sert, pp. 48–51; Giedion, 'The Need for a New Monumentality', pp. 25–39.

'battle against period revivalism' while acknowledging that 'functionalism was not enough', and concluding that modernism

> has only achieved the first negative stage of the struggle for a contemporary architectural language. The second positive stage has still to be undertaken, the development on an idiom rich and flexible enough to express all the ideas that architecture – especially representational architecture – ought to be capable of expressing.[15]

For Pevsner, aware of resistance to a new architecture, the picturesque was a means to make modernism familiar. Remarking that the picturesque and 'the modern revolution . . . had all the fundamentals in common' he also wished to distinguish between interwar and postwar modernism.[16] Noting an increasing sensitivity to place and 'a new faith in nature' that recalled Thomson, Pevsner drew attention to the picturesque in order to question one modernism – universal, mechanical and insensitive – in favour of another that was local, empirical and environmentally aware.[17] Denying that picturesque modernism was nostalgic, he evoked Locke to conclude: 'In planning and architecture today, "each case on its merit" is the functional approach.'[18]

Pevsner's praise for the picturesque met extensive criticism. Alan Colquhoun, with a certain modernist intransigence, claimed that Pevsner had focused on aesthetics to the detriment of function, which Pevsner denied, repeating his opinion that the 'aesthetic value' of the picturesque, and of modernism, were 'stimulated by the disciplines of function and technique'.[19] But Pevsner's most ardent critic, due to their close association, was Reyner Banham, whose PhD he had supervised. Banham admired the picturesque, appreciating 'a controlling sensibility that combined toughness of conception with tenderness towards the "genius of the place"'.[20] But he was shocked by his former tutor's emphasis on its continuing relevance, declaring Pevsner's support for the 'empiricism and compromises' of the picturesque to be a denial of his life's work.[21]

In opposition to the picturesque and in support of an alternative modernism, Banham promoted a new architectural movement – The New Brutalism – in *The Architectural Review*'s December 1955 issue.[22] As precedents he cited the anti-formal and non-hierarchical tendencies in Jean Dubuffet's *art brut* and Michel Tapié's *Un art autre*, 1952, which he transformed into *Une architecture autre*. The principles of brutalism are, Banham concludes, '1. Memorability as an image; 2. Clear exhibition of structure; and 3. Valuation of materials "as found".'[23] The second and third principles affirmed the modernist concern for truthful and unadorned structures and materials. The first principle was less expected, given modernism's

15 Hastings et al, 'In Search of a New Monumentality', p. 117.

16 Pevsner, 'Twentieth-Century Picturesque: An Answer to Basil Taylor's Broadcast', p. 229.

17 Pevsner, 'The Lure of Rusticity', p. 27.

18 Pevsner, 'The Genius of the Place', p. 233. Refer to Macarthur and Aitchison, pp. 1–43.

19 Colquhoun, p. 2; Pevsner, 'Twentieth-Century Picturesque: An Answer to Basil Taylor's Broadcast', p. 229, quoted in Pevsner, 'Twentieth Century Picturesque: Reply to Alan Colquhoun', p. 2. For an attempt to relate modernism and the picturesque in compositional terms refer to Hitchcock, pp. 9, 12, 220.

20 Banham, 'Kent and Capability', p. 89.

21 Banham, 'Revenge of the Picturesque', p. 267.

22 In 'The New Brutalism' Banham does not refer to the picturesque directly but to Basil Taylor's criticism, to which Pevsner responded. In *The New Brutalism*, Banham details his attack on the picturesque. Banham, 'The New Brutalism', p. 355; Banham, *The New Brutalism*, p. 43, Pevsner, 'Twentieth-Century Picturesque: An Answer to Basil Taylor's Broadcast', pp. 227–229.

23 Banham, 'The New Brutalism', p. 361.

Alison and Peter Smithson, Hunstanton Secondary Modern School, Norfolk, 1954. Interior. Courtesy of RIBA Library Photographs Collection.

supposed aversion to aesthetic discussions and Banham's famous conclusion to *Theory and Design in the First Machine Age*, 1960, which was based on his doctoral thesis: 'The architect who proposes to run with technology . . . may have to emulate the Futurists and discard his whole cultural load.'[24] Banham's attention to image memorability may have been, in part, a response to the profusion of mass-produced images in the postwar era,[25] as well as a reaffirmation of architects' long-held concern to creatively blur the relations between drawings and buildings. But the image he advocated is not applied; it is the direct result of structure and function, materials and technology. While some of his contemporaries believed that modernism had been too functional, Banham concluded that it had not been functional enough. Instead of the metaphorical functionalism that he too often found in early modernism, he promoted a literal functionalism. Identifying Alison and Peter Smithson as brutalism's key architects, Banham praises the directness of

24 Banham, *Theory and Design in the First Machine Age*, pp. 329–330.

25 Zimmerman, p. 221.

129

their first significant building, Hunstanton Secondary Modern School in northwest Norfolk, close to Houghton, which he describes as

almost unique among modern buildings in being made of what it appears to be made of . . . Water and electricity do not come out of unexplained holes in the wall, but are delivered to the point of use by visible pipes and manifest conduits.[26]

26 Banham, 'The New Brutalism', p. 357.

Banham's one criticism was Hunstanton's formal composition. Concerned that a design should reflect the logical disposition of its functions, he was suspicious of symmetry, as was Pevsner for similar reasons, and his preference for a memorable, asymmetrical image may indicate a suppressed debt to the picturesque and his doctoral supervisor. Banham attributed Hunstanton's symmetry to the influence of Rudolf Wittkower, who in *Architectural Principles in the Age of Humanism*, 1949, hoped to stimulate architects to develop 'new and unexpected solutions to this ancient problem' of proportion and its symbolic meaning to society.[27] But the Smithsons disputed the timing of Wittkower's influence and may instead have read Colin Rowe's 'The Mathematics of the Ideal Villa', 1947. Comparing the Platonic form and Arcadian setting of Palladio's Villa Rotonda, 1569, and Villa Foscari, c.1560, to those of Le Corbusier's Villa Savoye, Poissy, 1931, and Villa Stein, Garches, 1927, Rowe helped to promote a further Palladian revival.[28] Together, Wittkower and Rowe were the catalyst for a classical resurgence in modernism. By 1952 the Smithsons described *Architectural Principles* as 'the most important work on architecture published in England since the war'.[29] Pevsner's only rejoinder was to caustically remark that Hunstanton School 'is entirely unbrutal. It is symmetrical, clean, precise'.[30]

27 Wittkower, p. 135.

28 Rowe refers to Isaac Ware's 1738 English translation of *I quattro libri dell' archittetura* and the original French edition of *Précisions*, 1930. Rowe, 'The Mathematics of the Ideal Villa', pp. 2–14.

29 Alison and Peter Smithson, 'Correspondence: Architectural Principles in the Age of Humanism', p. 140.

30 Pevsner, 'The Anti-Pioneers', p. 298.

The Smithsons claimed that Alison Smithson was the first person to use the term 'brutalism' in 1953, and Banham's article on the subject was a response to their one-page statement in the January 1955 issue of *Architectural Design* in which they describe 'The New Brutalism' as 'the only possible development *for this moment* from the Modern Movement'.[31] As precedents the Smithsons emphasise Le Corbusier's use of primitive *béton brut* (raw concrete) in the early 1950s, which Banham also mentions, and the 'reverence for the natural world and, from that, for the materials of the built world' in traditional Japanese architecture.[32]

31 Alison and Peter Smithson, 'Banham's Bumper Book on Brutalism', p. 1590; Alison and Peter Smithson, 'The New Brutalism', p. 1.

32 Banham notes that the Smithsons had not visited Japan at that time. Alison and Peter Smithson, 'The New Brutalism', p. 1; Banham, 'The New Brutalism', p. 356; Banham, *The New Brutalism*, p. 46.

33 Lasdun, in Davies and Lasdun, 'Thoughts in Progress: The New Brutalism', pp. 111–112. Refer to Calder, pp. 59–68.

It was at this stage that Denys Lasdun entered the debate, deriding weak-willed postwar architecture, mocking the Festival of Britain and welcoming brutalism's contribution as being more worthwhile than '90 per cent of the architectural theorizing that is going on at present'.[33] Lasdun was then in his early forties, and about a decade older than the Smithsons. In the 1930s he had worked for Berthold Lubetkin's Tecton, returning there to become a partner after the war. By the mid-1950s, he had progressed from the early Corbusianism of his house in Newton Road, west London, 1937, to the more sculpturally and materially expressive cluster block, Keeling House, that he designed and built in Bethnal Green, east London. In Britain, due to his prestigious commissions, Lasdun would become the architect most identified with brutalism, more even than the Smithsons. But dismissing the term as dogmatic, Lasdun never applied it to his own work and vehemently disliked being called a brutalist. Neither did he consider Le Corbusier to be one.

Lasdun praised Wittkower, and remarked with regard to Hunstanton: 'This is a good building because it observes, with an uncompromising rigour, the classic properties in its proportions and in the disposition of its masses and volumes. The more specifically brutalist elements, such as the untreated materials and the exposed pipes and ducts and conduits, do not add anything at all as far as I can see.'[34] In an immediate, dismissive riposte, the Smithsons claimed that Lasdun's critique was just stylistic, while their concern was to draw an ethical 'rough poetry out of the confused and powerful forces which are at work' in a complex 'mass production society'.[35]

In *The New Brutalism: Ethic or Aesthetic,* 1966, Banham reflected on the movement's development and acknowledged the Smithsons' disregard for *The Architectural Review*'s promotion of the picturesque in 1947:

> Such an approach, which 'judges every case on its merits', etc, stands on a firm tradition of British Liberalism, democracy and common law, but it seemed of absolutely trivial value to a younger generation to whom the given elements of the planning situation seemed to be social chaos, a world in ruins, the prospect of nuclear annihilation, and what appeared to be a complete abandonment of architectural standards on the part of their elders.[36]

After this initial opposition, which the Smithsons confirmed in an otherwise withering book review, Banham documented the Smithsons' increasing engagement with the picturesque, citing their competition design for Coventry Cathedral in 1951 as a turning point.[37] But Banham underestimated the speed and extent of the Smithsons' conversion to the picturesque. Even at Hunstanton, which was first designed in 1949 and completed in 1954, there are references to the English landscape garden, including a ha-ha at the entrance, recalling a Palladian house and its setting.[38]

To promote the conjunction of modernism and the picturesque, *The Architectural Review* had included building reviews alongside articles on 'Fonthill

34 Lasdun, in Davies and Lasdun, 'Thoughts in Progress: Summing Up III – The "Objects Found" Philosophy', p. 436; Lasdun, in Davies and Lasdun, 'Thoughts in Progress: The New Brutalism', pp. 111–112.

35 Alison and Peter Smithson, 'The New Brutalism: Alison and Peter Smithson Answer the Criticisms on the Opposite Page', p. 113.

36 Banham, *The New Brutalism*, p. 12.

37 Banham, *The New Brutalism*, p. 12; Banham, 'Revenge of the Picturesque', p. 273; Alison and Peter Smithson, 'Banham's Bumper Book on Brutalism', p. 1590.

38 Alison and Peter Smithson, *Alison and Peter Smithson: The Shift*, p. 36.

Alison and Peter Smithson,
Hunstanton Secondary
Modern School, Norfolk,
1954. View from the ha-ha.
Courtesy of Architectural
Press Archive/RIBA Library
Photographs Collection.

James Wyatt, Fonthill
Abbey, Wiltshire, 1796.
View of the South Front, in
John Rutter, *Delineations
of Fonthill and its Abbey*,
1823, plate 12.

Abbey', 'The Lure of Rusticity' and related themes.[39] As a second home to their one in London, in 1958 the Smithsons bought a property in Wiltshire, furthering their fascination for the picturesque by transforming a small dilapidated cottage into Upper Lawn Pavilion, a new '"folly" implanted' within the late eighteenth-century estate of ruined Fonthill Abbey,[40] which Turner had painted while it was under construction.[41]

The Smithsons applied the theory of the picturesque widely, including to car travel.[42] Designed in 1955, their favourite was the Citroën DS, which they characterised as brutalist.[43] *AS in DS: An Eye on the Road*, 1983, is Alison Smithson's account of earlier journeys between their urban and rural homes and around England, focusing on the country rather than the city. She often remarked: 'A book is like a small building to us.'[44] This one is cut to the plan-shape of the car that made it possible, at 1:18 scale and a size common to toy cars and architectural guidebooks.[45] Photographs of the DS in front of Upper Lawn Pavilion pay homage to Le Corbusier's 1921 mass-production '"Citrohan" (not to say Citroën). That is to say, a house like a motor-car' and his habit of photographing a favoured car in front of his houses of that era.[46] Writing in 1957, Roland Barthes remarked that *La Déesse* – the Goddess – 'marks a change in the mythology of cars . . . it is now more *homely* . . . conceived as comfort rather than performance'.[47] Panoramic windows, pneumatic suspension, front wheel drive, 3125mm between the front and rear axles and a chassis-cloaking body combine to create a smooth and spacious ride: Alison Smithson's 'private room on wheels'.[48]

Le Corbusier's appreciation of the machine aesthetic had further relevance. In his analogy of cars to temples in *Vers une architecture*, 1923 – published in English as *Towards a New Architecture*, 1927 – there is an echo of Plato's praise for the beauty of 'solids produced on a lathe or with ruler and square'.[49] If a car can be a building *La Déesse* qualifies as both a mobile home and a touring temple.

In his introduction, Peter Smithson describes *AS in DS* as a 'Primer' for the 'sensibility resulting from the moving view of landscape'.[50] Comforted in 'our own-climate-cell', Alison Smithson concludes that observation at a distance and at speed can still be engaged.[51] Rather than characterise this sensibility as new, she locates its origins in the eighteenth-century landscape, which was also explored through movement: 'With landscape, we are most encumbered by established English sensibilities; and so deeply involved we have in front of our eyes almost a pre-formed vision, the where-with-all to relive the whole spirit of the English picturesque.'[52]

39 Bronkman, pp. 149–157; Pevsner, 'The Lure of Rusticity', p. 27.

40 Alison and Peter Smithson, *The Charged Void*, p. 238.

41 In 1798, two years into its lengthy construction, the architect James Wyatt commissioned Turner to paint *A Projected Design for Fonthill Abbey* to convince and delight William Beckford, his patron. The painting was exhibited at the Royal Academy with only the architect credited. In the following year Beckford invited Turner to depict the Abbey under construction. Fonthill Abbey was completed in 1807. In 1823 Beckford sold it due to financial pressures.

42 The Smithsons' interest in driving extended to urban design. Multiple urban centres were connected by motorways in 'Cluster City', which they first presented at CIAM's tenth conference at Dubrovnik in 1956. Alison and Peter Smithson, 'Cluster City', pp. 332–336.

43 The architect Flaminio Bertoni was the designer. Alison and Peter Smithson, 'Banham's Bumper Book on Brutalism', p. 1591.

44 Alison Smithson, quoted in Peter Smithson, 'Think of it as a Farm!', p. 97.

45 Citroën paid for the book to be cut to this size and shape.

46 Le Corbusier, p. 222.

47 Barthes, 'The New Citroën', p. 89.

48 Alison Smithson, *AS in DS*, p. 111.

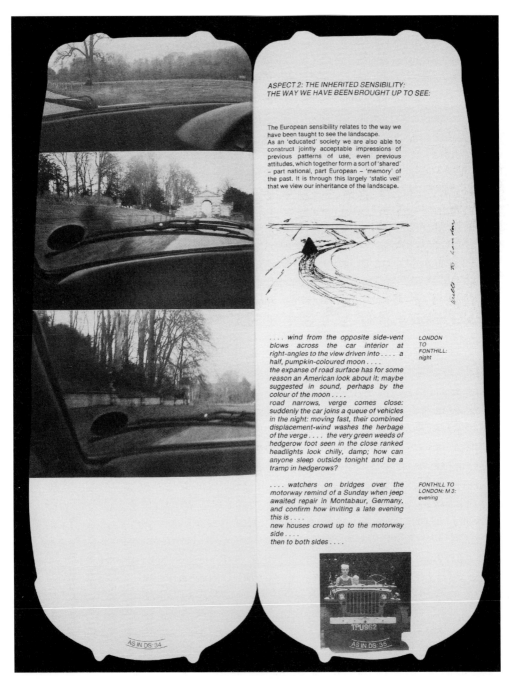

Alison Smithson, *AS in DS: An Eye on the Road*, 1983, pp. 34–35. First published in 1983 by Delft University Press, reprint in 2001 by Lars Müller Publishers, Switzerland. Courtesy of the Smithson Family Collection.

Alison and Peter Smithson, Upper Lawn Pavilion, 1959–. View of the north façade and Citroën DS, 1962. Courtesy of the Smithson Family Collection.

49 Le Corbusier, pp. 31, 124, 125, 130, 135; Plato, *Philebus*, p. 51.

50 Peter Smithson, 'A Sensibility Primer', p. 1; Alison Smithson, *AS in DS*, p. 47.

51 Alison Smithson, *AS in DS*, pp. 47, 111.

52 Alison Smithson, *AS in DS*, p. 151.

A narrative illustrated with pictorial representations, *AS in DS* follows Colonna's model as well as that of the autobiographical, visual and spatial diary combining design and history, as in Kent's Italian notebook. *AS in DS* is about the picturesque and of the picturesque: it affords many views literally and in interpretation. In words, drawings, maps and photographs – many produced in the DS – diary entries describe nature and weather and, emphasising the association of ideas, refer to travels, peoples and events in the past and present from Thomas Gainsborough to Apollo 13. Each diary entry describes an 'as found' condition in a vivid and immediate manner that is typical of brutalism and the picturesque:

> a brush-stroke of duck-egg blue setting-off aggressive grey clouds; a foretaste of the stupendous water-sharp-colours of the view that never fails to please . . . the sun behind and to the right, shows to perfection massed bare woods and ivy clad trunks.[53]

53 Alison Smithson, *AS in DS*, p. 39.

Views through side and rear view mirrors appear frequently in *AS in DS*, recalling a favoured instrument of the picturesque. In a Gainsborough sketch, c.1750, a seated artist holds the Claude Glass in his left hand and sketches with

Thomas Gainsborough,
Sketch of an Artist with a
'Claude Glass', c.1750.
Courtesy of the British
Museum.

his right. Praising 'the *general effect*, the *forms of the objects*, and the *beauty of tints*, in one complex view', Gilpin even describes the merits of using the Claude Glass in a fast-moving carriage: 'We are rapidly carried from one object to another. A succession of high-coloured pictures is continually gliding before the eye. They are like the visions of the imagination; or the brilliant landscapes of a dream.'[54] The Claude Glass was just one instrument carried by an eighteenth-century

54 Gilpin, *Remarks on Forest Scenery,* vol. 2, p. 225.

picturesque tourist. Others included pens, pencils, watercolours, sketchbooks, guides, a pedometer, water-flask, telescope and barometer. Together, they equate to the instrumentation available to Alison Smithson in the DS. A car driver looks forward through the windscreen and backwards through mirrors. But a Claude Glass draws the eye to the reflected landscape not the path ahead. In 1805 a Lakeland traveller who stumbled near the summit of Helvellyn was found with a Claude Glass by his side, becoming 'the first man to die in search of the picturesque'.[55] As a passenger, Alison Smithson could concentrate on the view and not worry about the drive.

Although she appreciated its compositional possibilities, her concern for the picturesque was not only visual. As a 'teaching document' Alison Smithson intended *AS in DS* to improve understanding of specific landscape conditions, such as weather, topography, natural history and use, and to encourage designs that would respond with thoughtful invention. She notes the delicate adjustments of an old road to site and seasons. In contrast, 'a modern road might lead a passenger to suspect that the road's engineer has no long knowledge of the route, nor the tricks

Alison and Peter Smithson, Upper Lawn Pavilion, 1959–. View through the patio window to the Fonthill woods to the north, 1995, taken after the Smithsons left Fonthill. Courtesy of Georg Aerni.

55 Hamblyn, p. 172. Refer to 'The Story of Gough and his Dog' in Rawnsley, pp. 153–208; Maillet, p. 271, n. 5.

56 Alison Smithson, *AS in DS*,
p. 91, refer to p. 11.

57 Alison and Peter Smithson,
'Cluster City', p. 332.

58 Zweinger-Bargielowska,
pp. 234–242.

of micro-climate, nor sufficient interest to have travelled "his" route to discover its seasonal weather mutations'.[56] In the subtlety of the old landscape, she identifies a model for a new architecture. Like Pevsner, the Smithsons associated the picturesque with an attitude to function that was indebted to empiricism, writing in 1957 that 'today the word functional does not merely mean mechanical, as it did 30 years ago. Our functionalism means accepting the realities of the situation, with all their contradictions and confusions, and trying to do something with them'.[57]

Such an opportunity soon arose. After 15 years, rationing in the UK finally ended in 1954, leading to rising prices.[58] But the consumer boom was so buoyant that in

Alison and Peter Smithson, *The Economist* Building, London, 1964. Street view. Courtesy of John Donat/ RIBA Library Photographs Collection.

1957 the incoming Conservative Prime Minister Harold Macmillan famously remarked that 'people have never had it so good'.[59] In 'Letter to America', 1958, Peter Smithson indicated his growing disenchantment with wasteful 'consumer-orientated society', emphasising instead the continuing relevance of the make-do-and-mend philosophy that had prevailed during rationing.[60] But just a year later, the Smithsons accepted the commission to design the central London headquarters for *The Economist* newspaper, a consistent advocate of free trade and globalisation. The Smithsons' decision was not so surprising when considered historically. For eighteenth-century advocates of the picturesque, British liberalism included economic liberalism.

As a catalyst to design, the Smithsons chose the polluted atmosphere of the capital city, which was still nicknamed the 'Big Smoke'. In response to 'The London Fog Inquiry', 1901, an editorial in *Nature* described atmospheric pollution as London's 'insidious enemy', recalling Evelyn's language 250 years earlier.[61] Atmospheric pollution in the city peaked in around 1900 and by 1950 was merely at the same level as in 1700. Air quality was often worst in winter, when cold, stagnant weather prevented the dispersal of pollutants. On Thursday 4 December 1952 a slow-moving anticyclone settled over the city. By the following night, it had stalled completely.[62] Sir Donald Acheson, once the Chief Medical Officer, recalled: 'I lost myself in a street in London which I knew like the back of my hand. I couldn't see anything, had no idea where I was'.[63] In a single day, the filters to the National Gallery's air conditioning system 'clogged at 26 times the normal rate and in one four-hour period they clogged at 54 times the normal rate'.[64] The cause of 4,000 deaths, the Great Smog of 1952 was a catalyst for the Clean Air Act of 1956, which was the first UK legislation to address pollution from domestic as well as industrial sources. The Act did not address the true pollutant – sulphur dioxide – but sulphur emissions were reduced because all domestic and most industrial consumption was transferred to electricity, gas and smokeless fuels, which combined with a further decrease due to industrial decline. But reductions in traditional pollutants were to some extent matched by an increase in other pollutants, such as road traffic. Even the interiors of homes and offices did not necessarily offer respite because improved draught exclusion standards allowed pollutants to linger, such as formaldehyde resins and dust mites' fungal spores.[65] As each adult breathes more than 10,000 litres of air per day, pollutants continued to circulate through lungs.

The Smithsons hired *The Architectural Review*'s Gordon Cullen to prepare 'Townscape' perspectives of *The Economist* building, and described the carved forms of Hawksmoor's St George's, Bloomsbury, 1731, as the city's 'climate register'.[66] Clad in the same Portland stone as the church, *The Economist* building

59 Macmillan, quoted in Fisher, p. 192.

60 The article was reprinted and credited to Alison and Peter Smithson in *Ordinariness and Light*, pp. 135–143. Alison Smithson, 'Patio and Pavilion', p. 11; Peter Smithson, 'Letter to America', p. 95.

61 The London County Council funded the Inquiry, which was prepared by the UK Meteorological Office. Refer to Shaw, p. 649.

62 Brimblecombe, *The Big Smoke*, p. 166. Refer to Brimblecombe and Bentham, pp. 243–245.

63 Acheson, quoted in Simons, p. 219.

64 Brimblecombe, *The Big Smoke*, p. 168, refer to pp. 170–171.

65 Brimblecombe and Bentham, pp. 255–256.

66 Alison and Peter Smithson, 1986, quoted in Salter and Wong, p. 9. Refer to Salter, in Salter and Wong, pp. 40–41.

Alison and Peter Smithson,
The Economist Building,
London, 1964. Plaza.
Courtesy of Architectural
Press Archive/RIBA Library
Photographs Collection.

absorbed and collected from the air the final soots from London's fireplaces. Anticipating the deep staining from the pollutants, the façade was detailed to channel rainwater from window sills to the column gutters, at which point the stone was scoured by the effects of rain and up-draught winds and its whiteness renewed. As a consequence the façade, which originally had little modulation of its structure, acquired great visual depth, understood through the control of the shadows of soot and the scouring of the stone

writes Peter Salter, who had worked for the Smithsons.[67]

67 Salter, in Salter and Wong, p. 40.

Critical of suburban sprawl, the Smithsons wished to express the differences between the city and the country while recognising their interdependence. In the country, they extended the Georgic dream at Upper Lawn Pavilion. Peter Smithson wanted 'to build like a farmer', drawing on local knowledge of a place 'not only the visual, but what a place smells like, how the wind hits it'.[68] Combining new and old, they replaced the dilapidated cottage with a two-storey house of similar vol-

68 Peter Smithson, *Conversations*, pp. 48–49.

Alison and Peter Smithson, Upper Lawn Pavilion, 1959–. Kitchen with ladder to first floor, June 1962. Courtesy of the Smithson Family Collection.

69 Alison and Peter Smithson, 'Folly at Fonthill, Wilts.', p. 482.

70 Alison and Peter Smithson, *The Charged Void*, p. 238; Alison and Peter Smithson, 'Folly at Fonthill, Wilts', p. 482. Refer to Peter Smithson, in conversation with Bruno Krucker, 28 September 2001, in Krucker, p. 40.

71 Peter Smithson, in Alison and Peter Smithson, *Upper Lawn, Solar Pavilion Folly*.

72 Alison Smithson, 'Patio and Pavilion', p. 11.

ume and incorporated existing fragments such as the garden wall, chimney, paving and well. Accessible up a steep climb, more a ladder than a staircase, the glazed first floor 'gazebo' offered views in all directions.[69] Services were limited. The kitchen had a sink and dishwasher but no fridge, oven or hob. Cooking occurred outside. Bedrooms were not defined; at night mattresses were unrolled and placed on the floor. A wood-burning stove provided limited warmth. The single-glazed expanse caused over-heating in summer and condensation and heat loss in winter. But these 'failings' were essential to the experience of the Smithsons' 'primitive' 'Solar Pavilion Folly', questioning familiar notions of domestic shelter and privacy.[70] Peter Smithson remarked that 'Upper Lawn was placed in an eighteenth century English landscape with the conscious intention of enjoying its pleasure . . . submitting to the seasons'.[71] The Smithsons accepted eighteenth-century levels of energy consumption as a means to engage the present through the past, testing the assumption that some loss in thermal comfort is amply compensated by, and even necessary to, a more complete experience of nature and weather.

Rather than nostalgic, the Smithsons saw the picturesque as relevant to contemporary urban and rural conditions. Alison Smithson remarked: 'I work with memory, and it allows me to make connections to the past, interpolations of the present and gives foresight – a most valuable facility for an architect – as to a possible future.'[72] Rather than Banham's untainted technological futurism, they favoured modernism's continuity with earlier centuries, celebrating the picturesque incorporation of difference that was also characteristic of brutalism. In eighteenth-century England, the genius of the place was made as much as found, the fusion of new ideas, forms and spaces with those already in place, which were themselves sometimes the result of earlier migrations. The same was true of brutalism.

In England in the early 1960s the expansion of higher education offered the opportunity to literally build on this debate at a larger scale. In the eighteenth century, Oxford and Cambridge were the only English universities. Coke did not go to a university while Walpole studied at Cambridge, returning to Houghton in 1698 to help his father manage the estate after the early deaths of his elder brothers. Oxford and Cambridge remained the only English universities until 1826 when University College London (UCL) was founded as London University with the purpose to offer a university education to students of any class, race or religion. William Wilkins' neo-classicism was deemed to be the architectural style most appropriate to its values. The first 'civic' university was a catalyst for the creation of King's College London, a Church of England alternative to 'the Godless institution in Gower Street'. In 1836 UCL and King's were the founding colleges of a new university, which assumed the name originally taken by UCL: University of London. In the next phase of expansion, 'redbrick' universities were founded before the First World War in major cities such as Birmingham and Manchester. In 1961 the Conservative government set up a Committee on Higher Education chaired by Professor Lord (Lionel) Robbins, which after two years' deliberation recommended the creation of a number of new universities. In fact, by the time of the report, seven universities were already in development under the remit of the Universities Grants Committee (UGC). Emphasising the coexistence of teaching and research in a residential community, these 'plateglass' universities were located in smaller provincial towns and cities of a comparable size and character to Oxford and Cambridge – Brighton, Canterbury, Colchester, Lancaster, Norwich, Warwick and York – rather than major cities, the usual sites of civic and redbrick universities, which had larger student populations and a more dispersed academic community.

The new universities were the first in Britain to be fully controlled by the national government. Synonymous with the welfare state, they aimed to extend access to all people with 'the qualifications and the willingness to pursue higher education', as the Robbins Report concluded.[73] Heir to the liberal Enlightenment, the idea of a British welfare state was established in 1942 when the Inter-Departmental Committee on Social Insurance and Allied Services under the chairmanship of Sir William Beveridge presented its report to the wartime coalition government led by the Conservative Prime Minister, Winston Churchill. The Labour party's landslide victory in 1945 brought the report's conclusions to fruition, and the welfare state as realised aimed to extend access to good schools, universities and hospitals to the whole population, but did not intend a fundamental transformation of capitalism or attempt to address financial inequalities between rich and poor. Consistent with such an approach, the welfare state established the National Park and Access to the Countryside Act, 1949, while not questioning private land ownership.[74]

The idea of a university in Norwich was first proposed in the early twentieth century and was revived after the Second World War. As support for new universities grew, the initial working title – University of Norwich – was discarded because the local Promotion Committee believed that a university with regional backing was more likely to be accepted, and the UGC approved the University of East Anglia (UEA) in 1960. Of all the cities that acquired a new university, Norwich was the most isolated, literally as well as culturally. Lacking a convenient supply of coal, it had not prospered like the northern cities that developed in the late eighteenth century. After the industrial revolution and the expansion of worldwide trade, Norfolk stagnated, becoming sparsely populated and 'on the way to nowhere'.

In an increasingly global market, British agriculture could not match the much larger farms in North America and elsewhere. The proportion of the national

73 Robbins, p. 265.

74 Worpole and Orton, pp. 9–12.

population working on farms decreased, as did the land devoted to arable farming, which became more focused on East Anglia. Agriculture remained important to the Norfolk economy, while also emphasising its backwardness.[75] A Norfolk farmworker's house in the early 1960s still 'had no electricity or running water', the 'privy was outside' and the 'family bath was a large tin one brought in from the shed, and placed in the kitchen every Friday evening'. Afterwards, the tepid water was discarded in the garden where vegetables were grown for the family, who 'also kept pigs and geese; they would keep one pig and sell the others to the butcher before wintertime'.[76]

Norfolk's grand eighteenth-century estates continued into the twentieth century. The Whigs had initially been absorbed into the Liberal Party in the mid-nineteenth century and were no longer an identifiable political force in the mid-twentieth century, when Labour and the Conservatives were the principal parties. But in an obituary for Bert Hazell, who was Norfolk secretary of the Farm Servants' Union and then Labour MP for North Norfolk, Edward Coke, seventh Earl of Leicester, remarked: 'I respected Hazell. He was the MP who came into the one constituency in England where, in 1964, it was so feudal that it had to be explained to the electors that the ballot was secret.'[77] The aristocratic descendants of Walpole, Coke and Townshend still resided at Houghton, Holkham and Raynham respectively. But their prime concern was to maintain rather than expand their estates. Just as 'the landed estate was the economic engine of Georgian England – locus of its capital accumulation, technical innovation and social modernization,' so too was the university in welfare state England, particularly in a county such as Norfolk.[78]

In the 1720s the journey from London to Norfolk took four days; by the 1960s it was just a few hours. In the mid-twentieth century, a railway network served the county, connecting small towns and ports. But in 1963 'The Reshaping of British Railways' proposed the closure of a third of all lines and stations on the basis of cost and efficiency. Commissioned by a Conservative government and largely implemented by a Labour one, Dr Richard Beeching's report indicated cross-party bias towards car ownership that was typical of the time. Many smaller stations were lost but the one to Norwich was not threatened. By road, the journey to north-west Norfolk followed similar routes to those undertaken by Coke and Walpole. The car journey to the county town was simple but comparatively slow, as Norfolk was one of the few English counties not included in the postwar motorway boom.

Despite, or perhaps because of, a certain rural backwardness, the idea of creating a university in Norwich was the most ambitious transformation of Norfolk's culture and economy. While the universities of Oxford and Cambridge had been the focus of their towns for centuries, the urban sites available to the new

75 Williamson, *An Environmental History of Wildlife in England*, pp. 139–141.

76 Freakley, p. 11.

77 Edward Coke, seventh Earl of Leicester, quoted in Dalyell.

78 Cosgrove, 'Airport/Landscape', p. 222.

universities were less desirable. But, citing the benefits of urban renewal and social integration, *The Architects' Journal* endorsed a run-down city-centre site that then included Norwich's identifiable, if modest, red-light district.[79] But the response of Sir Cecil Syers, Secretary of the UGC, was dismissive: 'If all Norwich has to offer is the Ber Street site, there will be no university there.'[80] Instead, and at no cost to the fledgling UEA, the city council offered a site at Earlham on Norwich's southwest periphery, affirming the UGC's requirement for a parkland educational campus in which academic departments, student residences and sports facilities were adjacent to each other.

In 1964 Banham, who had sided with *The Architects' Journal* in supporting a city centre campus, offered an acerbic assessment of life for a newly arrived academic in and around Norwich, his childhood home:

> It is quite a cushy ecology for a certain type of intellectual – you can still pick up a piece of gracious property to live in at prices below national averages, and some gracious sticks of antique furniture to go in it; there is a gracious network of art-lovers and music-addicts and some gracious places like the Assembly House for them to congregate in. A man with a modicum of money or talent behind him and an entertaining wife beside him can have a very nice life in Norwich in a sickening sort of way.[81]

A year later the author and academic Malcolm Bradbury moved from a redbrick to a plateglass university, lured by UEA's enthusiasm for interdisciplinary research and contemporary writing.[82] He soon remarked to David Lodge, his friend and former colleague at the University of Birmingham: 'It's said in various quarters in Norwich that the town and the university are rather notably provincial; but we shall see.'[83] Kenneth Clark struck a more optimistic note at the end of the concluding episode of *Civilisation*, 1969, his seminal BBC series on western art, architecture and philosophy:

> I am at one of our new universities, the University of East Anglia . . . I should doubt if so many people have been as well fed, as well read, as right-minded, as curious and as critical as the young are today.

In his final words Clark remarked:

> one mustn't overrate the culture of what used to be called top people before the wars. They had charming manners but they were as ignorant as swans. They knew a little about literature, less about music, nothing about art and less than nothing

79 Editors, 'Sites for Norwich University', p. 744; Editors, 'Universities: Genuine Urban or Fake Suburban', pp. 745–746.

80 Syers, quoted in Sanderson, p. 74.

81 Banham, 'How I Learnt to Live with the Norwich Union', pp. 101–102.

82 Bradbury, 'Creative Writing and the University'.

83 Bradbury, letter to David Lodge, autumn 1966, courtesy of Dominic Bradbury.

about philosophy. The members of a music group or an art group at a provincial university would be 10 times better informed and more alert.[84]

[84] Clark, *Civilisation*, episode 13, 'Heroic Materialism', BBC 2, 1969.

The focus of the campus, Earlham Hall, is a large house built of local materials – brick and flint – with a late sixteenth-century core and significant later additions. Eighteenth-century Earlham had a rural rather than a suburban location as Norwich barely extended beyond the city walls. Once owned by a descendant of Francis Bacon, the Hall was later leased to the Gurneys, an influential Quaker family who in the 1790s created a park along the River Yare, which meanders to the west and south of the house, offering views down to the water and onto the farmland beyond. Typical of a late eighteenth-century picturesque landscape, Earlham emphasised sweeping topography rather than emblematic monuments because the expressive garden was then assumed to place fewer restrictions on the imagination. William Faden's 1797 map of Norfolk indicates an extensive park, while an 1829 estate map suggests that the cultivated park to the north and 'ornamented farmland' to the south were conceived as an aesthetic whole.[85] Later in the nineteenth century a perimeter tree line was planted along the park's southern boundary, dividing it from the fields and plantations beyond. In his semi-autobiographical novel *Lavengro: The Scholar, the Gypsy, the Priest,* 1851, George Borrow remembers Earlham, where he fished as a boy: 'pleasant is that valley, truly a goodly spot'.[86] A friend of Henry James and Edith Wharton, the biographer and novelist Percy Lubbock was a later resident. His memoir, *Earlham,* 1922, offered a picture of life beside the River Yare: 'it twinkles over gravel and watercress to the brick archway of the bridge, turns suddenly black and silent in the fishing-pool, and winds idly away through the Earlham meadows, a full-fed stream, deep enough to carry us in our broad-beamed old boat'.[87]

[85] Williamson, *The Archaeology of the Landscape Park,* p. 228.

[86] Borrow, p. 156.

[87] Lubbock, p. 179.

The plateglass universities' commitment to self-improvement was indebted to empiricism and their landscape settings reaffirmed the association of self-understanding with experience of the natural world. Identification with an ancestral estate was equally compelling. Many of the locations chosen for the seven new universities possessed a historic house, which was often each institution's first base. A country estate was traditionally assumed to be socially and culturally superior to the merchants' houses in the towns and ports, a prejudice that the new universities maintained. Referring to his official residence – Wood Hall, a seventeenth-century house a few miles to the west of UEA – the university's first Vice-Chancellor, Frank Thistlethwaite, remarked: 'It seemed desirable . . . to be quartered in a house which was known to, and accepted by the county, rather than in some town house in the centre of Norwich'.[88]

[88] Thistlethwaite, quoted in Muthesius, p. 139.

In the postwar era there was a desire to reaffirm Britain's past but the nineteenth century – which early modernists had denounced more than any other as bourgeois, repressive and hypocritical – was ignored once again and for similar reasons as before. Instead, in a decade known for cultural and social experimentation, an eighteenth-century parkland setting was seen as particularly appropriate for a new welfare state university precisely because of its association with British liberalism, and reassertion in the 1940s and 1950s as a totem of national identity. In Norfolk, such a site had special resonance because the county is known for some of England's grandest eighteenth-century estates. Thistlethwaite remarked of Earlham: 'There emanated from its associations with the Bacon and Gurney families and the Norwich circle a *genius loci* which could not fail to imbue students with a sense of their cultural inheritance.'[89]

In 1960, Rowe remarked of Thistlethwaite's alma mater: 'Cambridge is fundamentally 17th century, republican and Whig and anything which is all these things is by definition critical of the status quo.'[90] Such a questioning spirit encouraged UEA and its Vice-Chancellor to challenge as well as appreciate England's oldest universities. UEA's motto is 'Do Different' and, from the outset, it was known for interdisciplinary research, which the established universities did little to encourage. The desire to progress as well as preserve extended to the university's gowns. Rather than approach Ede & Ravenscroft, the reputed Cambridge-based supplier, Thistlethwaite commissioned bold modernist designs from the designer and photographer Cecil Beaton.[91]

While eighteenth-century England advocated liberalism, only a small proportion of the population was allowed a university education, the right to vote, and access to a picturesque estate. In contrast, the welfare state aimed to open these rights and pleasures to all classes, legitimising its values and forms by reference to ancient heritage and modern purpose.

As architect of the new university, Lasdun had a London address and a national reputation, just like Kent two centuries before.[92] Soon after his appointment Lasdun and his wife, Susan, spent the weekend with Sir Roy and Lady Harrod at their house at Holt, northwest of Norwich. Billa Harrod – who had been Christopher Hussey's girlfriend and then John Betjeman's fiancée before she became Harrod's wife – recommended *The Shell Guide to Norfolk*, 1957, which she had co-authored with C.L.S. Linnell, and later sent Lasdun a Christmas card adorned with her own snapped photograph of the architect admiring Repton's nearby tomb at Aylsham.[93] As author of *The Picturesque: Studies in a Point of View*, 1927, and architectural editor of *Country Life*, Hussey was influential in associating national identity with the landed estate, which became a favourite tourist venue of the postwar

89 Thistlethwaite, 'The Founding of the University of East Anglia: A Reminiscent Chronicle', November 1963, p. 10, Lasdun Archive, RIBA Drawings and Archives Collections, Victoria and Albert Museum, London.

90 Rowe, in Tusa et al., p. 25.

91 Dormer and Muthesius, p. 119.

92 In 1961 Lasdun had submitted designs for student residences at St John's College, Cambridge, which were not selected, but he impressed Thistlethwaite, then a fellow and member of the building committee. Cambridge Architectural Research Ltd, p. 5.

93 Billa Harrod, letter to Lasdun, 22 March 1962, Lasdun Archive.

Christmas Card from
Billa and Roy Harrod to
Denys and Susan Lasdun,
featuring Denys Lasdun
photographed at the tomb
of Humphry Repton.
Courtesy of Lasdun Archive/
RIBA Library Photographs
Collection.

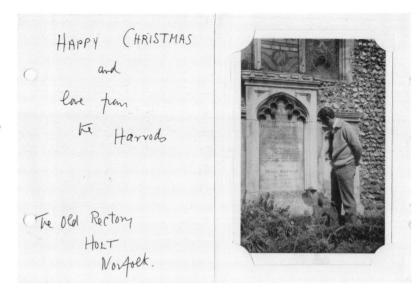

HAPPY CHRISTMAS
and
love from
the Harrods

The old Rectory
HOLT
Norfolk.

car-owning middle class, expanding a practice that Gilpin had helped to promote.[94] Often accompanied by Billa, the Lasduns toured Norfolk, visiting Holkham,
Houghton and Repton's park at Sheringham. In a blue exercise book Lasdun noted
local people and places, including Borrow and Lubbock's recollections of Earlham,
while Susan Lasdun recalls that Norfolk was then such 'a backwater it was like
going back to the eighteenth century'.[95]

At Holkham, the Hall remained but the landscape was significantly changed
from Coke and Kent's day. A nine-mile brick wall and extensive plantations encir-
cled the estate, diminishing views to the coast. Creating a further barrier, an
extensive pine forest resisted wind and wave erosion, steadying the dunes against
the sea and protecting the reclaimed marshes and parkland to the south.[96] As
the pines were planted densely, the result was a dramatically dark and undulating landscape with only fungi and mosses flourishing among a carpet of pine
needles. The forest proved temporarily insufficient against the catastrophic 1953
flood when the sea breached the park wall and destroyed the railway line, leaving the marshes underwater for 11 weeks. In the mid-1960s, Hazell was the
first member of the House of Commons to initiate a debate on coastal erosion.[97]
After visiting Holkham in that decade, Colvin acknowledged that the pines were
an effective means to stabilise the dunes, much more so than any grass, and
proposed that they be planted elsewhere along the east coast where erosion was
a serious threat.[98]

94 Daniels, *Fields of Vision*, pp.
101–103.

95 Lady (Susan) Lasdun, in
conversation with Jonathan Hill, 16
August 2012.

96 The forest of Austrian, Corsican,
Maritime and Scots pines was
planted in the second half of the
nineteenth century; its western edge
marks the limit of the Holkham
estate. *Holkham National Nature
Reserve*, unpaginated; Soissons,
p. 60; Wade Martins, *A Great Estate
at Work*, p. 83.

97 Dalyell.

98 Colvin, *Land and Landscape*,
1970, pp. 260–261.

Due to the efforts of Brown in the 1760s and Repton later in the century, the park was more open and consistent than before.[99] To promote a design, Repton presented each client with a 'Red Book' in which comparative drawings contrasted the existing site with his picturesque proposal. His Holkham 'Red Book', 1789, includes a proposal for 'a Room . . . reserved for a sea view', probably the North Lodge.[100] But by the time of Lasdun's visit, Kent's North and South Lawns, Seat on the Mount, and North and South Lodges were all absent, as were the avenues through Obelisk Wood. The Triumphal Arch, Temple and Obelisk were Kent's only surviving garden structures, while the axial avenue also remained. The Temple had housed a succession of estate workers in the nineteenth century but was a ruin by the 1930s before it was later restored, as W. O. Hassall, librarian to successive Earls of Leicester, recalled:

> One evening I counted over 300 bats emerge for their nocturnal duties from a hole in the roof, which they shared with a long-established swarm of bees. The trees were encroaching ever nearer and were full of the sound of wood pigeons.[101]

At an early press conference to discuss his design for Earlham, Lasdun emphasised his intention 'not to wreck for all time the most wonderful landscape in which we find ourselves . . . it's a very, very beautiful place'.[102] Drawing an analogy between design and use, eighteenth-century designers conceived the picturesque landscape while walking the site, and imagined its future occupants in motion too. According to Repton: 'The spot from whence the view is taken, is in a fixed state to the painter; but the gardener surveys his scenery while in motion; and . . . sees objects in different situations'.[103] Repeating this practice soon after receiving the UEA commission, Lasdun walked the site 'in all seasons, in mist, snow, wind and sun', even surveying it from a helicopter.[104] Snow was in abundance because the first winter after his appointment was the coldest since 1739–1740, when Kent was transforming Holkham.

In a key design decision with picturesque connotations, Lasdun decided that the various architectural elements 'were to be disposed on this site with loving care for the configuration and contours of the landscape, its prospect and aspect', recalling the first chapter – 'The Prospect' – in Hussey's seminal study of the picturesque.[105] Acknowledging a local influence, Lasdun remarked:

> The site – itself an organism: water, marsh, slope, trees, meadow, parkland – is set in East Anglian landscape: and Norwich is close to the east. If Repton had been asked to do this university on this landscape, he would have said, 'Keep it that way'.[106]

99 Soissons, pp. 40, 89; Williamson, *The Archaeology of the Landscape Park*, p. 102; Williamson, 'The Development of Holkham Park', p. 71.

100 Repton, quoted in Williamson, 'The Development of Holkham Park', p. 68.

101 Hassall, 'The Temple at Holkham, Norfolk', p. 1310.

102 Lasdun, 'About Anglia'.

103 Repton, p. 96.

104 Alexander Redhouse and Peter McKinley, 'UEA, Denys Lasdun and Partners', lecture, 15 February 1966, quoted in Sanderson, p. 147.

105 Lasdun, 'His Approach to Architecture', p. 273; Hussey, pp. 1–17.

106 Lasdun, 'His Approach to Architecture', p. 273.

107 The monograph was published in 1962. Refer to Daniels, *Fields of Vision*, p. 107; Daniels, *Humphry Repton*.

Hussey's analysis of Repton was brief but Lasdun's praise came just a few years after Dorothy Stroud's monograph re-asserted Repton's reputation.[107] Although he had no involvement with Earlham, Repton was an appropriate local inspiration, and had designed a garden for Bartlett Gurney at Northrepps, north of Norwich, in the early 1790s.

Lasdun's reference to Repton indicated not only the potential he saw in the site but also his empathy for East Anglia and England. In an early press conference he advocated a regional as well as national architecture, telling the *Eastern Daily Press*,

> There will be no question of trying to create a university for Norwich at long distance . . . The greater modern movements fired my youth but now I am past my youth and I think for myself . . . I am very much concerned with rather special values, solely, or mostly, applying to England.[108]

108 Lasdun, 1962, quoted in Dormer and Muthesius, p. 156.

Like Pevsner, Lasdun's personal history stimulated a deep concern for national identity. He 'wanted to belong', remarks Susan Lasdun.[109] According to his son, James,

109 Lady (Susan) Lasdun, in conversation with Jonathan Hill, 22 August 2012.

> as the sole bearer of his Russian name, he had something altogether sui generis about him and wasn't terribly interested in his own prehistory . . . He was Jewish but not really, having been brought up with no sense of Jewish identity. He was English but not really, being Jewish. And he was Christian but not really, having lapsed almost as soon as he converted.

Despite studying at two elite institutions – Rugby School and the Architectural Association (AA) – he felt 'an embattled outsider'. Questioning the hierarchy of words above images in English society, he challenged the assumption that images only acquire validity if accompanied by words. But prone to melancholy, Lasdun believed that he lacked 'the deep literary culture' that 'was a prerequisite for being taken seriously as an artist in England, regardless of one's field'.[110]

110 James Lasdun, pp. 54–60.

Founded in 1847, the AA is Britain's oldest school of architecture although the Royal Academy offered architecture courses first. Full-time architectural education only came to replace apprenticeships at the start of the twentieth century, and Lasdun studied at the AA in the early 1930s, when UK architects became registered professionals. The professions were conceived in the nineteenth century as a response to the fluctuations of a rampant industrialised economy, which created a vastly expanded market with many new trades and the

subdivision of existing ones. To the apparent benefit of practitioners and con-
sumers, the state offered a profession legal protection in return for the safe
management of its activities. Established a decade before the AA, the RIBA
delayed demands for professional registration until the 1920s, when its member-
ship had increased to include half of British architects. Wishing to deny the RIBA
complete control, the government protected the term 'architect' but not architectural practice, and established a separate body to monitor the profession in
the Architects (Registration) Act 1931, although RIBA members dominated its
committee.[111] Consequently, the profession that Lasdun entered was focused on
building design and supervision, more so than in the eighteenth century when
disciplinary boundaries were imprecise and Kent conceived buildings, chairs,
gardens, paintings and theatre sets.

UEA had initially approached Leslie Martin to be its architect. He was then
head of the architecture school at Cambridge, where Thistlethwaite had studied
and lectured before moving to Norwich. Given the small size of his office, Martin
proposed that he would conceive an overall plan in which other architects would
design specific buildings, a principle that the university retained in later years.
But at the start, with Thistlethwaite's support, Harold Mackintosh – first Viscount
Mackintosh of Halifax, Chairman of the Promotion Committee and first Chancellor
of UEA – preferred 'there to be one mind and one style throughout the university',
a decision that matched the early modernist mind-set if not the picturesque one.[112]

Modernist architecture had not found favour in Britain between the two World
Wars but its social agenda – devoid of any early radicalism – was amenable to the
welfare state. In 1963 Thistlethwaite touched upon this acquiescence in writing of

> an obligation to think through afresh the design of a university in academic and
> in architectural terms. I suppose our thinking has been governed by two princi-
> ples . . . one the principle of flexibility and the other what I might call the principle
> of coherence.[113]

Identifying flexibility as a means to redeem and transform functionalism, postwar
architects advocated a model that combined flexibility and coherence but was
anything but new. In *Megastructure: Urban Futures of the Recent Past*, 1976,
Banham mentions early examples that incorporated multiple functions in a single
form, such as Old London Bridge, 1209–1831, and an Italian hill-town, Urbino.
Citing Ralph Wilcoxon's four-part definition – modularisation, unlimited extension,
permanent structural framework and transient infill units – he identifies projects
by Le Corbusier as more recent and relevant inspirations, including the Plan Obus

[111] The principle of a separate regulatory body continued in the subsequent Architects Act 1997, in which the Architects' Registration Board (ARB) replaced the Architects Registration Council for the United Kingdom (ARCUK).

[112] Mackintosh, quoted in Dormer and Muthesius, p. 49. Refer to Cambridge Architectural Research Ltd, p. 5.

[113] Thistlethwaite, in Lasdun, 'About Anglia'.

for Algiers, 1931. Describing megastructures as the 'Dinosaurs of the Modern Movement', Banham recognises a forlorn attempt to answer present problems with past failures. Acknowledging their monolithic self-image, the institutions of the welfare state readily commissioned megastructures, none more so than the plateglass universities. But emphasising the unified purpose of an academic population, Banham concludes that a university could not serve as a test case for more complex urban conditions. A singular form suited architects' sense of visual order but was impractical and insensitive to the varied and changing demands of a city.[114]

Functionalism was a useful concept for early twentieth-century modernists but there was no coherent theorisation of architectural determinism at the time and little indication that it was rigorously applied to a design. In the postwar era, the fiction of flexibility had replaced 'the fiction of function'.[115] Architects equated flexibility with technical adjustments. But they were rarely made, either because they were not simple to achieve or were irrelevant to changing needs. Banham remarked that Lasdun's designs for UEA 'have the unmistakeable air of megastructure, even though they fulfil few of the structural or adaptive norms thought to be essential to the concept'.[116] Writing in 1965, with implicit criticism of projects such as Peter Cook's Plug-In City of 1963–1964, Lasdun rejected the modernist obsession with the transformative potential of technology: 'What we shall build in East Anglia is an organism which is architecturally complete and incomplete, which can grow and change but which does not produce a wilderness of mechanisms.'[117]

In the late 1960s, as Lasdun's design began to take shape, students praised the university's 'self-conscious newness' and credited the architect – 'we all knew the name of Lasdun' – although many disliked the concrete.[118] Outside a big city, a university was one of the few places where some of the radical effects of the 1960s could be immediately experienced. In Norwich, the peripheral Earlham campus emphasised the isolation of town and gown. On her visit to UEA in 1968, a small group of students declared Princess Margaret a 'Vietnam murderer' and set fire to the Union Jack. Her response was light-hearted: 'Oh good! I've been protested against'. A visit by the Queen later that year was deliberately undermined by an outdoor seminar on 'Democracy in the University', which more than 200 students attended.[119] Local reaction was particularly hostile because four generations of British monarchs had lived at Sandringham, the Royal Family's English country estate in northwest Norfolk, close to Houghton and Holkham.[120] At UEA the principal student protests occurred at the start of the 1970s, when the university's mismanagement of drug allegations led to student break-ins and strikes. In 1970, students refused to pay money into the university's Barclays account due

114 Banham, *Megastructure*, pp. 7–9, 130–132, 142–199.

115 Anderson, p. 21.

116 Banham, *Megastructure*, p. 132.

117 Lasdun, 'His Approach to Architecture', p. 273.

118 UEA students, quoted in Dormer and Muthesius, p. 105.

119 Sanderson, pp. 189–191.

120 Queen Elizabeth II and the Royal family used a beach hut among the pines at Holkham, which had been donated by Thomas Coke, fifth Earl of Leicester. In 2003 a fire destroyed the beach hut but it is not known if the arsonist knew that it belonged to the Queen.

to the bank's business in apartheid South Africa. In a conservative county, local opinion was negative once again due to the bank's connections with the Gurney family, whose bank had been absorbed into Barclays.[121] By 1972, reflecting a less optimistic decade, Keva Coombes, President of the UEA Students' Union, knew where to lay the blame: 'the architecture has a subtle effect on people – it destroys their sense of community'.[122]

At the same time, Malcolm Bradbury, by then co-founder with Angus Wilson of UEA's pioneering MA in Creative Writing programme, was completing what would become his best-known novel – *The History Man*, 1975 – set in the fictional plateglass University of Watermouth at the start of the 1972 academic year, when 'the Swinging Sixties' became 'the Sagging Seventies'.[123] A liberal humanist critique of Marxist radicalism, Bradbury's narrative focuses on Howard Kirk, a sociology lecturer who assumes that the ends justify the means and history is on his side. According to Bradbury, the 'hero-villain' of *The History Man* is

> a rogue of rogues . . . But at least Howard believed – even if it was chiefly for his own advantage – in all the things that still do matter. He believed in history, society, philosophy, ideas, human progress, mental discovery, all that's left of the Enlightenment Project.[124]

The novel's title is usually associated with its principal character but it equally refers to the author. While Kirk's confidence in his inevitable destiny is paradoxically a-historical, Bradbury's conception of history is dialogical.

The author and his principal character both criticise the new university's architecture. The Finnish nationality of the architect, Jop Kaakinen, emphasises the social democratic ideals of his 'pious modernismus': 'black plastic chairs, their seats moulded to the shape of some average universal buttock . . . a zealous equality prevails in the air, and the place has become a little modern state'.[125] Kirk is equally dismissive: 'Not radical enough'.[126] But connecting Kaakinen to Kirk, Bradbury blames both Watermouth's 'still expanding dream in white concrete' and the moral ambiguity of his principal character on the dehumanising 'ideological scepticism' of modern, industrialised society, of which 'postmodern consumer culture' is the latest stage.[127]

Focused on an ancient hall to the west of the conurbation and assembled on a repetitive module – 'possibly the only successful large-scale industrialised precast reinforced concrete building complex yet built', according to the Smithsons – UEA has more than a passing resemblance to the University of Watermouth.[128] But in autumn 1967 Bradbury wrote to Lodge: 'The new building now makes us seem

121 Dormer and Muthesius, pp. 104–108; Sanderson, pp. 196–206; Upjohn, p. 1323.

122 Coombes, quoted in Sanderson, p. 214.

123 Bradbury, 'Welcome Back to the History Man'.

124 Bradbury, 'Welcome Back to the History Man'.

125 Bradbury, *The History Man*, pp. 49, 62–65.

126 Bradbury, *The History Man*, p. 49.

127 Bradbury, *The History Man*, pp. 49, 3; Bradbury, 'Welcome Back to the History Man'.

128 Alison and Peter Smithson, *Without Rhetoric*, p. 30.

129 Bradbury, letter to David Lodge, autumn 1967, courtesy of Dominic Bradbury.

130 Sanderson, p. 441; Dominic Bradbury, email to Jonathan Hill, 20 December 2011.

131 Lasdun, 'His Approach to Architecture', p. 273.

like a big university, with all the advantages and disadvantages. On the whole they look just now like advantages.'[129] Confirming the admiration that Bradbury expressed to Lasdun when they first met, Dominic Bradbury writes of his father: 'I always thought that he was fond of Lasdun's work at the UEA and proud of the new identity that it gave the university.'[130] Rather than associate Lasdun with a dehumanising modernism it is probable that Bradbury recognised shared concerns. Like *The History Man*, Lasdun's edited volume, *Architecture in an Age of Scepticism*, 1984, emphasises the continuing relevance of liberal humanism when it enters into a critical and constructive dialogue with contemporary society.

Remarking that 'the brief from the academics rightly posed the question, "how should young people live in a new university?"' Lasdun contrasted his design with the authority and hierarchy of an established university, and drew on picturesque precedent to make this distinction.[131] The entrance to UEA lies to the south of Earlham Road, which leads to the city centre. Along the entrance avenue, Lasdun

Denys Lasdun, UEA Development Plan, 1962. Courtesy of Lasdun Archive/ RIBA Drawings and Archives Collection.

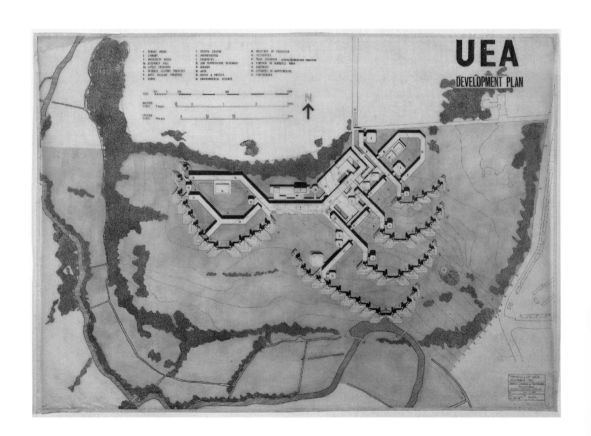

placed a beech hedge in a ha-ha, emphasising the uninterrupted parkland views. To the south of Earlham Hall and just beyond the tree belt that defined the edge of the park, the university begins at the northern edge of the ornamented farmland, where the flat site ends and the slope begins.[132] Entered from the rear, the university's principal orientation is down towards the river and its marshy banks, offering views to the fields beyond as in the eighteenth century. Cars and buses are left at the campus entrance and the site is pedestrian. Placed at an oblique angle to the contours, a teaching accommodation spine and aerial pedestrian walkway snake along the ridge for nearly 500 metres. Teaching blocks are attached to the spine's north elevation. Monolithic single-function buildings, such as the library, are to the southeast. Student housing completes the sequence, arranged in an array of ziggurats that step down towards the sloping riverside lawn speckled with tree clumps. Lasdun proposed five terraces comprising 46 ziggurats but only the Norfolk and Suffolk terraces were constructed. Their north elevations are blank, emphasising the southern orientation. Bisecting each ziggurat, a steep staircase steps down six floors from the aerial walkway to the lawn. Suggesting a social structure within the student housing, each landing leads to a breakfast room at the prow. Corridors to the left and right, which are just 2.08 metres high, provide access to study bedrooms. The low, dark corridors dramatically emphasise the transition to the southern vista, which is seen from the private and communal rooms. Adding to its original 165-acre site, the university later bought 100 acres on the south side of the Yare to protect the view.

Proposing the full extent of the university in 15 years' time, Lasdun's UEA development plan of December 1962 has three scales: 1:1250, a 'walking scale' of 3 miles per hour and a 'cycling scale' of 10 miles per hour. In the picturesque, the eye is drawn to a monument or natural feature but the path is not direct or singular. Even when the visitor is static, movement is implicit because any view is understood in relation to other potential views and is but one part of a complex whole. Arranged across the slope, UEA offers oblique views that associate physical movement with the strides and leaps of the imagination, as Lasdun made clear: 'every moment of walking is a moment of thinking'.[133]

UEA does not strictly adhere to a specific picturesque era. Recalling Repton as well as Kent, Lasdun exploited the site's latent qualities to subtly reconfigure its topography. Following Repton but not Kent, he included no statues and monuments, although his concern for myths and metaphors evoked the emblematic garden in other ways, notably in the terms he used to describe his design.[134] UEA's craggy aesthetic also brings to mind Repton's quip that Knight saw 'no delight but in the scenes of Salvator Rosa'.[135]

132 The ornamented farmland was used as a municipal golf course before UEA acquired it.

133 Lasdun, 'His Approach to Architecture', p. 273.

134 Repton, p. 259.

135 Repton, p. 101.

In some picturesque estates, such as Rousham, a garden building's location to the north, south, east or west informed its style, so that the garden could be understood as a microcosm of the world.[136] At Holkham, the estate's dual orientation established a dialogue between culture and nature, and between contrasting conceptions of nature, as a negotiation between evolving and interdependent philosophical traditions: the Enlightenment and romanticism.

Evident in the eighteenth century, the hybridisation of Enlightenment and romantic sensibilities continued into subsequent centuries, defining mid-twentieth-century modernism. Susan Lasdun writes that her husband was 'deeply impressed with the magnificence of the axial avenue at Holkham and how merely by planting, grandeur and power can be eloquently expressed'.[137] Lined with Holm Oaks of Mediterranean origin that recall the pleasures of the Grand Tour, the avenue runs due north until a tree-clad ridge reveals a panoramic view, and the route then winds down to a building sequence that in the eighteenth century included the Hall, Seat on the Mount and North Lodge, and then onto the harbour and sea beyond. UEA, as Lasdun imagined it, exactly inverts this sequence, beginning with a tree-lined linear avenue that runs due south until it reaches a 'nodal point' that reveals 'panoramic views' across the university and towards the river.[138] Completing the building sequence in the 1962 development plan, one terrace of ziggurats is to the west, pointing south like an arrow. To the east a sequence of four ziggurats are aligned north to south, increasing in length as they approach the Yare. Aerial walkways thread through the site, creating a more varied and picturesque movement sequence than was actually built. The southern ziggurat meets the Yare, bridging the north bank and enclosing a harbour and boathouse. Footbridges cross the river to the east and west, and an open-air elliptical amphitheatre with circular stage is cut into the slope a little further to the east.

In eighteenth-century Britain, references to ancient Rome emphasised one empire's desire to acquire authority from another, and to surpass it too. In the mid-twentieth century, Britain was adjusting to a new role and references to empire were of less relevance than a reassuring historical continuity. As well as a response to the topography of a sloping site, it is likely that UEA's southern orientation refers not only to ancient and Renaissance Rome, as at Holkham, but also to ancient Greece, which became a strong influence on British architecture in the 1790s. It also recalls the influence of classical antiquity on Lasdun's heroes: Hawksmoor, Soane and Le Corbusier.[139] The north is referred to in terms of climate rather than direction:

Pevsner never said that there was a British tradition but there were English ways of doing things, which I agree with. I see all English architects in the European

136 Coffin, 'The Elysian Fields of Rousham', p. 419.

137 Lady (Susan) Lasdun, email to Jonathan Hill, 9 August 2012.

138 Lasdun, UEA Development Plan, December 1962, Lasdun Archive.

139 Hawksmoor and Kent were not as different as contemporary disagreements suggested; both favoured the ruin, Palladian motifs, heavy rustication, and the juxtaposition of forms and scales. Refer to Worsley, pp. 202–204, 216–217.

tradition but making an architecture nevertheless English. The tradition has been adapted to our culture, to our climate, light, materials and genius loci, *and that's what makes it English.* [140]

The final image in William Curtis' 1994 monograph shows Lasdun absorbed in reading as he leans against one of the massive stepped seats in the ancient Greek theatre at Epidauros. Lasdun's comment on the National Theatre, 1976, equally applies to UEA: 'If it does not sound too romantic, the building itself is the . . . theatre'.[141] Alluding to the landscape setting of early theatres, horizontal stratification – a geometrical expression of a social organisation – was one of his recurring themes.[142] At UEA the ziggurats' low ceilings emphasise the analogy to a stepped theatre. A flush parapet and sunken drainage trough protect the outer edge of the terraces so that no balustrade is necessary.[143] If the ziggurats are the seating, the lawn to the south is the stage and the water and fields the backdrop, recalling the open-air theatre in ancient Greece. The relationship of actors to audience can be inverted because the ziggurats are also the stage on which daily life is performed, a permanent architectural backdrop, as in Palladio's Teatro Olimpico.[144]

In the first monograph published on Lasdun – *A Language and a Theme*, 1976 – 10 of the 12 images of UEA are exterior views, and later publications

Denys Lasdun, UEA, 1968. View looking southeast towards the River Yare from behind the ziggurats. Courtesy of Richard Einzig/ Arcaid Images.

[140] Lasdun, 'Is there a British Tradition?', p. 43.

[141] Lasdun, quoted in Connell, p. 10.

[142] Lasdun, 'The Architecture of Urban Landscape', p. 139.

[143] But the university added window latches to prevent students using the terraces.

[144] Curtis, 'A Language and a Theme', pp. 17–18.

Denys Lasdun, UEA, 1968.
View looking southwest
towards the River Yare
from behind the ziggurats.
Courtesy of Richard Einzig/
Arcaid Images.

Denys Lasdun, UEA, 1968.
Interior of typical ziggurat
study bedroom. Courtesy
of Richard Einzig/Arcaid
Images.

also largely ignore the interiors: 'My concept was urban: buildings linked with walkways, square and street, free of traffic, rather like an Italian Renaissance hill town . . . freeing the maximum acreage of the Earlham site as decorative parkland with the hint of Humphry Repton.'[145] In this sense, the architect created the hill as well as the town. As the sloping lawn rises nearly 25 metres from the river to the ridge and the buildings rise a further 30 metres, the university is one of the higher hills in the famously flat lowlands of east Norfolk, and visible from some distance. Meandering through this landscape, the Yare is one of the principal navigable rivers in the Norfolk Broads and leads to the North Sea some 15 miles to the east of UEA. Employing coastal, landscape and urban metaphors, Lasdun remarked that the 'architectural hills and valleys' of an 'academic city' are an 'outcrop of stone on the side of a hill leading down to a river' and 'landlocked harbour'.[146]

As with Coke and Kent two centuries before, it is unlikely that Lasdun only had the Norfolk coast in mind. Influencing the eighteenth-century picturesque, the seventeenth-century paintings in Holkham's Landscape Room imagine a pastoral Arcadia of temples and amphitheatres, rolling coastal and river landscapes and relaxed inhabitation that evoke the rural life praised by Virgil and Pliny in classical antiquity. These forms and metaphors are found at UEA too.

Allusions to a Virgilan landscape were particularly poignant when seen in relation to 1960s farming practices. Emblematic of the burgeoning environmental movement, Rachel Carson in *Silent Spring*, 1962, famously denounced the effect of pesticides on wildlife as the numbers of many mammals, birds, insects and plants decreased significantly.[147] Remarking that 'I became interested in designing buildings which responded almost ecologically to unique and specific situations', Lasdun recommended Colvin as UEA's landscape architect and she was appointed in 1966.[148] Elected President of the Institute of Landscape Architects in 1951 – the first woman to head a UK design or environmental profession – Colvin is associated with the development of modernist landscape architecture in Britain. But in *Land and Landscape*, 1947, she remarks:

> It may be true, as Christopher Tunnard claims, that no new style in garden design equivalent to modern architecture has yet appeared, and that older styles slavishly reproduced are inappropriate. But architecture is dealing with completely new materials as well as new needs, whereas the natural materials of landscape (land and vegetation) and the basic human needs which landscape fulfils are ageless.[149]

While acknowledging humanity's considerable influence she questioned the degree to which any landscape can be described as 'man-made':[150]

145 Lasdun, in response to Frank Thistlethwaite, 'Origins: A Personal Reminiscence of UEA's Foundation', 2000, Lasdun Archive.

146 Lasdun, 'The Architecture of Urban Landscape', p. 146; Lasdun, quoted in Curtis, *Denys Lasdun*, p. 96; Lasdun, 'His Approach to Architecture', p. 273.

147 Carson, pp. 277–297.

148 Lasdun, 'The Architecture of Urban Landscape', p. 135.

149 Colvin, *Land and Landscape*, 1947, p. 62.

150 Colvin, *Land and Landscape*, 1947, p. 7.

We should think of this planet, Earth, as a single organism, in which humanity is involved. The sense of superior individuality which we enjoy is illusory. Man is a part of the whole through evolutionary processes, and is united to the rest of life through the chemistry of lungs and stomach; with air, food and water passing in constant exchange between the soil and the tissues of plant and animal bodies.[151]

151 Colvin, *Land and Landscape*, 1970, p. 2.

152 Colvin, *Wonder in a World*, p. 32.

153 Colvin, *Wonder in a World*, pp. 5–6, 7–8, refer to p. 3.

154 Colvin, *Wonder in a World*, p. 2. Refer to Jacques, pp. 88–101.

155 Colvin, *Wonder in a World*, p. 26.

156 Hal Moggridge, in conversation with Jonathan Hill, 11 November 2013.

157 Denys Lasdun & Partners, Architects, with Davis, Belfield & Everest, Quantity Surveyors, 'Report on Landscape and Playing Fields, UEA', November 1965, pp. 4–6, Colvin & Moggridge, Landscape Architects, Archive.

158 Colvin, 'Interim Landscape Report and Approximate Estimate of Cost, UEA', December 1967, pp. 1–2, 21, Colvin & Moggridge Archive.

159 Hal Moggridge, in conversation with Jonathan Hill, 11 November 2013.

160 Lasdun, 'Report on Landscape and Playing Fields, UEA', November 1965, p. 7, Colvin & Moggridge Archive.

161 Colvin, 'Interim Landscape Report and Approximate Estimate of Cost, UEA', December 1967, p. 22, Colvin & Moggridge Archive.

In *Wonder in a World*, 1977, a book privately printed when she was 80, Colvin evokes a biblical narrative: 'The myth of Eden seems to be echoing today: man ate of the forbidden fruit and lost his heritage of the garden.'[152] For this loss, Colvin blames the myopia of Enlightenment understanding: 'The landscape yields to the botanist the sight of rare plants and flowers, to the geologist it yields history, to the lover appreciation of love . . . Religion is still primitive, but so also is science . . . Fallibility is the human condition.'[153] Emphasising a holistic and metaphysical appreciation of nature, and culture within nature, Colvin recognises a 'contact or communication between the individual mind and the universal subconscious, through means (which I believe to be) natural and physical':[154] Expressing a keenly ecological agenda, she concludes that 'survival is within our choice should we decide to change our way of life and follow natural law instead of dominating it in our greedy self-interest. For this we should have to accept that we are but a "fragment of totality"'.[155] Hal Moggridge, who became her business partner in 1969 and collaborated on UEA, characterises Colvin as 'a romantic, as am I'.[156]

On her appointment, Colvin received Lasdun's November 1965 detailed report on UEA's landscape, which includes an inventory of existing trees, an appendix on the transplantation of young trees threatened by construction, and proposals for new plantations.[157] Confirming Lasdun's intentions, Colvin looked to maintain the site's rich variety of natural habitats, including hedgerows, marshes, meadows, riverbanks and woods, not least because they would be particularly stimulating for the university's Schools of Biological Sciences and Environmental Sciences, which established the UK's pre-eminent Climatic Research Unit under Hubert H. Lamb's direction in 1971–1972.[158] As far as possible, she wanted the landscape to be 'a self-conserving system' remarks Moggridge.[159]

Lasdun's 1962 development plan depicts the river diverted north to meet the ziggurats but his 1965 landscape report also suggests a 'Broad' as an alternative.[160] In Colvin's 1967 landscape report the 'Broad' is already a 'wide expanse of water' and it was later enlarged into a substantial lake, further integrating the ornamented farmland into the picturesque park.[161] The rising ground was made to gently dip close to the base of the ziggurats so that they appear to rise directly from the land like the rocky outcrops that Lasdun intended. Nearer to the

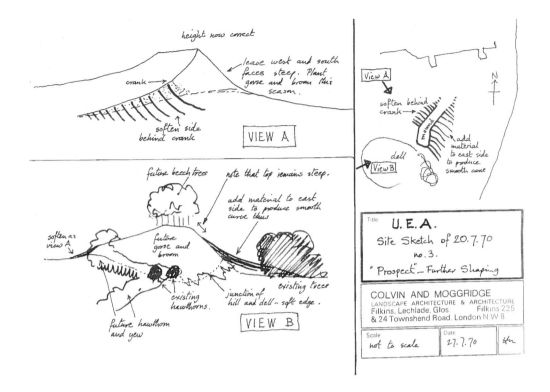

Colvin & Moggridge, landscape architects for Phase 1 of UEA, 1970. Site sketch. Courtesy of Colvin & Moggridge.

university buildings Colvin recommended that fine grass would be closely mown, while further away it would be of a rougher texture, left long and only 'scythed occasionally', contrasting a cultivated lawn to a wild meadow.[162] Colvin also refers to 'the dell', 'a large hollow, perhaps an old chalk pit' with 'a small wood of natural growth at its southern end', which 'is of ecological interest, containing self-sown deciduous' trees of various ages.[163] She suggests that one part of this 'wilderness' could accommodate the open-air elliptical amphitheatre depicted in this location in Lasdun's 1962 development plan. A sketch section shows the wooded hill as a backdrop to the stage.[164] Introducing a further emblem of the picturesque, Colvin & Moggridge proposed a 'Prospect' on a newly sculpted hill immediately to the north of the dell.[165] To the south a further 'wilderness' 'would include waterlogged reed beds, new plantations of cricket bat willows, a large lake (the Broad) and a small area of unkempt meadow'.[166]

Colvin and Thistlethwaite became good friends and she stayed with the Vice-Chancellor when she visited UEA. At his encouragement, she wrote to him in 1968, once again asserting that the planting regimes of earlier landowners were a responsibility inherited by the welfare state.[167] Remarking that 'Repton may have

162 Colvin, 'Interim Landscape Report and Approximate Estimate of Cost, UEA', December 1967, p. 17, dwg. 511/R/5, Colvin & Moggridge Archive.

163 Colvin, 'Interim Landscape Report and Approximate Estimate of Cost, UEA', December 1967, p. 27, Colvin & Moggridge Archive.

164 Colvin, 'Interim Landscape Report and Approximate Estimate of

165 Colvin & Moggridge, 'Site Sketch no. 3. "Prospect" – Further Shaping', 20 July 1970, drawn by Moggridge, Colvin & Moggridge Archive.

166 Colvin & Moggridge, 'Landscape Recommendations to Accompany Development Plan 1970, UEA: First Draft', January 1970, p. 5, Colvin & Moggridge Archive.

167 Colvin, letter to Thistlethwaite, 4 November 1968, Colvin & Moggridge Archive.

168 Colvin, *Land and Landscape*, 1970, p. 128; Colvin, *Trees for Town and Country*, n. 16; Colvin, 'Interim Landscape Report and Approximate Estimate of Cost, UEA', December 1967, p. 11, Colvin & Moggridge Archive.

169 Residential Accommodation, April 1964, UEA Special Collections, quoted in Sanderson, p. 163.

170 Pevsner, *The Englishness of English Art,* pp. 163–164.

been the first person' to recognise 'that there was a sort of natural appropriateness, depending on opposite rather than on similar qualities, between the forms of architecture and the forms of nature', she was concerned to preserve a group of mature Spanish Chestnuts. The 'tree has a curious, gaunt habit with heavy lateral branches that droop with age, and a flattened head of angular branches at the summit' that contrasts with, and thus complements, the ziggurats.[168]

In UEA's carefully composed skyline the service blocks surmounting the ziggurats contain water tanks that initiate a poetic narrative described in a 1964 report: 'rainwater is collected in gutters in the roof of each floor, discharged from one to the next at the prow of each breakfast room and drained to the River Yare'.[169] Expressing the flow of water, an extruded concrete gargoyle completes the prow of each floor. Rising behind the ziggurats, the articulated rooftops of the teaching blocks are particularly evident in the science departments, which include cranked ventilation ducts, sculpted water tanks and a cantilevered lecture theatre. In *Civilisation*, the ziggurats seen from the River Yare are the setting for Clark's concluding narration. In Curtis's monograph, the frontispiece shows the same view in a photograph by Richard Einzig – part of a set of fine black-and-white images of the campus taken by the photographer – emphasising the analogy between the stepped theatres of the book's first and last images. Acknowledging its importance, this photograph also appears in *A Language and a Theme* and *Architecture in an Age of Scepticism,* as well as in *Megastructure*. Einzig's photograph recalls Pevsner's association of a nation with its climate: 'moisture . . . lays a haze over man and building, dissolving their bodily solidity'.[170] Across the marshy meadow, the craggy silhouette is seen in the misty evening glow of a vast Norfolk sky scattered with high drifting clouds. To the left, the sparse foliage of a large tree frames the view, very much in the manner that Claude would frame his own picturesque subjects through left-of-centre overhanging leaves and branches, inspiring both eighteenth-century and twentieth-century advocates of the picturesque. Between the ziggurats and the tree, two isolated figures – one walking, the other cycling – depict the movement scales of Lasdun's 1962 development plan.

Already in 1957 Lasdun had remarked that his intention was to create 'high intensity, monumental, poetic buildings'.[171] His design for UEA recalls such buildings from earlier eras. When seen from the Yare, a stepped ziggurat surmounted by a vertical service block acknowledges, in form but not function, an acropolis surmounted by a temple, which was a staple image of Le Corbusier's *Towards a New Architecture* and the AA's Beaux-Arts education when Lasdun was a student. Reflecting on a stepped and pinnacled medieval cathedral rising above moist fens, Lasdun remarked: 'We love Ely, one of the greatest buildings that this country

171 Lasdun, in Davies and Lasdun, 'Thoughts in Progress: Summing Up II', p. 395.

Denys Lasdun, UEA, 1968.
View of the ziggurats from
the River Yare. Courtesy
of Richard Einzig/Arcaid
Images.

Claude Lorrain, *A Sunset
or Landscape with Argus
Guarding Io*, c.1650.
Courtesy of the Collection
of the Earl of Leicester,
Holkham Hall, Norfolk/
Bridgeman Images.

163

172 Lasdun, 'A Sense of Place and Time', p. 221.

173 Lasdun, 'A Sense of Place and Time', p. 221.

174 In June and July 1972 Lasdun discussed the condition of Soane's cork models with Summerson, Lasdun Archive.

has ever produced.'[172] On a similar theme, he recalled an unbuilt proposal for Cambridge in which Hawksmoor 'felt that the East Anglian landscape could do with a vertical emphasis'.[173]

Admiring Soane, Lasdun discussed cork models with John Summerson, then curator of Sir John Soane's Museum, and followed Soane's practice in commissioning one of UEA.[174] Soane favoured cork because of its ability to convincingly represent the monumental stone ruins of classical antiquity and Lasdun clearly hoped to achieve a similar sense of mass with concrete, his preferred material. Seen across the lawn, the ziggurats acknowledge Soane's fascination for Vanbrugh and Hawksmoor's design for Blenheim Palace. To accompany his professorial lectures at the Royal Academy, Soane's pupils produced extensive drawings. One drawing sequence shows the palace in different light conditions. Through the mist, heavy with vapour, the north elevation appears in pale silhouette between the sky and ground, enabling Soane to remark that 'there is a constant variety of outline

175 Soane, quoted in Watkin, *Sir John Soane*, p. 373.

that pleases from whatever point it is viewed (as are viewed ancient temples)'.[175] UEA recalls Blenheim's picturesque silhouette as well as Vanbrugh's fascination for ruination, but while he intended that the palace would appear serene in contrast to the desolate manor, the ziggurats soon came to suggest past and future ruins.

Alison and Peter Smithson with Nigel Henderson, R. S. Jenkins and Eduardo Paolozzi, *Patio and Pavilion*, This is Tomorrow, Whitechapel Gallery, London, 1956. Courtesy of the Smithson Family Collection.

Born at Blenheim, Winston Churchill was a grandson of the seventh Duke of Marlborough. In 1940 he addressed the House of Commons for the first time as the newly appointed Prime Minister. Emphasising Britain's history as an island nation, as well as its association with nature, Churchill resolved to 'wage war, by sea, land and air'. The themes of national remembrance and renewal that Clark, Colvin and Pevsner emphasised in the 1940s later combined with the optimism of the welfare state to evoke both egalitarian monumentality and thoughts of potential ruination. Architects in the 1950s and 1960s remembered the aerial Blitz and acknowledged the nuclear threat of the Cold War. On 6 August 1945, the American Boeing B-29 Superfortress *Enola Gay* was the first plane to drop an atomic bomb, code-named 'Little Boy'. The devastation of Hiroshima left a flattened, rubble-strewn city, not sublime ruins for present and future generations, increasing the psychological need for monumental as well as ruined architectures.

In 1956 the Smithsons – working with Nigel Henderson, R. S. Jenkins and Eduardo Paolozzi – created *Patio and Pavilion*, one of twelve displays in *This is Tomorrow*, an exhibition at the Whitechapel Gallery, London.[176] The Pavilion was a shed of reused timber boarding with a corrugated plastic roof adorned with decayed and discarded objects. Responding to intellectual, emotional and physical needs in a simple and direct manner that was reminiscent of the primitive hut and appropriate to postwar austerity, *Patio and Pavilion* was astutely described as 'a frugal pastoral' by Lawrence Alloway.[177] But Banham criticised it as 'submissive to traditional values' and also remarked that it evoked remains 'excavated after the atomic holocaust'.[178] In the same year, at the Daily Mail Ideal Home exhibition in London, the Smithsons displayed their *House of the Future*, which imagined the home of a young, urban and childless couple in 1981. Walls, floors and ceilings were sculpted into a single, smoothly flowing surface. The internal temperature was constant and maintained automatically. At the press of a button the adjustable living room table would sink into the floor. Conscious of Hiroshima and the Cold War, the Smithsons implied that the *House of the Future* was a bomb shelter: 'All the food is bombarded with gamma rays – an atomic byproduct to kill all bacteria'.[179] Likening the *House of the Future* to the Citroën DS, they also implied a further interpretation of their favourite car: now a bunker as well as a home and a temple.[180]

Identifying differing reactions in Britain and Germany, W. G. Sebald – Professor of German Literature at UEA, which he joined in 1970 – concluded that the devastating Allied bombing campaign had little effect on postwar German consciousness because it was repressed and subjugated to German pragmatism: 'We do not

176 Collectively called Group Six, its members belonged to the Independent Group, which was active and influential in the 1950s. Theo Crosby curated the exhibition.

177 Alloway, quoted in Lippard, p. 36.

178 Banham, 'This is Tomorrow', p. 187; Banham, *The New Brutalism*, p. 65.

179 Alison and Peter Smithson, 'House of the Future', p. 99.

180 Beatriz Colomina notes that they associated the DS with House of the Future in hindsight and argues that a more likely influence was the Volkswagen Beetle, which they owned when they designed the *Ideal Home* exhibit. Colomina, p. 36; Alison and Peter Smithson, *Changing the Art of Inhabitation*, p. 115; Peter Smithson, 'Conglomerate Ordering', p. 186.

Alison and Peter Smithson, *House of the Future*, Daily Mail Ideal Home, London, 1956. Living room with sunken table, looking towards the patio and kitchen. Courtesy of John McCann/RIBA Library Photographs Collection.

Denys Lasdun chartering a helicopter to view the UEA site, 1963. Courtesy of Lasdun Archive/RIBA Library Photographs Collection.

feel any passionate interest in our earlier way of life and the specific features of our civilization, of the kind universally perceptible, for instance, in the culture of the British Isles.'[181] In the Second World War, Peter Smithson served with Queen Victoria's Own Madras Sappers and Miners in India and Burma, while Lasdun first served with the Royal Artillery and then transferred to the Royal Engineers Airfield Construction Company. At the D-day landings and later during the war he was involved in the design of airplane landing strips. 'I found those earth-moving machines extraordinarily exciting and I liked making hills, banks and ditches' was how Lasdun acknowledged UEA's debt to his wartime years.[182] Recalling aerial surveys, a photograph also records Lasdun's pleasure as he disembarks from a bright yellow helicopter hired to discover the university's best siting.

Michael Beloff coined the term 'plateglass universities' in reference to their architecture and accessibility, but UEA's principal material – concrete – suggests alternative metaphors, including references to wartime experiences.[183] Concrete was extensively employed in ancient Rome, while reinforced concrete was developed in the nineteenth century as a hybrid of fine and coarse aggregates, cement and water with steel reinforcement. In the Bauhaus publication *The New Vision*, 1928, László Moholy-Nagy criticised people 'who look for the essence of architecture in the meaning of the conception of shelter'.[184] Steel and glass seemed to best represent the early modernist concerns for transparency, lightness and impermanence. But, also in 1928, Giedion argued that the widespread use of concrete diminished national boundaries.[185] Descended from a Russian Jewish family, Lubetkin arrived in London early in the following decade. Of similar ancestry but British-born, Lasdun joined Tecton in 1938, the year in which the practice completed Finsbury Health Centre in reinforced concrete, the material representing the egalitarian healthcare policies of a progressive London borough.

An early pioneer, Auguste Perret described reinforced concrete as an 'antique material turned modern'.[186] Concrete was most popular among architects not in the early twentieth century when they dismissed history but in the postwar era when they rediscovered it, wishing to emphasise continuity between the past and the present. Architects selected concrete because of the meanings it suggested as much as any practical advantages it offered. Emphasising concrete's primitivism to recall both archaic forms and recent devastation, Le Corbusier characterised the angled rooflights at the monastery of Sainte-Marie de la Tourette, 1959, as 'cannons' and 'machine guns' while the monks described the pock-marked surfaces as 'stigmata of suffering'.[187] Of equal importance to its adoption as *the* material of mid-century modernism, concrete was associated with the new rights and responsibilities available in the welfare state, as in uniform study bedrooms piled high in a ziggurat.

[181] Sebald, pp. viii–ix, 5–12. Refer to Vidler, 'Air War and Architecture', pp. 29–40.

[182] Lasdun, in Dennis Sharp, 'Interview with Denys Lasdun', 1976, first draft, pp. 3, 6, Lasdun Archive.

[183] Beloff.

[184] Moholy-Nagy, p. 59.

[185] Giedion, *Building in France*, p. 152.

[186] Perret, quoted in Legault, p. 46.

[187] Le Corbusier, quoted in Forty, *Concrete and Culture*, p. 181; La Tourette monks, quoted in Legault, p. 47. Refer to Forty, *Concrete and Culture*, pp. 21–22, 37–39, 69–77, 160–164; Virilio, pp. 37–47.

Concrete's two construction processes, both employed at UEA, emphasise the dialogue between old and new. Standardised and repetitive, precast concrete is formed in a factory and quickly assembled on site, as in an industrial process, while in situ concrete is poured into purpose-made formwork in the open air, and closer to a craft process. A concrete building is a memorial to the weather as its constituent materials set and solidified and, bearing the imprint of its formwork, to the shapes and surfaces of a lost timber building. Building materials have specific attributes and relations with other materials, reacting to and affecting the weather, both locally in terms of a microclimate and globally. Concrete's environmental performance is complex. Its high thermal mass can help to maintain an even internal temperature in summer and winter. But, when chalk and clay are fused at high temperatures to form cement, high carbon dioxide emissions are a disturbing consequence. Lasdun was unaware of the seriousness of this problem, having designed UEA before global warming became widely acknowledged.

Whether in situ for the spine or precast for the ziggurats, UEA's concrete surfaces were smooth not rough, at least initially. But seen from the north, the student residences offered towering blank walls and a castellated profile. Associations with bastions and bomb shelters were unavoidable. To his son, Lasdun remarked: 'You know, James, there's something aphrodisiacal about the smell of wet concrete.'[188] However, he explained his choice in relation to its context: 'Of all the suitable materials available today concrete in its natural grey state appears to enhance the colours of the landscape to the greatest advantage.'[189] Students and academics in the 1960s remember that the fresh, pale concrete offered a strong contrast to the lush, green grass, as did the buff stone and brick at Houghton and Holkham respectively.[190]

But Lasdun liked 'sombre buildings' even when he was in Rome, and he was aware that massive materials tend to produce the most evocative and poignant ruins.[191] Ruination does not only occur after a building no longer has a function. Instead, it is also a continuing process that develops at differing speeds in differing places while a building is still occupied. Rather than occur consistently throughout a building, maintenance varies according to the needs of specific spaces, components and materials. Sometimes maintenance and repair can halt ruination or delay it somewhat, while accepting and accommodating partial ruination can question the recurring cycles of production, obsolescence and waste that feed consumption in a capitalist society.

Reinforced concrete weathers and stains on the outside and also ages from within. Concrete's tendency to form surface cracks allows water penetration to initiate alkali-silica reactions, causing steel to corrode and concrete to fracture

188 James Lasdun, p. 58.

189 Lasdun, quoted in Dormer and Muthesius, p. 70.

190 Kate Holeywell conducted interviews with UEA alumni and faculty for her doctoral research on creative writing at British universities, email to Jonathan Hill, 22 December 2011.

191 Lasdun, in 'Interview with Denys Lasdun', revised draft, 13 June 1979, p. 10, Lasdun Archive.

and break.[192] Susan Lasdun recalls that her husband was 'very romantic about rain-streaked concrete'.[193] Unlike La Tourette, UEA did not look primitive at first. Instead, it looked pristine and then aged quickly. Traditional atmospheric pollutants, such as sulphur dioxide, had deceased since the start of the twentieth century but there had been a significant increase in nitrogen dioxide fertiliser deposits, stimulating fungal growths on UEA's building surfaces.[194] Marked with algae, lichen and moss, UEA appeared archaic by the end of the twentieth century, suggesting wartime destruction as well as picturesque and ancient ruins like those depicted in Coke's Landscape Room, while appearing even older than Houghton and Holkham, buildings constructed over two centuries before. Fecund in a damp climate, dappled fungal blotches offered seasonal variation, merging with the blacks and greys of winter trees and contrasting with summer's vibrant colours. Algae, lichen and moss were consistent with Lasdun's conception of the ziggurats as rocky outcrops tucked into the slope above a moist, marshy river, and he enjoyed the romantic appeal of UEA's later appearance. Of the National Theatre, he remarked, 'I have always wanted to see the exterior with something growing on it – Virginia creeper would be ideal, changing colour with the seasons', adding, 'It will weather, it will streak, it will become part of nature. It will probably get lichen from the river, there will be trees around it.'[195] Of UEA, he concluded,

> As bits get chipped off and bits grow around it, I think it will become part of landscape . . . On a wet day it may look drab and forbidding, and they might scuttle away from it. On a sunny day it's magical, but then buildings are like that, they should be.[196]

The etymology of the term 'monument' refers to the Latin *monumentum*, which in turn derives from *monere*, meaning to remind, warn and advise, so that the monument's purpose is more complex and questioning than it is often assumed to be. In 'On the Modern Cult of Monuments: Its Character and its Origin', 1903, Alois Riegl identified the 'historical value' of a monument, which refers to a specific time and physical condition, and its 'age value', which relates to a general appreciation of the passage of time. Riegl concluded that in his era monuments were appreciated for their age value as a means to come to terms with decay and death, while their historical value was largely ignored.[197] Recalling the creative interdependence of the monument and the ruin in earlier historical models, UEA's partially decayed state in the late twentieth century came to combine both historical and age value.

192 Yates, pp. 110–118.

193 Lady (Susan) Lasdun, in conversation with Jonathan Hill, 16 August 2012.

194 Brimblecombe and Grossi. 'Damage to Buildings from Future Climate and Pollution', pp. 13–14; Brimblecombe and Grossi, 'Potential Damage to Modern Building Materials from 21st Century Pollution', p. 116; Peter Brimblecombe, email correspondence with Jonathan Hill, 1 and 4 September 2013.

195 Lasdun, in Simon Jenkins, 'Interview with Denys Lasdun', 19 April 1979, Lasdun Archive; Lasdun, quoted in Connell, p. 10.

196 Lasdun, in 'Interview with Denys Lasdun', revised draft, 13 June 1979, p. 11, Lasdun Archive.

197 Riegl, pp. 22–24, 29, 38.

Monuments to traumatic events are nearly as common as celebratory monuments. The purpose of the monument is not only to remind us of the past; it can also remind us of the values the future should fulfil or reject.[198] But monuments can be ineffective means of collective remembrance, and their original meanings are soon forgotten or obscured unless they are continuously recalled and reaffirmed through everyday or ritualistic behaviour. Alongside the creation of monumental buildings that represent societal values, there is a process of forgetting in terms of the decay of meaning as well as the decay of material, which may result from natural processes or deliberate human actions.[199] In contrast to the static value of the symbolic monument, which mostly concerns remembrance, the allegorical ruin requires a person or a society to forget as well as remember so that meanings are open to an evolving process of adaptation and reinvention.

While ancient ruins are admired, modern ruins receive less appreciation. In part, this is because contemporary materials rarely match the stoic grandeur of earlier ruins, of which only the most substantial survive. But modern ruins are disturbing for other reasons too. In 1825 the high stone tower of Fonthill Abbey collapsed, just 18 years after it was completed to James Wyatt's design. In 1844 a visitor to the ruined Abbey remarked:

> *Ruins that have been such for ages, whose tenants have long since been swept away, recall ideas of persons and times so far back that we have no sympathy with them at all; but if you wish for a sight of all that is melancholy, all that is desolate, visit a modern ruin.*[200]

In an ancient ruin, decay occurred in the distant past, stimulating general thoughts of degradation and renewal in the present. In a modern ruin, active decay occurs before our eyes, stimulating particularly disturbing thoughts of our imminent degeneration and demise,[201] while also reinforcing the necessity of creative action today.

Exemplifying the emotive potential of architecture and landscape, and the possibility of growth as well as decay, the allegorical, monumental, modern, 'living' ruin looks to the future as well as the past, generating an appropriate image for a highly regarded and innovative university that today is best known for creative writing and climate change research. But algae, lichen and moss also turned a past image of the future – a new university – into one of swift decay that was sadly appropriate to the demise of free higher education, one of the emblems of the welfare state.

After the Second World War, most local authorities paid students' tuition fees and also contributed a maintenance grant towards living costs, which the 1962

198 Jackson, 'The Necessity for Ruins', p. 93.

199 Forty, 'Introduction', p. 16.

200 Lansdown, p. 40.

201 Pétursdóttir and Olsen, pp. 3–8.

Education Act made a legal obligation. But in 1988 the Conservative Education Secretary, Kenneth Baker, signalled a policy change with the quip: 'everyone's in debt these days, aren't they?'[202] The first state-supported student loans were for maintenance alone. But Labour's Teaching and Higher Education Act of 1998 introduced tuition fees, which led to a sequence of higher fees and larger loans. Imagining a parallel loss of principle, Bradbury remarked of Kirk, his 'hero-villain': 'No doubt in 1979 he would have voted for Thatcher, and in 1997 for Blair. He would be enjoying his vice-chancellorship at Batley Canalside University, and the life peerage has been a source of the greatest pleasure.'[203]

In 2003 – two years after Lasdun's death – the ziggurats, spine, aerial walkway and other elements of his design were listed Grade II*, initiating a refurbishment programme to the specification of English Heritage, the public body responsible for historic buildings. Ignoring that they had become part of the architecture, and were in accordance with the architect's intention, the university appointed a contractor to remove the algae, lichen and moss and apply an anti-fungal inhibitor. The buildings were new again, and much the worse for it.

UEA's quickly ruined state indicates the continuing shock of the sublime in the modern era, which in architecture has found expression in its relations with technology as well as art and nature. The technological sublime has been especially evident since industrialisation, as in Turner's paintings and Clark's recollection of aerial bombing on an industrial scale, which affirmed Price's close association of the picturesque and sublime.[204] In his speech to the 1963 party conference, the Leader of the Opposition, Harold Wilson, associated Labour with technological innovation in contrast to the governing Conservatives:

> In all our plans for the future, we are redefining and we are restating our socialism in terms of the scientific revolution . . . The Britain that is going to be forged in the white heat of this revolution will be no place for restrictive practices or outdated methods on either side of industry.[205]

An astute self-publicist, Wilson's words mimicked those of President John F. Kennedy two years earlier. Citing the successful Soviet rocket programme, Kennedy responded in belligerent rhetoric characteristic of the Cold War:

> if we are to win the battle that is now going on around the world between freedom and tyranny . . . I believe that this nation should commit itself to achieving the goal, before this decade is out, of landing a man on the moon and returning him safely to Earth.[206]

202 Baker, quoted in Bates.

203 Bradbury, 'Welcome Back to the History Man'.

204 Clark, quoted in Woodward, *In Ruins*, p. 212; Price, *An Essay on the Picturesque*, p. 76.

205 Labour Party Conference, 1 October 1963.

206 Kennedy.

Just eight years later, the Moon landing exemplified the technological sublime in the 1960s, both in the sense identified by Burke that a human construction – in this case the lunar module – could be sublime, and in the sense defined by Kant that the human ability to remain rational in the presence of terrifying natural phenomena, and thus transcend nature, is itself sublime.[207]

207 Kant, part 1, pp. 94–117.
Refer to Crowther, p. 52; Wiedmann, pp. 25–26.

Suggesting 'that at the dawn of romanticism, *Burke's* elaboration of the aesthetics of the sublime, and to a lesser extent *Kant's, outlined a world of possibilities for artistic experiments in which the avant-gardes would later trace their paths*', Jean-François Lyotard states: 'The sublime is perhaps the only mode of artistic sensibility to characterize the modern.'[208] He concludes that art's fundamental purpose remains the same as in the eighteenth century, to offer a 'pictorial or otherwise expressive witness to the inexpressible', including 'impending death'.[209] The influence of Barnett Newman's 'The Sublime is Now', 1948, led Lyotard to distinguish between the romantic sublime and the modern avant-garde sublime, which is concerned only with the present time and place, he contends.[210] But in *Modern Painting and the Northern Romantic Tradition*, 1975, Robert Rosenblum still places Newman within a romantic tradition, noting that 'the Jewish tradition of proscribing graven images' may have encouraged him to emphasise abstraction as the means to encounter the sublime.[211]

208 Lyotard, 'The Sublime and the Avant-Garde', pp. 206, 200.
209 Lyotard, 'The Sublime and the Avant-Garde', pp. 199, 204.
210 Barnett Newman, pp. 51–53.
211 Rosenblum, pp. 211–212.
Refer to Crowther, p. 54.

Indicating that there is a northern romantic tradition in architecture as well as art, UEA was conceived as a rugged landscape, manifesting qualities that Burke attributed to sublime nature – vastness, darkness and even deformity – and recalling his assertion that 'No work of art can be great, but as it deceives; to be otherwise is the prerogative of nature only.'[212] The 1960s is associated with technological innovation as well as social and cultural experimentation. But scientific progress did not mesmerise Lasdun; the technological Pop sensibility was primarily the work of a younger group of architects. Especially in UEA's decayed state at the cusp of the twenty-first century, technology evoked the sublime through failure.

212 Burke, p. 76.

In constructing metaphors and associations, conceiving design and use in relation to time and motion, and imagining UEA's future state, Lasdun emphasised the role of the allegorical imagination in architectural conception and perception. Associating designs with stories and histories, he remarked that each architect must devise his or her 'own creative myth', which should be 'sufficiently objective' and also have 'an element of subjectivity; the myth must be partly an expression of the architect's personality and partly of his time, partly a distillation of permanent truths and partly of the ephemera of the particular moment'.[213] The 'creative myth' can be a private inspiration or a public, collective narrative that is disseminated widely, either to architects, or to users, or to society as a whole. Emphasising that

213 Lasdun, 'The Architecture of Urban Landscape', p. 137.

'I don't mean myth in the sense that it is untrue,' Lasdun concluded: 'My own myth . . . engages with history'.[214]

In *Architecture in an Age of Scepticism*, Lasdun describes Le Corbusier's Pavilion Suisse, Cité Universitaire, Paris, 1931, as 'a seminal building' in which 'All the polemics of the machine aesthetic were brought together'.[215] But he also writes that by the 1950s the city's 'historical continuity was being lost' and architecture must rediscover its roots.[216] In ancient Greece, he recognised not only the origins of classicism, but also a poetic dialogue between built and natural forms. Like many architects of his generation, Lasdun's reassertion of classical principles was latent due to his education. In his teens he read J. C. Stobart's *The Glory that was Greece*, 1911, and *The Grandeur that was Rome*, 1912, and he studied at the AA when the strong Beaux-Arts influence led to projects such as 'An Embassy on a Rocky Promontory', which was seen alongside 'the early stirrings of modern architecture' that made the AA the first UK architecture school committed to modernism.[217] One of his tutors was Rowland Pierce, who designed Norwich City Hall, 1938, in partnership with Charles Holloway James. At the AA, Pierce emphasised Beaux-Arts planning and introduced Lasdun to the mass, monumentality and composition of Edwin Lutyens' designs. Asked to measure a specific building in his third year Lasdun chose Hawksmoor's Kensington Palace Orangery, 1705, from which he acquired 'a great understanding of the forces of structure and a sense of the weight of materials. This started a lifelong interest in an architect so singular and so profoundly concerned with the roots of architecture and the nature of space'.[218] As a birthday present in 1934 Lasdun received *The Architecture of Humanism: A Study in the History of Taste*, 1914, in which Geoffrey Scott focuses on the impact of the great classical works and celebrates the baroque: 'Architecture, simply and immediately perceived, is a combination, revealed through light and shade, of spaces, of masses and of lines.'[219] A year later, in a further birthday present, he highlighted Le Corbusier's description of architecture as 'a thing of art, a phenomenon of the emotions' and of 'masses' perceived 'in light'.[220]

While designing UEA, Lasdun was aware of contemporary theories on the classical foundation of modernist architecture, which were indebted first to Heinrich Wölfflin and then to his student Wittkower, who taught and influenced Rowe at the Warburg Institute, University of London. Committed to the German-speaking tradition of architectural history established in the nineteenth century, to which Pevsner and Giedion also belonged, Rowe continued the comparative formal-spatial analysis of buildings according to their effects on personal and social experience, and vice versa, and identified architectural styles and eras according to this method. Studying buildings of the late sixteenth and early twentieth centuries

214 Lasdun, in 'Interview with Denys Lasdun', revised draft, 13 June 1979, p. 9, Lasdun Archive; Lasdun, 'The Architecture of Urban Landscape', p. 139.

215 Lasdun, 'The Architecture of Urban Landscape', p. 134.

216 Lasdun, 'The Architecture of Urban Landscape', pp. 135, 137.

217 Richards, p. 43; Lasdun, 'Royal Gold Medallist Address', p. 221.

218 Lasdun, 'Royal Gold Medallist Address', p. 221.

219 Scott, p. 210.

220 Le Corbusier, pp. 23, 31. Refer to Curtis, *Denys Lasdun*, pp. 20–27.

in 'Mannerism and Modern Architecture', 1950, he identifies 'formal ambiguity' and 'deliberate inversion' in response to 'the very human desire to impair perfection'.[221] Quoting Le Corbusier, Rowe remarks: 'At one moment, architecture is "the art above all others which achieves a state of Platonic grandeur"; but, at the next, it becomes clear that this state, far from being changeless and eternal, is an excitement subsidiary to the personal perception of "the masterly, correct and magnificent play of masses brought together in light."'[222] Concluding that the 'whole modern movement appears to share' Le Corbusier's emphasis on subjective experience rather than ideal order, Rowe identifies 'the visual index of an acute spiritual crisis' in 'the present day'.[223]

Commenting on contemporary architects who 'seek to re-establish the full classical language' Lasdun sympathetically concluded: 'They have chosen a hard and difficult road where success is problematic and failure probable.'[224] Centuries before, confidence in natural reason had undermined the authority of the classical canon. But rather than wither, classicism continued as an evolving language open to new influences and mutations, as Rowe's analysis emphasised. Returning Lasdun's mostly positive appraisal of Hunstanton, and recognising a shared commitment to history and modernity, the Smithsons concluded that Lasdun's success at UEA was the result of 'the classical architect's skills . . . the traditional understanding about size, scale and measure'.[225] They were in a position to know. Peter Smithson had enrolled at the Royal Academy precisely to acquire a classical expertise, submitting as his entry for the 1949 Grand Prize a design for a university museum that acknowledged Mies' debt to classicism.[226]

Soon after his appointment as UEA's architect, Lasdun told the *Eastern Daily Press*: 'Hawksmoor was a far greater architect than Frank Lloyd Wright'.[227] Later he remarked that Hawksmoor's 'point of departure was Ancient Rome but he was convinced that departure from this was essential', concluding that Hawksmoor broke the rules of classical architecture to emphasise them more.[228]

> NH uses elements of classical and gothic (the only elements available to him) in a free, unprejudiced manner not just quoting them but reconstituting them in a new and original whole which is neither classical or gothic but is wholly original and wholly convincing.[229]

If Lasdun had replaced 'gothic' for 'modern' he could have equally applied this analysis to himself. He was concerned both to emphasise the classical foundation of modern architecture and also to disrupt and transform it in the manner of a modern Hawksmoor.

221 Rowe, 'Mannerism and Modern Architecture', pp. 33–35.

222 Rowe quotes from the 1927 edition of *Towards a New Architecture*; the pagination is the same as in the 1946 edition. Le Corbusier, pp. 102, 31, quoted in Rowe, 'Mannerism and Modern Architecture', p. 42.

223 Rowe, 'Mannerism and Modern Architecture', pp. 42–43.

224 Lasdun, 'The Architecture of Urban Landscape', p. 137.

225 Alison and Peter Smithson, *Without Rhetoric*, p. 30.

226 Powers, p. 65.

227 Lasdun, 3 March 1962, quoted in Dormer and Muthesius, p. 156.

228 Lasdun, 'Notes on a Lecture on Nicholas Hawksmoor', in Curtis, *Denys Lasdun*, p. 223.

229 Lasdun, 'Notes on a Lecture on Nicholas Hawksmoor', in Curtis, *Denys Lasdun*, p. 223.

Architects have used history in different ways, whether to indicate their continuity with the past or departure from it. From the Renaissance to the early twentieth century the architect was a historian in the sense that an architectural treatise combined design and history, and a building was expected to manifest the character of the time and knowingly refer to earlier historical eras. Modernism ruptured this system in principle if not always in practice. Advocating an architecture specific to the present and breaking from previous educational models, Gropius excluded the history of architecture from the Bauhaus syllabus, while in the 'Manifesto of Futurist Architecture', 1914, Antonio Sant'Elia and Filippo Tomasso Marinetti proclaimed: 'This architecture cannot be subject to any law of historical continuity.'[230] But even modernists who denied the relevance of the past relied on histories to validate modernism and articulate its principles. Books such as Pevsner's *Pioneers of the Modern Movement*, 1936, and Giedion's *Space, Time and Architecture*, 1941, identified a modernist prehistory to justify modernism's historical inevitability, rupture from the past and systematic evolution.[231]

To some degree, mid-century modernists merely reaffirmed an appreciation of history that was latent in a work such as Le Corbusier's *Vers une architecture*, but had been largely ignored. But the Second World War was a more scientific war than the First, and nuclear devastation undermined confidence in technological progress as a means of social transformation, notably for the generation of architects who had seen military service. In the search for stability in the uncertain aftermath of 1945, modernism's previously dismissive reaction to social norms and cultural memories was itself anachronistic. The consequence was not just to acknowledge early modernism's classical heritage but also to place a concern for history at the heart of architecture once again, affirming the liberal humanist tradition that modernism had once seemed to repudiate, and undermining the unnecessary opposition between tradition and innovation that modernism had once seemed to pose. To be ancient and modern was no longer a contradiction. Frances Yates – author of *The Art of Memory*, 1966 – described the National Theatre as an 'ancient truth in a new idiom', to Lasdun's 'enormous pleasure'.[232]

In early 1961 the RIBA hosted two lectures, in which the speakers, both historians, acknowledged a mutual debt despite their previous differences, leading its President to quip: 'I hope we have not got to the stage when Pevsner speaks only to Banham and Banham speaks only to God.'[233] Just one year after he proposed that the architect should 'run with technology', Banham suggested a similar agenda for the historian in his lecture 'The History of the Immediate Future'.[234] Acknowledging 'the occupational risks of prophecy', he adopted a scientific analogy:

230 Sant'Elia and Marinetti, p. 35.

231 Vidler, *Histories of the Immediate Present,* pp. 4–5.

232 Frances Yates, letter to Lasdun, 17 May 1976, Lasdun Archive; Lasdun, letter to Frances Yates, 21 May 1976, Lasdun Archive.

233 William Holford, in Pevsner, 'Modern Architecture and the Historian or The Return of Historicism', p. 239; Banham, 'The History of the Immediate Future', p. 252; Pevsner, 'Modern Architecture and the Historian or The Return of Historicism', p. 230.

234 Reyner Banham, *Theory and Design in the First Machine Age*, pp. 329–330.

History is to the future as the observed results of an experiment are to the plotted graph. That is, you plot on the graph the results of which you are sure, you seek for a line, an algebraic curve, that connects them convincingly and you produce it beyond the last certain point to see where it will lead.[235]

A prospect of the future is implicit in many histories but in Banham's lecture it was explicit: 'History is our only guide to the future.'[236] Once established, modernism was supposed to remain triumphant.[237]

Seemingly contradicting his earlier conjunction of modernism and the picturesque, Pevsner remarked in 1961 that at 'the beginning of the twentieth century, there arose a generation of giants, who created a new style of architecture, entirely independent of the past' and later concluded: 'It seemed folly to think that anybody would wish to abandon' modernism.[238] But the precursors to the newly established modernist canon were ripe for revival and reinterpretation, like any earlier architecture. In his RIBA lecture Pevsner acknowledged the influence of his modernist histories, and took the blame for unwittingly encouraging the 'return' of 'such a dominating faith in history that it chokes original action and the action which replaces it is inspired by the past'.[239] In a BBC radio broadcast later that decade he contrasted contemporary architecture with his *Pioneers of the Modern Movement*, which was reprinted as *Pioneers of Modern Design* in 1949 and revised in 1960. Once again recognising his 'embarrassing' influence on architects who revived styles that he had discarded, Pevsner identified 'an anti-Pioneers style . . . alarmingly harking back to art nouveau and to expressionism'.[240] Acknowledging 'neo-expressionism' as the more pervasive, he nominated postwar Le Corbusier as its key figure and criticised the Royal College of Physicians, London, 1964, even though he had 'the greatest respect for Denys Lasdun', its architect.[241] Pevsner first denigrated the 'over-powering . . . brutality' of the new style and then, despite his personal distaste, recognised its contemporary relevance as 'a successor to my international modern of the 1930s, a postmodern style I would be tempted to call it, but the legitimate style of the 1950s and 1960s'.[242] Unable, or unwilling, to recognise that brutalism was subject to modernist and picturesque influences, Pevsner characterised it as a brief interlude associated with the anxious aftermath of war: 'phases of so excessively high a pitch of stimulation can't last. We can't, in the long run, live our day-to-day lives in the midst of explosions.'[243]

Lasdun is not usually described as a postmodernist. His architectural references were multiple, including classicism, modernism, the baroque and the picturesque. But he took history seriously and did not employ historical motifs in the casual and superficial manner of some postmodernists. Lasdun's concern for myths is charac-

235 Banham, 'The History of the Immediate Future', p. 252.

236 Banham, 'The History of the Immediate Future', p. 252.

237 Pevsner's lecture was given a month before Banham's. In the responses to Pevsner's lecture, W. A. Allen had remarked: 'If I turn to history at all, I see it rather like a curve on a graph which by its shape may reveal the direction things are likely to take.' Allen, in Pevsner, 'Modern Architecture and the Historian or The Return of Historicism', p. 238.

238 Pevsner, 'Modern Architecture and the Historian or The Return of Historicism', p. 230; Pevsner, 'The Anti-Pioneers', p. 295.

239 Pevsner, 'The Return of Historicism', p. 271. Refer to Pevsner, 'Modern Architecture and the Historian or The Return of Historicism', p. 230.

240 Pevsner, 'The Anti-Pioneers', pp. 295, 305.

241 Pevsner, 'The Anti-Pioneers', p. 298.

242 Pevsner, 'The Anti-Pioneers', p. 299.

243 Pevsner, 'The Anti-Pioneers', p. 307.

Denys Lasdun, Royal College of Physicians, London, 1964. Courtesy of Henk Snoek/RIBA Library Photographs Collection.

teristically postmodern but his reference to 'permanent truths' is not, contradicting Lyotard's definition of the '*postmodern* as incredulity toward metanarratives'.[244] However, Lyotard included the postmodern within the modern. Acknowledging the process by which a new artwork questions an earlier one, his categorisation is dynamic and not specific to an era: 'A work can become modern only if it is first postmodern. Postmodernism thus understood is not modernism at its end but in the nascent state.'[245] In this sense, Lasdun became postmodern to remain modern. But given that so many of his references were from earlier centuries and without irony, it seems equally appropriate to conclude that he became premodern to remain modern.

Early Italian modernists did not reject historical references to the extent of other CIAM members and in 1961 Pevsner focused his criticism on postwar Italian architects for furthering this concern, citing Ernesto N. Rogers.[246] In 1959 Banham had dismissed 'the Italian retreat from modern architecture' as 'infantile regression', while at the CIAM conference in the same year Peter Smithson specifically criticised the historical references in Rogers' recently completed Torre Velasca, Milan, somewhat disingenuously given his growing concern for the picturesque.[247] But Lasdun proclaimed:

> *If you look at the modern Italian work, for example, it is at least clear that architects have engaged in terrible battle with architecture and certainly many of*

244 Lyotard, *The Postmodern Condition*, p. xxiv.

245 Lyotard, *The Postmodern Condition*, p. 79.

246 Pevsner, 'Modern Architecture and the Historian or The Return of Historicism', pp. 231–233.

247 The last conference of the Congrès International d'Architecture Moderne was held at Otterlo in The Netherlands. Rogers' firm was Banfi, Belgiojoso, Peressutti and Rogers (BBPR). Banham, 'Neo-Liberty', p. 235; Oscar Newman, pp. 94–95.

them have been disastrously defeated; but most English architects seem to have reached a gentlemanly understanding with their art that they should leave each other strictly alone. [248]

Critical of international modernism, Rogers promoted appreciation of national and regional architectural cultures. Advocating 'continuity' in 1954, he emphasised that 'No work is truly modern which is not genuinely rooted in tradition, while no ancient work has a modern meaning which is not capable of somehow reflecting our modern temper.' [249] To explain his conception of a building in dialogue with its physical and natural surroundings and contributing to an evolving historical continuity, Rogers quoted from 'Tradition and the Individual Talent', 1917, in which T.S. Eliot emphasises that the present alters our understanding of the past as much as the past influences the present. Admired by Rogers and equally indebted to Eliot's essay, Lasdun noted the value that the poet placed on innovation as well as tradition: 'The existing monuments form an ideal order among themselves, which is modified by the introduction of the new (the really new) work of art among them.' [250] Including Palladio, Wren and Le Corbusier in one evolving 'architectural tradition', Lasdun transformed Eliot's words into his own:

> *Context is not only topographical and physical, it is also historical . . . My concern for context is as an agent of architectural transformation. The place you build actually has formative influences on the nature of the building. And when the building is there it has formative influences and effects on the place it is made.* [251]

Confirming the prevalence of such ideas in postwar architecture, Vincent Scully concluded in 1969 that the architect will 'always be dealing with historical problems – with the past and, a function of the past, with the future. So the architect should be regarded as a kind of physical historian . . . the architect builds visible history'. [252] As a design is a reinterpretation of the past that is meaningful to the present, each building or landscape is a new history. The architect is a historian twice over: as a writer and as a designer.

In postwar Britain, the return of history meant the return of the ruin, the enduring emblem of an evolving tradition from the picturesque and romanticism to picturesque and romantic modernism. Equating a history to a ruin, Walter Benjamin remarked: 'Allegories are, in the realm of thoughts, what ruins are in the realm of things.' [253] Our understanding of the past is inevitably partial. Laying bare the processes of construction and decay, a history is both a ruin of the past and a speculative reconstruction in the present. Equally, the novel's origins in the

248 Lasdun does not name the Italian architects to whom he refers. Lasdun, in Davies and Lasdun. 'Thoughts in Progress: Summing Up III – The "Objects Found" Philosophy', p. 436.

249 Rogers, p. 2.

250 Eliot, pp. 26–27, filed in Lasdun Archive.

251 Lasdun, 'Draft, Suggested Theme – The Late Show, BBC', 8 July 1992, Lasdun Archive; Lasdun, in 'Interview with Denys Lasdun', agreed draft, 27 June 1979, p. 4, Lasdun Archive.

252 Scully, p. 257. For a less subtle discussion of the 'reawakened' 'interest in history', refer to Giedion, 'History and the Architect', pp. 106–110.

253 Benjamin, *The Origin of German Tragic Drama*, p. 178.

fictional autobiography ensure that a 'life in ruin' is a recurring literary metaphor, representing potential as well as loss, and a challenge to the protagonist, whether he or she is incarcerated on an island or in a prison as in Defoe's two best-known novels, for example.

Histories and novels each display a concern for the past, present and future. The historian acknowledges that the past is not the same as the present, while the novelist inserts the reader in a place and time that feels very present even if it is not. Whether implicit or explicit, a critique of the present and a prospect of the future are evident in histories and novels. They both need to be convincing but in different ways. Although no history is completely objective, to have any validity it must appear truthful to the past. A novel may be believable but not true. But recognising the overlaps between two literary genres, Bradbury notably describes his novel *The History Man*, as 'a total invention with delusory approximations to historical reality, just as is history itself'.[254]

As a design is equivalent to a history, we may expect the designer as well as the historian 'to have a certain quality of *subjectivity*' that is 'suited to the objectivity proper to history', as Paul Ricouer concludes.[255] But the designer does not usually construct a history with the rigour expected of a contemporary historian, and we expect the designer to display other qualities of subjectivity as well, whether personal or cultural.

A design is also equivalent to a novel, convincing the user to suspend disbelief. Lasdun's design for UEA is a social and cultural history of a nation, which acknowledges a debt to earlier migrations and appreciates new influences. Equally it is a fictional autobiography, indicating the society to which he wished to belong. Part-historian, part-novelist, the architect is *The History Man*. We expect a history or a novel to be written in words, but they can also be cast in concrete or seeded in soil. An architectural book can be a history and a novel, and so can a building or a landscape.

254 Bradbury, 'Author's Note', *The History Man*. Refer to Lowenthal, pp. 210–237.

255 Ricoeur, 'Objectivity and Subjectivity in History', p. 22.

conclusion

conclusion

Derived from the Latin *nascere*, meaning 'to be born', the term 'nature' has numerous meanings in which the principal distinction is between, first, a concept through which humans define themselves in relation to what they think they are not, and, second, the phenomena and processes of which humanity is a part, as in Charles Darwin's theory of evolution in *The Origin of Species*, 1859, for example.[1]

1 Darwin, *The Origin of Species*, p. 109.

The term 'landscape' initially referred to land managed and cultivated by an agrarian community. Expanding its meaning, by the sixteenth century it also referred to a picture of nature and in the eighteenth century it was further applied to a prospect of actual nature, which in 1770 Whately so vehemently stated was 'as superior' to a mere 'painting, as a reality to a representation'.[2] In each of these meanings, 'landscape' acknowledges a human intervention, indicating why the prefix 'natural' is applied to a landscape that is seemingly unaffected by humanity even though this has been impossible for centuries. Such a landscape is culturally defined, reflecting what we have learned to see as natural, notably so in Britain, the first industrialised nation.[3]

2 Whately, p. 1.

3 Gilbert Meason used the term 'landscape architecture' in *On the Landscape Architecture of the Great Painters of Italy*, 1828, as did John Claudius Loudon in his edited collection of Repton's writings, *The Landscape Gardening and the Landscape Architecture of the Late Humphry Repton, Esq*, 1840. Rather than the design of landscapes, Meason and Repton most likely referred to architecture in a landscape setting. The slightly earlier term *architecte-paysagiste* is credited to Jean-Marie Morel. Disponzio, pp. 135–159.

The earliest meaning of the term 'culture' also referred to agriculture, and endured in everyday discourse from the Middle Ages to the late eighteenth century. Originating in the early sixteenth century, a further meaning emphasised that the successful and prosperous cultivation of land enabled a person to become cultured and cultivated. Both meanings were in use in the eighteenth century, but the association of culture with humanity not nature acquired prominence in the nineteenth century. Jonathan Bate describes the picturesque landscape as 'a symptom of the growing division between' the two 'senses of the word "culture"'.[4] But as it was conceived holistically in social, aesthetic, agricultural and ecological terms, the eighteenth-century Georgic estate can, alternatively, be understood as a key moment when both meanings of nature and of culture were interdependent in the term 'landscape'.

4 Bate, *The Song of the Earth*, pp. 3–5, 11–12.

5 Refer to Corner, 'Eidetic Operations and New Landscapes', p. 158; Corner, 'Terra Fluxus', p. 30; Cosgrove, 'Airport/Landscape', p. 223; Cosgrove, *Geography and Vision*, p. 1; Cosgrove, *Social Formation and Symbolic Landscape*, p. 15; Mostafavi, 'Why Ecological Urbanism? Why Now?', p. 50; Waldheim, 'Landscape as Urbanism', p. 39; Williams, p. 120.

The picturesque has been accused of many crimes. An emphasis on pictorial composition can force nature to imitate art, and may imply that certain social relations and environmental transformations are natural too.[5] But to dismiss the picturesque as merely a prospect on property, as some critics have done, is to ignore the complex painting history that informed the eighteenth-century estate and to disregard the subtlety of picturesque designs, which draw attention to the problems as well as the pleasures of vision. The picturesque is a deceptive, and even inaccurate, term because it emphasises one aspect of the eighteenth-century garden to the detriment of its other qualities, such as the importance of the senses and the seasons to design, experience, understanding and the imagination.

Conceiving a design as both a history and a fiction is not exclusive to the analogy of architecture to landscape. But it is central to this tradition because of the simultaneous and interdependent emergence of new art forms, each of them a creative and questioning response to empiricism's detailed investigation of subjective experience and the natural world: the picturesque landscape, the analytical history and the English novel, which its early advocates conceived as a fictional autobiography and characterised as a history not a story. The conjunction of art forms stimulated a lyrical environmentalism that profoundly influenced subsequent centuries.

While a prospect of the future is implicit in many histories and novels, it is explicit in a design, which is always imagined before it is built. Creative architects have often looked to the past to imagine the future, studying an earlier architecture not to replicate it but to understand and transform it, revealing its relevance to the present. Twenty-first century architects need to appreciate the shock of the old as well as the shock of the new.

The drawings for UEA were hand-made. Black ink was drawn directly onto tracing paper, with each drawing pen offering a specific line width. When a change was necessary, ink was gently erased with a razor blade, and a rubber then removed surface blemishes so that the tracing paper was ready for another ink line. Numerals and text were applied either with a drawing pen and stencil or as adhesive letters, placed one by one. A dyeline printer produced a monochrome copy on white paper, with a lingering ammonia aroma. The simplicity of the drawing process limited its visual complexity but encouraged conceptual clarity, as in the UEA development plan, 1962. Consultants and contractors communicated by phone and post as the fax machine was not yet commercially available.

Today, most architects draw on the computer and digital media have profoundly changed the ways that people communicate. Architectural authorship has always been a negotiation. The means of digital design emphasise this more, with each consultant and contractor contributing to the same 3D drawing. Rather than each drawing type reflecting the division of labour, a design drawing may also be a fabrication drawing. Bringing drawing closer to building and the ambiguities of architectural authorship to the fore, the conjunction of design and fabrication questions the history of the architect and division of labour in a manner that recalls the thirteenth century as well as the twenty-first.

Sharing the same information at the same time can facilitate local collective action, while on a regional or global scale it encourages the interconnectedness of peoples and places. But at the same time, digital media can detach that information, and the people who view it, from an awareness of history, society and place, encouraging an a-contextual formalism that has, so far, been the pervading characteristic of architecture that claims distinctly digital origins. Rather than new, the prevalent aesthetic preferences of digital designs are those of formally expressive twentieth-century decades. The principal difference between then and now is that it is possible to build what was previously just drawn. Increased computational ability allows complex forms to be calculated and constructed, shifting the economics of building production towards customisation rather than repetition.

Architects tend to fetishise newness and new technologies, and readily succumb to technological determinism. Just as early twentieth-century modernists eulogised industrial production and some 1960s modernists praised technological systems, a number of early twenty-first-century architects celebrate digital computation, distinguishing between a finite design object with one author and an open-ended design process with many contributors, which they respectively characterise as old and new. But new technologies rarely match architects' technological dreams. Many familiar twenty-first-century technologies are actually rather old, as was also the case in the early twentieth century. In *The Shock of the Old*, 2008, David Edgerton writes:

> *Culture has not lagged behind technology, rather the reverse; the idea that culture has lagged behind technology is itself very old and has existed under many technological regimes. Technology has not generally been a revolutionary force; it has been responsible for keeping things the same as much as changing them.*[6]

6 Edgerton, p. 212.

Rather than a simple linear progression from one technology to another, the result is more often an interdependent network of influences between differing media and technologies. For example, the advent of the printed book informed but did not displace architecture's representational role and stimulated a productive interdependence between books and buildings that remains important to architects' practice and status.

In many industries, a number of technologies – old and new – remain relevant and useful. Rather than fundamentally transform architects' practice, the advent of digital media is but one contributing factor to their evolving status. Rather than one model of architectural authorship replacing another, new and old models exist alongside each other. Just as a building can be both archaic and modern, design can incorporate a hybrid of old and new themes and techniques, not simply because they are useful but because they have social and cultural meaning. Already in the late eighteenth century and again in the mid-twentieth century, architects acknowledged *disegno* and industrial production as well as the picturesque, while design, construction and use were conceived temporally in terms of the ruin, and the creative influences of natural as well as human forces were appreciated.

In 'The Death of the Author', 1968, Barthes dismisses the assumption that the author alone determines the meaning of a text, and emphasises that words often contradict the author's intentions, concluding that 'the birth of the reader must be at the cost of the death of the Author'.[7] Recognising that each reader remakes a text anew, Barthes argues for the writer who is especially aware of the reader, with both having a role in the creation of meaning. Extending his earlier argument, he writes in *Camera Lucida*, 1980, that 'language is by nature, fictional' and concludes: 'No writing can give me . . . certainty. It is the misfortune (but also perhaps the voluptuous pleasure) of language not to be able to authenticate itself'.[8] Similarly, drawings, models, buildings and landscapes offer the 'voluptuous pleasure' of ambiguity not certainty, even though production drawings and an accompanying written specification have a contractual purpose.

An early eighteenth-century architect or patron could 'read' garden monuments with some degree of certainty and consistency due to their emblematic language, while the associative possibilities of a late eighteenth-century landscape were as open and expressive as its sweeping lawns. But the most significant picturesque landscapes, such as Holkham and 12–14 Lincoln's Inn Fields, are emblematic as well as expressive, and thus richer in their associative potential. Since modernism's suppression of the figurative and representational, and postmodernism's failure to take them seriously, most buildings and landscapes have been expressive alone, which limits the types of novels and histories they can tell. For all his concern for history, Lasdun relied on the associative possibilities of movement, material and form to tell his tale.

The emblems of an eighteenth-century picturesque landscape have less meaning today. But a combination of new and old figurative languages with con-temporary relevance and culturally diverse meanings would allow landscape – and architecture as landscape – to be emblematic as well as expressive once again, and thus further stimulate the user's imagination as well as that of the architect.

Architecture is most often experienced habitually, when it is rarely the focus of attention. But, as empiricism made evident, habit is not passive. Instead, it is a questioning intelligence acquired through experience and subject to continuing re-evaluation. Rather than necessarily a deviation from habit, a creative use can instead establish, affirm or develop a habit that is itself unexpected and evolving. In contrast to a singular focused activity such as reading, use is a particular type of awareness in which a person performs, sometimes all at once, a series of complex activities, some habitual, others not, that move in and out of conscious attention. Just as the reader makes a book anew through reading, the user makes a build-ing anew through using. Certain texts are more resistant to the reader because of

7 Barthes, 'The Death of the Author', p. 148. Refer to Foucault, 'What is an Author?', pp. 120–121, 131–136.

8 Barthes, *Camera Lucida*, pp. 87, 86.

their social or cultural importance. For example, a new interpretation of a religious text may be suppressed if it is made public. It is also more difficult for the user to affect some buildings than others. It is usually harder to transform a workplace than a home, whether through a physical transformation, a change of use, or an unexpected association.

A landscape's comparative lack of functional definition, and the sensual immediacy of the changing weather and seasons, may allow it to retain our attention more readily than a building and incorporate a range of unexpected activities with greater ease. All buildings change slowly and subtly, but an architecture that is conceived as analogous to an ever-changing landscape will be more temporally aware than other buildings and will require constant re-evaluation, encouraging particularly questioning and creative relations between objects, spaces and users at varied times, scales and dimensions.

Since the seventeenth and eighteenth centuries, the weather and climate have been essential to the evolving tradition in which architecture is synonymous with landscape. The history of poetic and practical responses to atmospheric pollution is now centuries old. But despite this history, and the burgeoning environmental movement in the 1960s, anthropogenic climate change was not widely acknowledged by scientists until the mid-1970s. In Britain and the many nations where 'romantic modernism' remains an abiding influence[9] and the monumental living ruin is a poignant and positive model, their increasing relevance depends on climate change, which is now the principal means to consider the relations between nature and culture.

Paradoxically, many of the contemporary 'solutions' to climate change reaffirm a faith in technological progress that has been a principal cause of anthropogenic climate change, and they are unlikely to be implemented due to insufficient scientific knowledge and political inertia generated by the conflicting agendas of countries and corporations.[10] In a parallel scenario, the rhetoric of sustainability tends to reduce architecture to a technical issue and the architect to a technocrat, employing a debased empiricism devoid of the poetic and practical implications of Evelyn and Colvin's environmental research.

Climate always changes, whether by human agency or other means. The dangers posed by anthropogenic climate change are real and need to be addressed when and where possible. But climate change is not only a scientific concern. In formulating designs that are equivalent to histories and novels, the tradition of architecture as landscape is compatible with a complex, creative and contextual engagement with climate change that is not only driven by fear and may stimulate cultural, social and environmental benefits, whether at a local, national or regional level.

9 Norberg-Schulz, p. 154.

10 Glover, pp. 22–23, 28–30, 86–88, 246–251; Hulme, p. 363; Merchant, p. 2; Smith, 'Foreword', pp. xi–xv; Smith, 'Nature at the Millennium', pp. 281–283.

In a further contemporary response to anthropogenic climate change, the continuing value of the term 'nature' has been questioned because it is assumed to affirm nature's separation from culture and encourage a fascination for unfettered nature that allows some sites to be protected and others to be overdeveloped. However, eradicating the term will aid rather than hinder nature's exploitation because commercial, industrial and national interests would be without restraint. As an idea, 'nature' is a human construction. But the places, species and phenomena that we include within nature are real and not solely subject to our imagination and will. Just because we have named something does not mean that we have made it or even understand it, however extensive our influence.

Contemporary technologies – whether mechanical, digital or craft – influence urban and rural landscapes. For example, a modern-day tractor is guided by a satellite navigation system for accuracy and efficiency. At a casual glance, a landscape may appear to be subject to human order, and no more natural than another 'cultural' artefact. But despite the reduction of wildlife habitats and proliferation of pesticides, each landscape is teeming with life forms that are subject to their own rhythms and intertwined in a complex network of relations with other life forms, including humanity.[11] The English origin of the term 'wilderness' is self-willed land.[12] In 1881 Darwin remarked: 'Worms have played a more important part in the history of the world than most persons would at first assume.'[13] In a similar vein, Edward O. Wilson states that 'insects are the little things that run the world'.[14] Thriving everywhere, they so greatly outnumber humans that their combined weight outweighs the human population by six times, and their history with the plant world is 400 million years older.[15] Even in a suburban garden there are likely to be around 1,500 insect species and a much larger total population. Human decisions influence other life forms but they do not control them.

The term 'coproduction' explains nature–culture relations and the cities, landscapes and weathers we inhabit.[16] Equally, people are natural as well as cultural beings. Just as the intermingling of natural and cultural forces creates the contemporary weather, a landscape or building results from the relations between nature and culture that arise during its conception, production and use. As architecture, landscape and the weather are each a product of nature–culture relations, they inform, affect and influence each other in a complex developmental process that is never one way.

The term 'author' has sustained over half a century of criticism because it has been associated with sole authority. But rather than a term such as agency, which may dissipate creativity, the 'coproduction' of multiple authors recognises that natural forces, as well as cultural ones, together create a building or landscape. Authorship

11 Williamson, *An Environmental History of Wildlife in England*, pp. 187–188.

12 Dave Foreman, referred to in Merchant, p. 230.

13 Darwin, *Formation of Vegetal Mould*, p. 305. Refer to Bennett, pp. 95–98.

14 Wilson, quoted in Grissell, p. 124.

15 Grissell, pp. 35, 144, 234.

16 Steve Rayner refers to 'coproduction' and Jane Bennett refers to 'distributed agency', while Carolyn Merchant recognises a 'partnership' in which 'both humans and nature are active' and nature is not gendered. Herbert Marcuse conceives nature as active, sometimes humanity's 'ally', sometimes hostile. Rayner, p. 287; Bennett, p. 38; Merchant, pp. 223–231; Marcuse, pp. 65, 69.

is not necessarily self-reflective. An insect, bird or worm may not be self-aware in the sense that we usually ascribe to human authorship, but its decisions are not mechanical and instead depend on the conditions it encounters. Acknowledging that authorship involves accidents as well as intentions, the contemporary sciences of climate change, ecology and complexity theory are consistent with the idea of nature as author. Sometimes competing, sometimes affirming, each author may inform or deny the other, as in a feisty dialogue of distinct voices and unexpected conclusions in which authorship is temporal and shared. In the conjunction of architecture and landscape – and design, history and fiction – nature is not just a protagonist, but may be a co-author too.

bibliography

Addison, Joseph, and Richard Steele. *The Spectator*. London: George Routledge, 1891, 3 vols.

Adorno, Theodor W., and Max Horkheimer. *Dialectic of Enlightenment*. Trans. John Cumming. London and New York: Verso, 1977. First published in 1944.

Albert, William. *The Turnpike Road System in England, 1663–1840*. Cambridge: Cambridge University Press, 1972.

Alberti, Leon Battista. *On the Art of Building in Ten Books*. Trans. Joseph Rykwert, Neil Leach and Robert Tavernor. Cambridge, MA and London: MIT Press, 1988. *De re aedificatoria* was written in around 1450 and published in 1485. Giacomo (James) Leoni first translated it into English as *Ten Books on Architecture* in 1726.

Alpers, Svetlana. *The Art of Describing: Dutch Art in the Seventeenth Century*. Chicago: University of Chicago Press, 1983.

Anderson, Stanford. 'The Fiction of Function'. *Assemblage*, no. 2, February 1987, pp. 19–31.

Andrews, Malcolm. *Landscape in Western Art*. Oxford: Oxford University Press, 1999.

Angelicoussis, Elizabeth. 'Walpole's Roman Legion: Antique Sculpture at Houghton'. *Apollo*, vol. 169, no. 562, February 2009, pp. 24–30.

Anonymous. *The Norfolk Congress: Or, A Full and True Account of Their Hunting, Feasting and Merrymaking; being singularly delightful and likewise very instructive to the Publick*. London: R. Lightbody, 1728.

Ayres, Philip. *Classical Culture and the Idea of Rome in Eighteenth-Century England*. Cambridge: Cambridge University Press, 1997.

Ayres, Philip. 'Introduction'. In Shaftesbury, *Characteristicks*, pp. xiii–xxxviii.

Bacon, Francis. 'Novum Organum'. *The Oxford Francis Bacon*. Oxford: Clarendon Press, 2004, vol. 11, pp. 52–447. First published in 1620.

Bacon, Francis. *Sylva Sylvarum: Or A Natural History, in Ten Centuries*. London: Thomas Lee, 1676. First published in 1627.

Ballantyne, Andrew. *Architecture, Landscape and Liberty: Richard Payne Knight and the Picturesque*. Cambridge: Cambridge University Press, 1997.

Banham, Reyner. *A Critic Writes: Essays by Reyner Banham*. Berkeley, Los Angeles and London: University of California Press, 1996.

Banham, Reyner. 'The History of the Immediate Future'. *Journal of the Royal Institute of British Architects*, vol. 68, no. 7, May 1961, pp. 252–260, 269. Based on a lecture given at the RIBA on 7 February 1961.

Banham, Reyner. 'How I Learnt to Live with the Norwich Union'. In Banham, *A Critic Writes*, pp. 100–104. First published in 1964.

Banham, Reyner. 'Kent and Capability'. In Banham, *A Critic Writes*, pp. 87–90. First published in 1962.

Banham, Reyner. *Megastructure: Urban Futures of the Recent Past*. London: Thames & Hudson, 1976.

Banham, Reyner. 'Neo-Liberty: The Italian Retreat from Modern Architecture'. *The Architectural Review*, vol. 125, no. 747, April 1959, pp. 231–235.

Banham, Reyner. *The New Brutalism: Ethic or Aesthetic*. London: Architectural Press, 1966.

Banham, Reyner. 'The New Brutalism'. *The Architectural Review*, vol. 118, no. 708, December 1955, pp. 355–361.

Banham, Reyner. 'Revenge of the Picturesque: English Architectural Polemics, 1945–1965'. In Summerson, *Concerning Architecture*, pp. 265–273.

Banham, Reyner. *Theory and Design in the First Machine Age*. London: The Architectural Press, 1960.

Banham, Reyner. 'This is Tomorrow'. *The Architectural Review*, vol. 120, no. 716, September 1956, pp. 186–188.

Baridon, Michel. 'Ruins as a Mental Construct'. *Journal of Garden History*, vol. 5, no. 1, January–March 1985, pp. 84–96.

Barrell, John. *The Dark Side of the Landscape: The Rural Poor in English Painting 1730–1840*. Cambridge: Cambridge University Press, 1980.

Barthes, Roland. *Camera Lucida*. Trans. Richard Howard. London: Fontana, 1982. First published in French in 1980.

Barthes, Roland. 'The Death of the Author'. In Barthes, *Image – Music – Text*, pp. 142–148. First published in 1968.

Barthes, Roland. *Image – Music – Text*. Trans. Stephen Heath. London: Flamingo, 1984.

Barthes, Roland. *Mythologies*. Trans. Annette Lavers. London: Paladin, 1973. First published in 1957.

Barthes, Roland. 'The New Citroën'. In Barthes, *Mythologies*, pp. 88–90.

Bate, Jonathan. 'Living with the Weather'. *Studies in Romanticism*, vol. 35, Fall 1996, pp. 431–447.

Bate, Jonathan. *Romantic Ecology: Wordsworth and the Environmental Tradition*. London and New York: Routledge, 1991.

Bate, Jonathan. *The Song of the Earth*. London: Picador, 2000.

Bates, Stephen. 'Tuition Fees: From "Free" University Education to Students Owing Thousands'. *The Guardian*, 12 October 2010. http://www.guardian.co.uk/education/2010/oct/12/tuition-fees-student-finance-history (retrieved 12 August 2012).

Batey, Mavis. *Alexander Pope: the Poet and the Landscape*. London: Barn Elms, 1999.

Baudelaire, Charles. *Selected Writings on Art and Artists*. Trans. P. E. Charvet. Harmondsworth: Penguin, 1972.

Baudelaire, Charles. 'What is Romanticism?', 1846. In Baudelaire, *Selected Writings*, pp. 52–54.

Bellamy, Liz. 'Money's Productivity in Narrative Fiction'. In Caserio and Hawes, pp. 180–195.

Beloff, Michael. *The Plateglass Universities*. London: Secker and Warburg, 1968.

Benjamin, Andrew, ed. *The Lyotard Reader*. Oxford: Basil Blackwell, 1989.

Benjamin, Walter. 'The Author as Producer'. In Benjamin, *Reflections*, pp. 220–238. First published in 1934.

Benjamin, Walter. *Illuminations: Essays and Reflections*. Ed. Hannah Arendt. Trans. Harry Zohn. New York: Schocken Books, 1969.

Benjamin, Walter. *The Origin of German Tragic Drama*. Trans. John Osborne. London and New York: Verso, 1998. Completed in 1928.

Benjamin, Walter. *Reflections: Essays, Aphorisms, Autobiographical Writings*. Ed. Peter Demetz. Trans. Edmund Jephcott. New York: Schocken Books, 1978.

Benjamin, Walter. 'The Work of Art in the Age of Mechanical Production'. In Benjamin, *Illuminations*, pp. 217–252. First published in 1936.

Bennett, Jane. *Vibrant Matter: A Political Ecology of Things*. Durham, NC and London: Duke University Press, 2010.

Black, Jeremy. *The British Abroad: The Grand Tour in the Eighteenth Century*. London: Sandpiper Books, 1999.

Black, Jeremy. *Eighteenth-Century Britain 1688–1783*. London: Palgrave Macmillan, 2008, 2nd edition.

Black, Jeremy. *Walpole in Power*. Stroud: Sutton Publishing, 2001.

Black, Scott. 'Romance Redivivus'. In Caserio and Hawes, pp. 246–261.

Blackett-Ord, Carol. 'Letters from William Kent to Burrell Massingberd from the Continent, 1712–1719'. *Walpole Society Annual*, vol. 63, 2001, pp. 75–109.

Boia, Lucian. *The Weather in the Imagination*. London: Reaktion, 2005.

Borrow, George. *Lavengro: The Scholar, the Gypsy, the Priest*. London: Gabriel Wells, 1923. First published in 1851.

Bradbury, Malcolm. 'Creative Writing and the University: Andrew Wilkinson Lecture'. http://www.malcolmbradbury.com/uea_and_creative_writing.html (retrieved 17 December 2012).

Bradbury, Malcolm. *The History Man*. London: Secker and Warburg, 1975.

Bradbury, Malcolm. 'Welcome Back to the History Man'. http://www.malcolmbradbury.com/fiction.html (retrieved 17 December 2012).

Braun, Bruce, and Noel Castree, eds. *Remaking Reality: Nature at the Millennium*. London and New York: Routledge, 1998.

Brettingham, Matthew, Jr. *The Plans, Elevations and Sections of Holkham in Norfolk, The Seat of the late Earl of Leicester*. London: J. Haberkorn, 1761.

Brettingham, Matthew, Jr. *The Plans, Elevations and Sections of Holkham in Norfolk, The Seat of the late Earl of Leicester. To which are added, The Ceilings and Chimney-Pieces; and also, A Descriptive Account of the Statues, Pictures, and Drawings; Not in the Former Edition*. London: T. Spilsbury, B. White and S. Leacroft, 1773.

Brewer, John. *The Pleasures of the Imagination: English Culture in the Eighteenth Century*. New York: Farrar, Straus and Giroux, 1997.

Brimblecombe, Peter. *The Big Smoke: A History of Air Pollution in London Since Medieval Times*. London and New York: Routledge, 1988.

Brimblecombe, Peter, ed. *The Effects of Air Pollution on the Built Environment*. London: Imperial College Press, 2003.

Brimblecombe, Peter. 'Interest in Air Pollution Among the Early Fellows of the Royal Society'. *Notes and Records of the Royal Society of London*, vol. 32, no. 2, March 1978, pp. 123–129.

Brimblecombe, Peter, and Graham Bentham. 'The Air that We Breathe: Smogs, Smoke and Health'. In Hulme and Barrow, pp. 243–261.

Brimblecombe, Peter, and Carlotta M. Grossi. 'Damage to Buildings from Future Climate and Pollution'. *APT Bulletin: Journal of Preservation Technology*, vol. 38, no. 2/3, 2007, pp. 13–18.

Brimblecombe, Peter, and Carlotta M. Grossi. 'Potential Damage to Modern Building Materials from 21st Century Pollution'. *The Scientific World Journal*, vol. 10, 2010, pp. 116–125.

Brindle, Steven. 'Kent and Italy'. In Weber, pp. 89–109.

Bronkman, H.A.N. 'Fonthill Abbey'. *The Architectural Review*, vol. 95, no. 570, June 1944, pp. 149–157.

Brown, David Blayney. *Romanticism*. London and New York: Phaidon, 2001.

Brown, John Croumbie, ed., trans. *French Forest Ordinance of 1669*. Edinburgh: Oliver and Boyd and London: Simpkin, Marshall and Co., 1883.

Brown, Laurence. 'Atlantic Slavery and Classical Culture at Marble Hill and Northington Grange'. In Dresser and Hann, pp. 91–101.

Bryant, Julius. 'From "Gusto" to "Kentissime": Kent's Designs for Country Houses, Villas and Lodges'. In Weber, pp. 183–241.

Burke, Edmund. *A Philosophical Enquiry into the Origin of our Ideas of the Sublime and Beautiful*. Ed. J. T. Boulton. London: Routledge and Kegan Paul, 1958. First published in 1757.

Butlin, Martin, and Evelyn Joll. *The Paintings of Turner*. New Haven and London: Yale University Press, 1984, 2 vols.

Cairns, Stephen, and Jane M. Jacobs. *Buildings Must Die: A Perverse View of Architecture*. Cambridge, MA and London: MIT Press, 2014.

Calder, Barnabas. '"A Terrible Battle with Architecture": Denys Lasdun in the 1950s, Part 2'. *ARQ*, vol. 12, no. 1, 2008, pp. 59–68.

Cambridge Architectural Research Ltd. 'Conservation Development Strategy for the University of East Anglia', issue 1, April 2006. http://www.uea.ac.uk/polopoly_fs/1.50472!conservation%20strategy.pdf (retrieved 1 November 2014).

Cameron, William J. ed. *Poems on Affairs of State: Augustan Satirical Verse, 1666–1714*. New Haven: Yale University Press, 1971.

Campbell, Colen. *Vitruvius Britannicus, or the British Architect*. New York: Benjamin Blom, 1970. First published in three volumes between 1715 and 1725.

Carpo, Mario. *The Alphabet and the Algorithm*. Cambridge, MA and London: MIT Press, 2011.

Carson, Rachel. *Silent Spring*. Boston: Houghton Mifflin, 1987. First published in 1962.

Carter, Philip. *Men and the Emergence of Polite Society, Britain 1660–1800*. Harlow: Pearson, 2001.

Caserio, Robert L., and Clement Hawes, eds. *The Cambridge History of the English Novel*. Cambridge: Cambridge University Press, 2012.

Casson, Hugh, Brenda Colvin and Jacques Groag. *Bombed Churches as War Memorials*. Cheam: Architectural Press, 1945.

Castell, Robert. *The Villas of the Ancients Illustrated*. London: Robert Castell, 1728.

Cereghini, Elisabetta. 'The Italian Origins of Rousham'. In Mosser and Teyssot, pp. 320–322.

Cholmondeley, David, and Andrew Moore. *Houghton Hall: Portrait of an English Country House*. New York: Skira Rizzoli, 2014.

Claridge, John. *The Shepherd of Banbury's Rules to Judge of the Changes of the Weather, Grounded on Forty Years' Experience*. London: W. Bickerton, 1744.

Coffin, David. 'The Elysian Fields of Rousham'. *Proceedings of the American Philosophical Society*, 1986, no. 130, pp. 406–423.

Coffin, David. *The English Garden: Meditation and Memorial*. Princeton: Princeton University Press, 1994.

Cohen, Jean-Louis, and G. Martin Moeller Jr, eds. *Liquid Stone: New Architecture in Concrete*. Basel: Birkäuser, 2006.

Coke, Thomas. 'An Account of a Meteor Seen near Holkam in Norfolk, Aug 1741. Transmitted to the Royal Society by the Right Honble Thomas Lord Lovell, F.R.S.' *Philosophical Transactions*, 1742–1743, vol. 42, pp. 183–184.

Colomina, Beatriz. 'Unbreathed Air 1956'. In Van den Heuvel and Risselada, pp. 31–49.

Colonna, Francesco. *Hypnerotomachia Poliphili: The Strife of Love in a Dream*. Trans. Joscelyn Godwin. London: Thames & Hudson, 1999. First published in 1499.

Colquhoun, Alan. 'Twentieth Century Picturesque: Letter to the Editors'. *The Architectural Review*, vol. 116, no. 691, July 1954, p. 2.

Colvin, Brenda. *Land and Landscape*. London: John Murray, 1947.

Colvin, Brenda. *Land and Landscape: Evolution, Design and Control*. London: John Murray, 1970.

Colvin, Brenda. 'A Planting Plan'. In Casson, Colvin and Groag, pp. 23–30.

Colvin, Brenda. *Trees for Town and Country*. London: Lund Humphries, 1972. First published in 1947.

Colvin, Brenda. *Wonder in a World*. Privately printed, 1977.

Congreve, William. *Incognita: Or, Love and Duty Reconcil'd. A Novel*. London: Peter Buck, 1692.

Connell, Brian. 'Denys Lasdun: Building a Landscape for Figures'. *The Times*, 24 March 1975, p. 10.

Conrads, Ulrich, ed. *Programs and Manifestoes on 20th-Century Architecture*. Cambridge, MA: MIT Press 1970.

Copley, Stephen. 'William Gilpin and the Black-Lead Mine'. In Copley and Garside, *The Politics of the Picturesque*, pp. 42–61.

Copley, Stephen, and Peter Garside. 'Introduction'. In Copley and Garside, *The Politics of the Picturesque*, pp. 1–12.

Copley, Stephen, and Peter Garside, eds. *The Politics of the Picturesque: Literature, Landscape and Aesthetics Since 1770*. Cambridge: Cambridge University Press, 1994.

Corner, James. 'Eidetic Operations and New Landscapes'. In Corner, *Recovering Landscape*, pp. 152–169.

Corner, James, ed. *Recovering Landscape: Essays in Contemporary Landscape Architecture*. New York: Princeton Architectural Press, 1999.

Corner, James. 'Terra Fluxus'. In Waldheim, *The Landscape Urbanism Reader*, pp. 21–33.

Cornforth, John. *Early Georgian Interiors*. New Haven and London: Yale University Press, 2004.

Cornforth, John. 'The Genesis and Creation of a Great Interior'. In Moore, pp. 29–40.

Cornforth, John. 'The Growth of an Idea'. *Country Life*, 14 May 1987, pp. 162–168.

Cornforth, John. *Houghton, Norfolk*. Derby: Heritage House Group Ltd, 2007.

Cosgrove, Denis E. 'Airport/Landscape'. In Corner, *Recovering Landscape*, pp. 220–231.

Cosgrove, Denis E. *Geography and Vision: Seeing, Imagining and Representing the World*. London and New York: I. B. Tauris, 2008.

Cosgrove, Denis E. *Social Formation and Symbolic Landscape*. Madison: University of Wisconsin Press, 1998.

Cowan, Brian. 'Reasonable Ecstasies: Shaftesbury and the Languages of Libertinism'. *The Journal of British Studies*, vol. 37, no. 2, April 1998, pp. 111–138.

Crary, Jonathan. *Techniques of the Observer: On Vision and Modernity in the Nineteenth Century*. Cambridge, MA and London: MIT Press, 1990.

Crewe, Maurice. 'The Fathers of Scientific Meteorology – Boyle, Wren, Hooke and Halley: Part 2'. *Weather*, vol. 58, no. 4, pp. 135–139.

Crinson, Mark, and Claire Zimmerman, eds. *Neo-Avant-Garde and Postmodern Architecture in Britain and Beyond*. New Haven and London: Yale University Press, 2010.

Crowther, Paul. 'Barnett Newman and the Sublime', *Oxford Art Journal*, vol. 7, no. 2, 1984, pp. 52–59.

Curry, Patrick. *Prophecy and Power: Astrology in Early Modern England*. Cambridge: Polity Press, 1989.

Curtis, William. *Denys Lasdun: Architecture, City, Landscape*. London: Phaidon, 1994.

Curtis, William. 'A Language and a Theme: The Architecture of Denys Lasdun & Partners'. In Denys Lasdun, *A Language and a Theme,* p. 9–19.

Dalyell, Tam. 'Bert Hazell: Trade Union Leader and Labour MP who Championed the Cause of Agricultural Workers'. *The Independent on Sunday*, 21 January 2009. http://www.independent.co.uk/news/obituaries/bert-hazell-trade-union-leader-and-labour-mp-who-championed-the-cause-of-agricultural-workers-1452239.html (retrieved 12 December 2012).

Daniels, Stephen. *Fields of Vision: Landscape Imagery and National Identity in England and the United States*. Cambridge: Polity Press, 1993.

Daniels, Stephen. *Humphry Repton: Landscape Gardening and the Geography of Georgian England*. New Haven and London: Yale University Press, 1999.

Darley, Gillian. *John Evelyn: Living for Ingenuity*. New Haven and London: Yale University Press, 2006.

Darwin, Charles. *Formation of Vegetal Mould Through the Actions of Worms with Observations on their Habits*. London: John Murray, 1881.

Darwin, Charles. *The Origin of Species*. Oxford: Oxford University Press, 1996. First published in 1859.

Davies, John H. V., and Deny Lasdun. 'Thoughts in Progress: The New Brutalism'. *Architectural Design*, vol. 27, April 1957, pp. 111–112.

Davies, John H. V., and Deny Lasdun. 'Thoughts in Progress: Summing Up II'. *Architectural Design*, vol. 27, November 1957, pp. 395–396.

Davies, John H. V., and Deny Lasdun. 'Thoughts in Progress: Summing Up III – The "Objects Found" Philosophy'. *Architectural Design*, vol. 27, December 1957, pp. 435–436.

Davis, Lennard J. *Factual Fictions: The Origins of the English Novel*. Philadelphia: University of Pennsylvania Press, 1996. First published in 1983.

De Bolla, Peter. *The Education of the Eye: Painting, Landscape and Architecture in Eighteenth-Century Britain*. Stanford: Stanford University Press, 2003.

De Man, Paul. *The Rhetoric of Romanticism*. New York: Columbia University Press, 1984.

Dean, Ptolemy. *Sir John Soane and the Country Estate*. Aldershot: Ashgate, 1999.

Decker, Sir Matthew. *An Account of a Journey Done into Hartford, Cambridgeshire, Suffolk,*

Norfolk and Essex, From the 21st June to the 12th July, Being 22 Days, 1728. Held in the Wilton House Archives, Wiltshire.

Defoe, Daniel. *An Historical Narrative of the Great and Tremendous Storm, Which Happened on Nov. 26th, 1703*. London: W. Nicoll, 1769. First published in 1704.

Defoe, Daniel. *Moll Flanders*. New York: Norton, 2004. First published in 1722.

Defoe, Daniel. *Robinson Crusoe*. Oxford: Oxford University Press, 2007. First published in 1719.

Defoe, Daniel. *Roxana, or the Fortunate Mistress*. Ed. P. N. Furbank. London: Pickering and Chatto, 2009. First published in 1724.

Defoe, Daniel. *A Tour through the Whole Island of Great Britain.* London: J. M. Dent, 1962. First published in 1724–1726.

Dehs, Jorgen, Martin Weihe Esbensen and Claus Peder Pedersen, eds. *When Architects and Designers Write/Draw/Build/?: Essays on Architecture and Design Research*. Aarhus: Arkitektskolens Forlag, 2013.

Descartes, René. *Discourse on Method, Optics, Geometry and Meteorology*. Trans. Paul Olscamp. Indianapolis: Hackett Publishing Company, 2001. First published in 1637.

Dickens, Charles. *Bleak House*. Ed. Stephen Gill. Oxford and New York: Oxford University Press, 1996. First published in nineteen instalments between 1852 and 1853.

Dillon, Maureen. *Artificial Sunshine: A Social History of Domestic Lighting*. London: The National Trust, 2002.

Disponzio, Joseph. 'Jean-Marie Morel and the Invention of Landscape Architecture'. In Hunt and Conan, pp. 135–159.

Dobell, Clifford. *Antony van Leeuwenhoek and his 'Little Animals'*. London: John Bale, Sons and Danielsson, 1932.

Dorey, Helen. 'Crude Hints'. In Woodward, *Visions of Ruin*, pp. 53–78.

Dorey, Helen. *John Soane and J.M.W. Turner: Illuminating a Friendship*. London: Sir John Soane's Museum, 2007.

Dorey, Helen. 'Sir John Soane's Courtyard Gardens at Lincoln's Inn Fields'. *The London Gardener or the Gardener's Intelligencer*, 1999–2000, vol. 5, pp. 14–21.

Dormer, Peter, and Stefan Muthesius. *Concrete and Open Skies: Architecture at the University of East Anglia*. London: Unicorn, 2001.

Downie, J. A. 'Biographical Form in the Novel'. In Caserio and Hawes, pp. 30–45.

Dresser, Madge, and Andrew Hann, eds. *Slavery and the British Country House*. Swindon: English Heritage, 2013.

Dunster, David, ed. *John Soane*. London: Academy Editions and New York: St. Martin's Press, 1983.

Du Prey, Pierre de la Ruffinière. *John Soane: The Making of an Architect.* Chicago: University of Chicago Press, 1982.

Edis, Robert W. *Decoration and Furniture in Town Houses*. London: Macmillan, 1881.

Editors, The. 'Sites for Norwich University'. *The Architects' Journal*, no. 3396, vol. 131, p. 744.

Editors, The. 'Universities: Genuine Urban or Fake Suburban'. *The Architects' Journal*, no. 3396, vol. 131, pp. 745–746.

Edgerton, David. *The Shock of the Old: Technology and Global History Since 1900*. London: Profile, 2008.

Edwards, Sebastian, Andrew Moore and Chloë Archer. 'The Catalogue'. In Moore, *Houghton Hall*, pp. 82–150.

Eliot, T. S. *Points of View*. London: Faber and Faber, 1941.

Eliot, T. S. 'Tradition and the Individual Talent'. In T. S. Eliot. *Points of View*, pp. 23–34. First published in 1917.

Emmison, Frederick, and Roy Stephens, eds. *Tribute to an Antiquary: Essays Presented to Marc Fitch by Some of His Friends*. London: Leopard's Head Press, 1976.

Evelyn, John. 'An Abstract of a Letter From the Worshipful John Evelyn Esq.; Sent to One of the Secretaries of the R. Society concerning the Dammage Done to his Gardens by the Preceding Winter'. *Philosophical Transactions of the Royal Society*, vol. 14, 1684, pp. 559–563.

Evelyn, John. *Elysium Britannicum, or, The Royal Gardens*. Ed. John E. Ingram. Philadelphia: University of Pennsylvania Press, 2001.

Evelyn, John. *Fumifugium: Or, The Inconveniencie of the Aer and Smoake of London Dissipated*. Ed. Samuel Pegge. London: B. White, 1772. First published in 1661, with a slightly different title.

Evelyn, John. *Sylva, or A Discourse of Forest-Trees, and the Propagation of Timber in His Majesties Dominions*. London: Royal Society, 1664.

Ferguson, Niall. *Empire: How Britain Made the Modern World*. London: Penguin, 2004.

Field, Ophelia. *The Kit-Cat Club*. London: Harper Perennial, 2009.

Finberg, A. J. *The Life of J.M.W. Turner, RA*. Oxford: Clarendon Press, 1961. First published in 1939.

Fisher, Nigel. *Harold Macmillan*. London: Weidenfeld and Nicolson, 1982.

Fleming, James Rodger. *Historical Perspectives on Climate Change*. New York and Oxford: Oxford University Press, 1998.

Ford, Brimley, and John Ingamells. *A Dictionary of British and Irish Travellers in Italy, 1701–1800*. New Haven and London: Yale University Press, 1997.

Forty, Adrian. 'Architectural Description: Fact or Fiction?'. In Dehs, Esbensen and Pedersen, pp. 188–209.

Forty, Adrian. *Concrete and Culture: A Material History*. London: Reaktion, 2012.

Forty, Adrian. 'Introduction'. In Forty and Küchler, pp. 1–18.

Forty, Adrian. *Words and Buildings: A Vocabulary of Modern Architecture*. London: Thames & Hudson, 2000.

Forty, Adrian, and Susanne Küchler, eds. *The Art of Forgetting*. Oxford and New York: Berg, 1999.

Foucault, Michel. *The Foucault Reader*. Ed. Paul Rabinow. London: Penguin, 1984.

Foucault, Michel. *Language, Counter-Memory, Practice: Selected Essays and Interviews*. Ed. Donald F. Bouchard. Trans. Donald F. Bouchard and Sherry Simon. Oxford: Blackwell, 1977.

Foucault, Michel. 'On the Genealogy of Ethics: An Overview of Work in Progress'. In Foucault, *The Foucault Reader*, pp. 340–372.

Foucault, Michel. 'Technologies of the Self'. In Martin, Gutman and Hutton, pp. 16–49.

Foucault, Michel. 'What is an Author?'. In Foucault, *Language, Counter-Memory, Practice*, pp. 113–138. First published in 1969.

Freakley, Bob. 'Creaker no. 66: David Pease'. *Creake News*, no. 73, Winter 2013, pp. 10–12.

Gage, John, ed. *Collected Correspondence of J.M.W. Turner*. Oxford: Clarendon Press, 1980.

Gage, John. *Colour in Turner: Poetry and Truth*. London: Studio Vista, 1969.

Gage, John. *J.M.W. Turner: 'A Wonderful Range of Mind'*. New Haven and London: Yale University Press, 1987.

Garnham, Trevor. *Architecture Re-Assembled: The Use (and Abuse) of History*. London and New York: Routledge, 2013.

Garry, Mary-Anne. *Wealthy Masters – 'Provident and Kind': The Household of Holkham 1697–1842*. Dereham: Larks Press, 2012.

George, M. Dorothy. *London Life in the Eighteenth Century*. Chicago: Academy Chicago Publishers, 1984. First published in 1925.

Gibson, Trish. *Brenda Colvin: A Career in Landscape*. London: Francis Lincoln, 2011.

Giedion, Sigfried. *Architecture You and Me: The Diary of a Development*. Cambridge, MA and London: Harvard University Press, 1958.

Giedion, Sigfried. *Building in France, Building in Iron, Building in Ferro-Concrete*. Trans. J. Duncan Berry. Santa Monica: The Getty Center for the History of Art, 1995. First published in 1928.

Giedion, Sigfried. 'History and the Architect'. In Giedion, *Architecture You and Me*, pp. 106–119.

Giedion, Sigfried. 'The Need for a New Monumentality'. In Zucker, pp. 25–39.

Giedion, Sigfried, Fernand Léger and José Luis Sert. 'Nine Points on Monumentality'. In Giedion, *Architecture You and Me*, pp. 48–51.

Gilpin, William. *Observations Relative Chiefly to Picturesque Beauty, Made in the Year 1772, on Several Parts of England; Particularly the Mountains, and Lakes of Cumberland, and Westmoreland*. London: R. Blamire, 1786, 2 vols.

Gilpin, William. *Remarks on Forest Scenery, and other Woodland Views (Relative Chiefly to Picturesque Beauty), Illustrated by the Scenes of New-Forest in Hampshire*. London: R. Blamire, 1791, 2 vols.

Gilpin, William. *Three Essays: On Picturesque Beauty; on Picturesque Travel; and on Sketching Landscape: To Which is Added a Poem, on Landscape Painting*. London: R. Blamire, 1792.

Girouard, Mark. *Life in the English Country House: A Social and Architectural History*. New Haven and London: Yale University Press, 1978.

Glacken, Clarence J. *Traces on the Rhodian Shore: Nature and Culture in Western Thought from Ancient Times to the End of the Eighteenth Century*. Berkeley: University of California Press, 1967.

Glover, Leigh. *Postmodern Climate Change*. London and New York: Routledge, 2006.

Goethe, Johann Wolfgang von. *Goethe on Art*. Trans. John Gage. London: Scholar Press, 1980.

Goethe, Johann Wolfgang von. 'On German Architecture (1772)'. In Goethe, *Goethe on Art*, pp. 103–112.

Golinski, Jan. *British Weather and the Climate of Enlightenment*. Chicago and London: University of Chicago Press, 2007.

Golinski, Jan. '"Exquisite Atmography": Theories of the World and Experiences of the Weather in a Diary of 1703'. *The British Journal for the History of Science*, vol. 34, no. 2, June 2001, pp. 149–171.

Gordon, Susan. 'The Iconography and Mythology of the Eighteenth-Century English Landscape Garden'. PhD thesis, University of Bristol, 1999.

Gregory, Richard. *Eye and Brain: The Psychology of Seeing*. Oxford: Oxford University Press, 1998.

Grissell, Eric. *Insects and Gardens: In Pursuit of Garden Ecology*. Portland: Timber Press, 2001.

Guilhamet, Leon. *Defoe and the Whig Novel: A Reading of the Major Fiction*. Newark: University of Delaware Press, 2010.

Hackney, Stephen. 'The Condition of Turner's Oil Paintings'. In Townsend, *Turner's Painting Techniques in Context*, pp. 50–54.

Hamblyn, Richard. *The Invention of Clouds: How an Amateur Meteorologist Forged the Language of the Skies*. London: Picador, 2001.

Hamilton, James. 'Earth's Humid Bubbles: Turner and the New Understanding of Nature'. In Richter-Musso and Westheider, pp. 52–64.

Hamilton, James. *Faraday: The Life*. London: Harper Collins, 2002.

Hamilton, James. *Turner: A Life*. London: Hodder and Stoughton, 1997.

Hamilton, James. *Turner and the Scientists*. London: Tate Gallery Publishing, 1998.

Hardy, John. 'The Interiors: The Furnishing of Holkham's Grand Apartment'. In Schmidt, Keller and Feversham, pp. 136–170.

Harris, Eileen. 'Sir John Soane's Library: "O, Books! Ye Monuments of Mind"'. *Apollo*, April 1990, pp. 242–247.

Harris, John. 'The Architecture of the House'. In Moore, *Houghton Hall*, pp. 20–28.

Harris, John. *William Kent 1685–1748: A Poet on Paper*. London: Sir John Soane's Museum, 1998.

Harrison, Charles. 'The Effects of Landscape'. In Mitchell, pp. 203–239.

Hart, Vaughan, and Peter Hicks. *Palladio's Rome: A Translation of Andrea Palladio's Two Guidebooks to Rome*. New Haven and London: Yale University Press, 2006.

Hassall, W. O. 'The Temple at Holkham, Norfolk'. *Country Life*, vol. 148, no. 3715, pp. 1310–1314.

Hassall, W. O. 'Views from the Holkham Windows'. In Emmison and Stephens, pp. 305–319.

Hastings, Hubert de Cronin, Osbert Lancaster, Nikolaus Pevsner and J. M. Richards. 'In Search of a New Monumentality: A Symposium'. *The Architectural Review*, vol. 104, no. 624, September 1948, pp. 11–128.

Hastings, Hubert de Cronin, Osbert Lancaster, Nikolaus Pevsner and J. M. Richards. 'The Second Half Century/The First Half Century'. *The Architectural Review*, vol. 101, no. 601, January 1947, pp. 21–36.

Hawes, Clement. 'Novelistic History'. In Caserio and Hawes, pp. 63–79.

Hell, Julia, and Andreas Schönle, eds. *Ruins of Modernity*. Durham, NC and London: Duke University Press, 2010.

Helsinger, Elizabeth. 'Turner and the Representation of England'. In Mitchell, pp. 103–125.

Herder, Johann Gottfried. *Outlines of a Philosophy of the History of Man*. Trans. T. Churchill. London: J. Johnson, 1799. First published as *Ideen zur Philosophie der Geschichte der Menschheit* in 1784–1791.

Heynen, Nik, Maria Kaika and Erik Swyngedouw, eds. *In the Nature of Cities: Urban Political Ecology and the Politics of Urban Metabolism*. London and New York: Taylor & Francis, 2006.

Hipple, John Walter. *The Beautiful, the Sublime and the Picturesque in Eighteenth-Century British Aesthetic.* Carbondale: Southern Illinois University Press, 1957.

Hipper, Kenneth. *Smugglers All: Centuries of Norfolk Smuggling*. Dereham: Larks Press, 2001.

Hiskey, Christine. 'The Building of Holkham Hall: Newly Discovered Letters'. *Architectural History*, vol. 40, 1997, pp. 144–158.

Hitchcock, Henry-Russell. *Modern Architecture: Romanticism and Regeneration*. New York: Hacker Art Books, 1970. First published in 1929.

Holkham National Nature Reserve. Norwich: The Nature Conservancy, 1972.

Holmes, Richard. *The Age of Wonder: How the Romantic Generation Discovered the Beauty and Terror of Science*. London: Harper Press, 2009.

Holtz, William V. *Image and Immortality: A Study of 'Tristram Shandy'*. Providence: Brown University Press, 1970.

Houfe, Simon, Alan Powers and John Wilton-Ely. *Sir Albert Richardson 1880–1964*. London: Heinz Gallery, 1999.

Howard, Luke. *The Climate of London, Deduced from Meteorological Observations Made at Different Places in the Neighbourhood of the Metropolis*. London: W. Phillips, 1818 and 1820, 2 vols.

Hulme, Mike. *Why We Disagree About Climate Change*. Cambridge: Cambridge University Press, 2009.

Hulme, Mike, and Elaine Barrow, eds. *Climates of the British Isles: Present, Past and Future*. London and New York: Routledge, 1997.

Hultzsch, Anne. *Architecture, Travellers, Writers: Constructing Histories of Perception 1640–1950*. London: Legenda, 2014.

Hunt, John Dixon. *Garden History: Issues, Approaches, Methods*. Washington, DC: Dumbarton Oaks, 1989.

Hunt, John Dixon. *Gardens and the Picturesque: Studies in the History of Landscape Architecture*. Cambridge, MA and London: MIT Press, 1992.

Hunt, John Dixon. *Greater Perfections: The Practice of Garden Theory*. London: Thames & Hudson, 2000.

Hunt, John Dixon. 'Landscape Architecture'. In Weber, pp. 365–391.

Hunt, John Dixon. *The Picturesque Garden in Europe*. London: Thames & Hudson, 2002.

Hunt, John Dixon. 'Verbal Versus Visual Meanings in Garden History: The Case of Rousham'. In Hunt, *Garden History,* pp. 151–181.

Hunt, John Dixon. *William Kent: Landscape Garden Designer*. London: Zwemmer, 1987.

Hunt, John Dixon, and Michel Conan, eds. *Tradition and Innovation in French Garden Art: Chapters of a New History*. Philadelphia: University of Pennsylvania Press, 2002.

Hunt, John Dixon, and Peter Willis, eds. *The Genius of the Place: The English Landscape Garden 1620–1820*. Cambridge, MA and London: MIT Press, 1988.

Hunt, John Dixon, and Peter Willis. 'Introduction'. In Hunt and Willis, *The Genius of the Place*, pp. 1–46.

Hussey, Christopher. *The Picturesque: Studies in a Point of View*. London: Frank Cass, 1983. First published in 1927.

Jackson, John Brinckerhoff. 'The Necessity for Ruins'. In Jackson, *The Necessity for Ruins and Other Topics*, pp. 89–102.

Jackson, John Brinckerhoff. *The Necessity for Ruins and Other Topics*. Amherst: University of Massachusetts Press, 1980.

Jacques, David. 'Modern Needs, Art and Instincts: Modernist Landscape Theory'. *Garden History*, vol. 28, no. 1, Summer 2000, pp. 88–101.

James, Charles Warburton. *Chief Justice Coke: His Family and Descendants at Holkham*. London: Country Life, 1929.

Jankovic, Vladimir. *Reading the Skies: A Cultural History of English Weather, 1650–1820*. Manchester: Manchester University Press, 2000.

Janowitz, Anne. *England's Ruins: Poetic Purpose and the National Landscape*. Oxford: Basil Blackwell, 1990.

Jarrett, Edward. 'Account of Thomas Coke's Grand Tour'. Held in the Bodleian Library, Oxford.

Jenner, Mark. 'The Politics of London Air: John Evelyn's *Fumifugium* and the Restoration'. *The Historical Journal*, vol. 38, no. 3, 1995, pp. 535–551.

Jones, Henry Bence. *The Life and Letters of Michael Faraday*. London: Longmans, 1870, 2 vols.

Jourdain, Margaret. *The Work of William Kent*. London: Country Life, 1948.

Kames, Henry Home, Lord. *Elements of Criticism*. Dublin: Sarah Cotter, 1762, 2 vols.

Kant, Immanuel. *Kant's Critique of Judgement*. Trans. J. H. Bernard. London: Macmillan, 1931. First published in 1790.

Kemp, Betty. *Sir Robert Walpole*. London: Weidenfeld and Nicolson, 1976.

Kennedy, John F. 'Special Message to the Congress on Urgent National Needs', 25 May 1961. http://www.jfklibrary.org/Research/Ready-Reference/JFK-Speeches/Special-Message-to-the-Congress-on-Urgent-National-Needs-May-25-1961.aspx (retrieved 1 October 2011).

Kent, William. 'Remarks by way of Painting and Archit.', 1714–1715. Held in the Bodleian Library, Oxford.

Klausmeier, Axel. 'Thomas Coke's Kitchen Garden'. In Schmidt, Keller and Feversham, pp. 72–75.

Knight, Richard Payne. *An Analytical Inquiry into the Principles of Taste*. London: T. Payne, 1805.

Knight, Richard Payne. *The Landscape, A Didactic Poem, in Three Books, Addressed to Uvedale Price, Esq*. Farnborough: Gregg International Publishers, 1972. First published in 1794.

Koerner, Joseph Leo. *Caspar David Friedrich and the Subject of Landscape*. London: Reaktion, 1990.

Krucker, Bruno. *Complex Ordinariness: The Upper Lawn Pavilion by Alison and Peter Smithson*. Zurich: ETH Zurich, 2002.

Laird, Mark. *A Natural History of English Gardening 1650–1800*. New Haven and London: Yale University Press, 2015.

Lamb, Hubert H. *Historic Storms of the North Sea, British Isles and Northwest Europe*. Cambridge: Cambridge University Press, 1991.

Lansdown, Henry Venn. *Recollections of the Late William Beckford*. Printed for private circulation, 1893.

Lasdun, Denys. 'About Anglia: Denys Lasdun Chosen to Design the New Norwich University, 1963'. http://www.eafa.org.uk/catalogue/213000 (retrieved 10 June 2012).

Lasdun, Denys, ed. *Architecture in an Age of Scepticism: A Practitioner's Anthology Compiled by Denys Lasdun.* London: Heinemann, 1984.

Lasdun, Denys. 'The Architecture of Urban Landscape'. In Denys Lasdun, *Architecture in an Age of Scepticism*, pp. 134–159.

Lasdun, Denys. 'His Approach to Architecture'. *Architectural Design*, vol. 35, June 1965, pp. 271–291.

Lasdun, Denys. 'Is there a British Tradition?'. *The Architectural Review*, vol. 175, no. 1946, May 1984, p. 43.

Lasdun, Denys. *A Language and a Theme: The Architecture of Denys Lasdun & Partners*. London: RIBA Publications, 1976.

Lasdun, Denys. 'Notes on a Lecture on Nicholas Hawksmoor'. In Curtis, *Denys Lasdun*, p. 223. Prepared in 1991.

Lasdun, Denys. 'Royal Gold Medallist Address'. In Curtis, *Denys Lasdun*, pp. 221–222. First published in 1977.

Lasdun, Denys. 'A Sense of Place and Time'. In Curtis, *Denys Lasdun*, pp. 220–221. First published in 1966.

Lasdun, Denys, & Partners. 'University of East Anglia'. *Architectural Design*, vol. 69, May 1969, pp. 245–268.

Lasdun, James. 'My Father'. *Modern Painters*, Winter 2003, pp. 54–61.

Laugier, Marc-Antoine. *An Essay on Architecture*. Trans. Wolfgang and Anni Herrmann. Los Angeles: Hennessey and Ingalls, 1977. First published as *Essai sur l'architecture* in 1753.

Leatherbarrow, David. 'Character, Geometry and Perspective: The Third Earl of Shaftesbury's Principles of Garden Design'. *Journal of Garden History*, vol. 4, no. 4, October–December 1984, pp. 332–358.

Le Camus de Mézières, Nicolas. *The Genius of Architecture; or, The Analogy of that Art With Our Sensations*. Trans D. Britt. Santa Monica: The Getty Center, 1992. First published as *Le génie de l'architecture; ou, l'analogie de cet art avec nos sensations*, 1780.

Le Corbusier. *Towards a New Architecture*. Trans. Frederick Etchells. London: Architectural Press, 1946. First published as *Vers une architecture*, 1923, and in English as *Towards a New Architecture*, 1927.

Lees-Milne, James. *Earls of Creation: Five Great Patrons of Eighteenth-Century Art*. London: Hamish Hamilton, 1962.

Lefaivre, Liane. *Leon Battista Alberti's Hypnerotomachia Poliphili: Re-Cognizing the Architectural Body in the Early Italian Renaissance*. Cambridge, MA and London: MIT Press, 1997.

Legault, Réjean. 'The Semantics of Exposed Concrete'. In Cohen and Moeller, pp. 46–56.

Li, Shiqiao. *Power and Virtue: Architecture and Intellectual Change in England 1660–1730*. London and New York: Routledge, 2007.

Lindsay, Jack. *The Monster City, Defoe's London, 1688–1730*. London: Granada, 1978.

Lippard, Lucy. *Pop Art*. London: Thames & Hudson, 1966.

Locke, John. *An Essay Concerning Human Understanding*. Ed. Peter H. Nidditch. Oxford: Clarendon Press, 1975. First published in 1690.

Locke, John. *A Letter Concerning Toleration*. London: A. Churchill, 1689.

Locke, John. 'A Register of the Weather for the Year 1692, Kept at Oates in Essex'. *Philosophical Transactions*, 1704–1705, vol. 24, no. 298, pp. 1917–1937.

Locke, John. *Some Thoughts Concerning Education*. London: A. and J. Churchill, 1693.

Locke, John. *Two Treatises of Government*. Ed. Peter Laslett. Cambridge: Cambridge University Press, 1988. First published in 1690.

Lowenthal, David. *The Past is a Foreign Country*. Cambridge: Cambridge University Press, 1985.

Lubbock, Percy. *Earlham.* London: Jonathan Cape, 1922.

Lukacher, Brian. *Joseph Gandy: An Architectural Visionary in Georgian England*. London: Thames & Hudson, 2006.

Lyotard, Jean-François. *The Post-Modern Condition: A Report on Knowledge*. Trans. Geoff Bennington, Brian Massumi and Regis Durand. Manchester: Manchester University Press, 1986. First published in French in 1979.

Lyotard, Jean-François. 'The Sublime and the Avant-Garde'. In Benjamin, *The Lyotard Reader*, pp. 196–211. First published in 1984.

Macarthur, John, and Mathew Aitchison. 'Pevsner's Townscape'. In Pevsner, *Visual Planning and the Picturesque*, pp. 1–43.

Macaulay, Rose. *Pleasure of Ruins*. London: Weidenfeld and Nicolson, 1953.

Mackley, Alan. 'Introduction'. In Mackley, *John Buxton Norfolk Gentleman and Architect*, pp. 1–32.

Mackley, Alan, ed. *John Buxton Norfolk Gentleman and Architect: Letters to his son 1717–1729*. Norwich: Norfolk Record Society, vol. 69, 2005.

Maillet, Arnaud. *The Claude Glass: Use and Meaning of the Black Mirror in Western Art*. Trans. Jeff Fort. New York: Zone Books, 2004.

Mallgrave, Harry Francis, ed. *Architectural Theory, Volume I: An Anthology from Vitruvius to 1870*. Oxford: Blackwell, 2006.

Manley, Gordon. 'Weather and Diseases: Some Eighteenth-Century Contributions to Observational Meteorology'. *Notes and Records of the Royal Society of London*, vol. 9, no. 2, May 1952, pp. 300–307.

Marcuse, Herbert. *Counterrevolution and Revolt*. Boston: Beacon Press, 1972.

Marsham, Robert. 'Celebrating the Tricentenary of Robert Marsham: A Jewel in the Wilderness', 2008. http://www.robertmarsham.co.uk/about-robert-marsham/a-jewel-in-the-wilderness (retrieved 27 December 2011).

Martin, Luther H., Hugh Gutman and Patrick H. Hutton, eds. *Technologies of the Self: A Seminar with Michel Foucault*. London: Tavistock, 1988.

Mason, Roger, ed. *Scotland and England, 1286–1815*. Edinburgh: John Donald, 1987.

McKeon, Michael. *The Origins of the English Novel 1600–1740*. Baltimore: Johns Hopkins University Press, 1987.

Merchant, Carolyn. *Reinventing Eden: The Fate of Nature in Western Culture*. New York and London: Routledge, 2003.

Middleton, Robin. 'Introduction'. In Le Camus de Mézières, pp. 17–64.

Millenson, Susan Feinberg. *Sir John Soane's Museum*. Ann Arbor: UMI Research Press, 1987.

Mitchell, W.J.T., ed. *Landscape and Power*. Chicago and London: University of Chicago Press, 2002, 2nd edition.

Moholy-Nagy, László. *The New Vision 1928 Fourth Revised Edition 1947 and Abstract of an Artist*. Trans. Daphne M. Hoffmann. New York: George Wittenborn, 1947. First published as *Von Material zu Architektur* in 1928.

Moore, Andrew. 'Creating a Seat in the Country, 1700–1745'. In Cholmondeley and Moore, pp. 49–70.

Moore, Andrew, ed. *Houghton Hall: The Prime Minister, the Empress and the Heritage*. London: Philip Wilson, 1996.

Moore, Andrew. 'The Making of Britain's First Prime Minister'. In Cholmondeley and Moore, pp. 33–47.

Moore, Andrew. 'The Making of Houghton Hall'. In Morel, et al., pp. 57–65.

Morel, Thierry. 'Houghton Revisited: An Introduction'. In Morel, et al., *Houghton Revisited*, pp. 31–43.

Morel, Thierry, Larissa Dukelskaya, John Harris and Andrew Moore. *Houghton Revisited: The Walpole Masterpieces from Catherine the Great's Hermitage*. London: Royal Academy of Arts, 2013.

Morris, Robert. *Lectures on Architecture*. London: J. Brindley, 1734.

Mortlock, D. P. *Holkham Library: A History and Description*. London: Roxburghe Club, 2006.

Mosser, Monique, and Georges Teyssot, eds. *The History of Garden Design: The Western Tradition from the Renaissance to the Present Day*. London: Thames & Hudson, 1991.

Mostafavi, Mohsen. 'Why Ecological Urbanism? Why Now?'. In Mostafavi and Doherty, pp. 12–53.

Mostafavi, Mohsen, and Gareth Doherty, eds. *Ecological Urbanism*. Baden: Lars Müller and Harvard University Graduate School of Design, 2010.

Mowl, Timothy. *William Kent: Architect, Designer, Opportunist*. London: Jonathan Cape, 2006.

Muthesius, Stefan. *The Postwar University: Utopianist Campus and College*. New Haven and London: Yale University Press, 2000.

Müller, Ulrich. 'Rousham: A Transcription of the Steward's Letters, 1738–42', *Garden History*, vol. 25, no. 2, Winter 1997, pp. 178–188.

Nebeker, Frederick. *Calculating the Weather: Meteorology in the 20th Century*. San Diego: Academic Press, 1995.

Newman, Barnett. 'The Sublime is Now'. *The Tiger's Eye*, vol. 1, no. 6, December 1948, pp. 51–53.

Newman, Oscar. *New Frontiers in Architecture, CIAM '59 in Otterlo*. New York: Universe Books, 1961.

Newton, Isaac. *Opticks*. New York: Dover, 1979. First published in 1704. This, the third edition, was published in 1723.

Nicholson, Kathleen. 'Turner, Claude and the Essence of Landscape'. In Solkin, *Turner and the Masters*, pp. 56–71.

Nicolson, Marjorie Hope. *Mountain Gloom and Mountain Glory: The Development of the Aesthetics of the Infinite*. New York: Norton, 1963.

Norberg-Schulz, Christian. *Nightlands: Nordic Building*. Cambridge, MA and London: MIT Press, 1996.

Olsen, Bjørnar, and Þóra Pétursdóttir, eds. *Ruin Memories: Materialities, Aesthetics and the Archaeology of the Recent Past*. London and New York: Routledge, 2014.

Palladio, Andrea. *The Four Books of Architecture*. Trans. Isaac Ware, 1738. New York: Dover, 1965. First published as *I quattro libri dell'archittetura* in 1570.

Palmer, Susan. 'From Fields to Gardens: The Management of Lincoln's Inn Fields in the Eighteenth and Nineteenth Centuries'. *The London Gardener or the Gardener's Intelligencer*, 2004–2005, vol. 10, pp. 11–28.

Panofsky, Erwin. '*Et in Arcadia Ego*: Poussin and the Elegiac Tradition'. In Panofsky, *Meaning in the Visual Arts*. pp. 295–320.

Panofsky, Erwin. *Meaning in the Visual Arts*. Chicago: University of Chicago Press, 1982. First published in 1955.

Parry-Wingfield, Catherine. *J.M.W. Turner, RA: The Artist and his House at Twickenham*. London: Turner's House Trust, 2012.

Parker, R.A.C. *Coke of Norfolk: A Financial and Agricultural Study, 1707–1842*. Oxford: Oxford University Press, 1975.

Pelletier, Louise. *Architecture in Words: Theatre, Language and the Sensuous Space of Architecture*. London and New York: Routledge, 2006.

Pepper, David. *Modern Environmentalism: An Introduction*. London and New York: Routledge, 1996.

Perry, Victoria. 'Slavery and the Sublime: The Atlantic Trade, Landscape Aesthetics and Tourism'. In Dresser and Hann, pp. 102–112.

Pétursdóttir, Þóra, and Bjørnar Olsen. 'Introduction: An Archaeology of Ruins'. In Olsen and Pétursdóttir, pp. 3–29.

Pevsner, Nikolaus. 'The Anti-Pioneers'. In Pevsner, *Pevsner on Art and Architecture*, pp. 293–307. Based on a broadcast in 1966.

Pevsner, Nikolaus. *The Englishness of English Art: An Expanded and Annotated Version of the Reith Lectures Broadcast in October and November 1955*. London: Architectural Press, 1956.

Pevsner, Nikolaus. 'The Genesis of the Picturesque'. *The Architectural Review*, vol. 96, no. 575, November 1944, pp. 139–146.

Pevsner, Nikolaus. 'The Genius of the Place'. In Pevsner, *Pevsner on Art and Architecture*, pp. 230–240. Based on a broadcast in 1955.

Pevsner, Nikolaus (Peter F. R. Donner). 'The Lure of Rusticity'. *The Architectural Review*, vol. 93, no. 553, January 1943, p. 27.

Pevsner, Nikolaus. 'Modern Architecture and the Historian or The Return of Historicism'. *The Architectural Review*, vol. 68, no. 6, April 1961, pp. 230–240. Based on a lecture given at the RIBA on 10 January 1961.

Pevsner, Nikolaus. *Pevsner on Art and Architecture: The Radio Talks*. Ed. Stephen Games. London: Methuen, 2002.

Pevsner, Nikolaus. 'The Return of Historicism'. In Pevsner, *Pevsner on Art and Architecture*, pp. 271–278. Based on a broadcast in 1961, and developed from Pevsner's RIBA lecture earlier that year, which was published as 'Modern Architecture and the Historian or The Return of Historicism'.

Pevsner, Nikolaus. 'Twentieth-Century Picturesque: An Answer to Basil Taylor's Broadcast'. *The Architectural Review*, vol. 115, no. 688, April 1954, pp. 227–229.

Pevsner, Nikolaus. 'Twentieth Century Picturesque: Reply to Alan Colquohoun'. *The Architectural Review*, vol. 116, no. 691, July 1954, p. 2.

Pevsner, Nikolaus. *Visual Planning and the Picturesque*. Ed. Matthew Aitchison. Los Angeles: Getty Research Institute, 2010.

Phillipson, Nicholas. 'Politics, Politeness and the Anglicisation of Early Eighteenth-Century Scottish Culture'. In Mason, pp. 226–246.

Plato. *Philebus*. Trans. J.C.B. Gosling. Oxford: Clarendon Press, 1975.

Plato. *Timaeus, Critias, Cleitophon, Menexenus, Epistles*. Trans. R. G. Bury. Cambridge, MA: Harvard University Press, 1929.

Plumb, J. H. 'Sir Robert Walpole and Norfolk Husbandry'. *Economic History Review*, 2nd series, vol. 5, no. 1, 1952, pp. 86–89.

Plumb, J. H. *Sir Robert Walpole: The King's Minister*. London: The Cresset Press, 1960.

Plumb, J. H. *Sir Robert Walpole: The Making of a Statesman*. London: The Cresset Press, 1956.

Pope, Alexander. *The Correspondence of Alexander Pope*, vols 1–5. Ed. George Sherburn. Oxford: Oxford University Press, 1956.

Pope, Alexander. *The Dunciad. As it is Now Changed by Mr. Pope. In Four Books*. Dublin: Philip Bowes, 1744.

Porter, Roy. *English Society in the Eighteenth Century*. London: Penguin, 1991.

Porter, Roy. *Enlightenment: Britain and the Creation of the Modern World*. London: Penguin, 2001.

Porter, Roy. *Flesh in the Age of Reason: How the Enlightenment Transformed the Way We See Our Bodies and Souls*. London: Penguin, 2004.

Powers, Alan. 'Albert Richardson: A Critical Survey'. In Houfe, Powers and Wilton-Ely, pp. 40–71.

Price, Uvedale. *An Essay on the Picturesque, as Compared with the Sublime and the Beautiful; and, on the Use of Studying Pictures for the Purpose of Improving Real Landscapes*. London: J. Robson, 1794. First published in Hereford in 1794.

Price, Uvedale. *Essays on the Picturesque, as Compared with the Sublime and the Beautiful; and, on the Use of Studying Pictures for the Purpose of Improving Real Landscapes*. London: J. Mawman, 1810, 3 vols.

Raphael and Baldassare Castiglione. 'The Letter to Leo X, c. 1519'. In Hart and Hicks, pp. 177–192.

Rattenbury, Kester, ed. *This is Not Architecture: Media Constructions*. London and New York: Routledge, 2002.

Rawnsley, H. D. *Past and Present at the English Lakes*. Glasgow: MacLehose and Sons, 1916.

Rayner, Steve. 'Domesticating Nature: Commentary on the Anthropological Study of Weather and Climate Discourse'. In Strauss and Orlove, pp. 277–290.

Repton, Humphry. *The Landscape Gardening and the Landscape Architecture of the Late Humphry Repton, Esq*. Ed. J. C. Loudon. Farnborough: Gregg International 1969. First published in 1840.

Reynolds, Joshua. *Letters of Sir Joshua Reynolds*. Ed. Frederick W. Hilles. Cambridge: Cambridge University Press, 1929.

Richards, J. M. *Memoirs of an Unjust Fella*. London: Weidenfeld and Nicolson, 1980.

Richardson, Charles James. *A Popular Treatise on the Warming and Ventilating of Buildings: Showing the Advantage of the Improved System of Hot Water Circulation*. London: John Weale Architectural Library, 1839, 2nd edition. First published in 1837.

Richardson, Margaret. *Building in Progress: Soane's View of Construction*. London: Sir John Soane's Museum, 1995.

Richietti, John. 'The Novel Before the "Novel"'. In Caserio and Hawes, pp. 14–29.

Richter-Musso, Inés, and Ortrud Westheider, eds. *Turner and the Elements*. Munich: Hirmer Verlag, 2011.

Ricoeur, Paul. *History and Truth*. Trans. Charles A. Kelbley. Evanston: Northwestern University Press, 1965.

Ricoeur, Paul. 'Objectivity and Subjectivity in History'. In Ricouer, *History and Truth*, pp. 21–40.

Riding, Christine. 'Making Waves'. In Riding and Johns, pp. 240–269.

Riding, Christine, and Richard Johns. *Turner and the Sea*. London: Thames & Hudson, 2013.

Riegl, Alois, 'On the Modern Cult of Monuments: Its Character and its Origin'. Trans. Kurt Forster and Dianne Ghirardo. *Oppositions* (Monument/Memory), ed. Kurt W. Forster, no. 25, 1982, pp. 21–51. First published in 1903.

Robbins, Professor Lord et al. 'Committee on Higher Education' (Robbins Report). London: Her Majesty's Stationery Office, 1963.

Rodner, William S. *J.M.W. Turner: Romantic Painter of the Industrial Revolution*. Berkeley, Los Angeles and London: University of California Press, 1997.

Rogers, Ernesto N. 'Continuità'. *Casabella Continuità*, no. 199, December 1953–January 1954, p. 2.

Rosenblum, Robert. *Modern Painting and the Northern Romantic Tradition: Friedrich to Rothko*. London: Thames & Hudson, 1975.

Rousseau, Jean-Jacques. *The Confessions of Jean-Jacques Rousseau*. Trans. J. M. Cohen. London: Penguin, 1953. First published in 1781.

Rowe, Colin. 'Mannerism and Modern Architecture'. In Rowe, *The Mathematics of the Ideal Villa and Other Essays*, pp. 29–51. First published in 1950.

Rowe, Colin. 'The Mathematics of the Ideal Villa'. In Rowe, *The Mathematics of the Ideal Villa and Other Essays*, pp. 1–27. First published in 1947.

Rowe, Colin. *The Mathematics of the Ideal Villa and Other Essays*. Cambridge, MA: MIT Press, 1976.

Ruskin, John. *Modern Painters*, vol. 1. London: George Allen, 1888. First published in 1843.

Ruskin, John. *Modern Painters*, vol. 3. London: Smith, Elder & Co., 1873. First published in 1856.

Ruskin, John. *Modern Painters*, vol. 4. London: George Allen, 1904. First published in 1856.

Ruskin, John. *Modern Painters*, vol. 5. London: George Allen, 1905. First published in 1860.

Ruskin, John. *The Seven Lamps of Architecture*. New York: Farrar, Straus and Giroux, 1984. First published in 1849.

Ruskin, John. *The Stones of Venice*. London: Smith, Elder and Co., 1851–1853, 3 vols.

Ruskin, John. *The Storm Cloud of the Nineteenth Century*. Orpington: George Allen, 1884.

Rykwert, Joseph. *The First Moderns: The Architects of the Eighteenth Century*. Cambridge, MA and London: MIT Press, 1980.

Saisselin, Rémy. 'Architecture and Language: The Sensationalism of Le Camus de Mézières'. *The British Journal of Aesthetics*, vol. 15, no. 3, Summer 1975, pp. 239–253.

Salmon, Frank. '"Our Great Master Kent" and the Design of Holkham Hall: A Reassessment'. *Architectural History*, vol. 56, 2013, pp. 63–96.

Salter, Peter, and Lorenzo Wong, eds. *Climate Register: Four Works by Alison and Peter Smithson*. London: Architectural Association, 1994.

Sanderson, Michael. *The History of the University of East Anglia, Norwich*. London: Hambledon and London, 2002.

Sant'Elia, Antonio, and Filippo Tomasso Marinetti. 'Manifesto of Futurist Architecture'. In Conrads, pp. 34–38. First published in 1914.

Savage, Nicholas. 'Kent as Book Illustrator'. In Weber, pp. 413–447.

Schama, Simon. *The Embarrassment of Riches: An Interpretation of Dutch Culture in the Golden Age*. London: Fontana, 1991.

Schmidt, Leo. 'Inventing Holkham'. In Schmidt, Keller and Feversham, pp. 80–103.

Schmidt, Leo. 'Thomas Coke, Earl of Leicester – the Builder of Holkham'. In Schmidt, Keller and Feversham, pp. 29–47.

Schmidt, Leo, with Christian Keller and Silke Langenberg. 'Building Holkham'. In Schmidt, Keller and Feversham, pp. 108–131.

Schmidt, Leo, Christian Keller and Polly Feversham, eds. *Holkham*. Munich: Prestel, 2005.

Scott, Geoffrey. *The Architecture of Humanism: A Study of the History of Taste*. London: Architectural Press, 1980. First published in 1924.

Scully, Vincent. *American Architecture and Urbanism*. London: Thames & Hudson, 1969.

Sebald, W. G. *On the Natural History of Destruction*. Trans. Anthea Bell. New York: Random House, 2004.

Sedgwick, Romney, ed. *Lord Hervey's Memoirs*. London: William Kimber, 1952.

Shaftesbury, Anthony Ashley Cooper, third Earl of. *Characteristicks of Men, Manners, Opinions, Times*. Ed. Philip Ayres. Oxford: Clarendon Press, 1999, 2 vols. First published as a three-volume collection in 1711.

Shaftesbury, Anthony Ashley Cooper, third Earl of. *The Life, Unpublished Letters, and Philosophical Regimen of Anthony, Earl of Shaftesbury*. Ed. Benjamin Rand. London: Swan Sonnenschein, 1900.

Shaw, W. N. 'The London Fog Inquiry'. *Nature*, no. 64, 31 October 1901, pp. 649–650.

Sicca, Cinzia Maria. 'On William Kent's Roman Sources'. *Architectural History*, vol. 29, 1986, pp. 134–157.

Simmel, Georg. *Essays on Sociology, Philosophy and Aesthetics*. Ed. Kurt H. Wolff. New York: Harper and Row, 1965.

Simmel, Georg. 'The Ruin'. In Simmel, *Essays on Sociology, Philosophy and Aesthetics*, pp. 259–266. First published in 1911.

Simons, Paul. *Since Records Began: The Highs and Lows of Britain's Weather*. London: Collins, 2008.

Smith, Neil. 'Foreword'. In Heynen, Kaika and Swyngedouw, pp. xi–xv.

Smith, Neil. 'Nature at the Millennium: Production and Re-enchantment'. In Braun and Castree, pp. 271–285.

Smith, Steven R. 'John Evelyn and London Air'. *History Today*, vol. 23, no. 3, March 1975, pp. 185–189.

Smithson, Alison. *AS in DS: An Eye on the Road*. Baden: Lars Müller, 2001. First published by Delft University Press in 1983.

Smithson, Alison. 'Patio and Pavilion, 1956, Reconstructed U.S.A. 1990'. *Places: A Quarterly Journal of Environmental Design*, vol. 7, no. 3, 1991, pp. 10–14.

Smithson, Alison, and Peter Smithson. *Alison and Peter Smithson: The Shift (Architectural Monographs 7)*. London: Academy Editions, 1982.

Smithson, Alison, and Peter Smithson. 'Banham's Bumper Book on Brutalism, Discussed by Alison and Peter Smithson'. *The Architects' Journal*. vol. 144, no. 24, 28 December 1966, pp. 1590–1591.

Smithson, Alison, and Peter Smithson. *Changing the Art of Inhabitation: Mies' Pieces, Eames' Dreams, the Smithsons*. London, Zürich and Munich: Artemis, 1994.

Smithson, Alison, and Peter Smithson. *The Charged Void: Architecture*. New York: Monacelli Press, 2001.

Smithson, Alison, and Peter Smithson. 'Cluster City: A New Shape for the Community'. *Architectural Review*, vol. 122, July–December 1957, pp. 332–336.

Smithson, Alison, and Peter Smithson. 'Correspondence: Architectural Principles in the Age of Humanism'. *Journal of the Royal Institute of British Architects*, vol. 59, no. 4, February 1952, p. 140.

Smithson, Alison, and Peter Smithson. 'Folly at Fonthill, Wilts.'. *Architectural Design*, vol. 33, October 1963, pp. 482–483.

Smithson, Alison, and Peter Smithson. 'House of the Future', *Daily Mail Ideal Home Exhibition, Olympia, 1956*, catalogue to the exhibition.

Smithson, Alison, and Peter Smithson. 'The New Brutalism'. *Architectural Design*, vol. 25, January 1955, p. 1.

Smithson, Alison, and Peter Smithson. 'The New Brutalism; Alison and Peter Smithson Answer the Criticisms on the Opposite Page'. *Architectural Design*, vol. 27, April 1957, p. 113.

Smithson, Alison, and Peter Smithson. *Ordinariness and Light: Urban Theories 1952–1960 and their Application in a Building Project 1963–1970*. London: Faber and Faber, 1970.

Smithson, Alison, and Peter Smithson. *Upper Lawn, Solar Pavilion Folly*. Barcelona: Edicions UPC, 1986.

Smithson, Alison, and Peter Smithson. *Without Rhetoric: An Architectural Aesthetic 1955–1972*. London: Latimer New Dimensions, 1973.

Smithson, Peter. 'Conglomerate Ordering'. In Webster, *Modernism Without Rhetoric,* pp. 182–193.

Smithson, Peter. *Conversations with Students: A Space for our Generation*. Eds Catherine Spellman and Karl Unglaub. New York: Princeton Architectural Press, 2005.

Smithson, Peter. 'Letter to America'. *Architectural Design*, vol. 28, March 1958, pp. 93–102. Reprinted and credited to Alison and Peter Smithson in *Ordinariness and Light,* pp. 135–143.

Smithson, Peter. 'A Sensibility Primer'. In Alison Smithson, *AS in DS*, p. 1.

Smithson, Peter. 'Think of it as a Farm! Exhibitions, Books, Buildings. An Interview with Peter Smithson'. In Rattenbury, pp. 91–98.

Smithson, Robert. *Robert Smithson: The Collected Writings*. Ed. Jack Flam. Berkeley and Los Angeles: University of California Press, 1966.

Smithson, Robert. 'A Tour of the Monuments of Passaic, New Jersey' (1967). In Smithson, *Robert Smithson*, pp. 68–74.

Soane, John. 'Crude Hints towards an History of my House in L(incoln's) I(nn) Fields'. In Woodward, *Visions of Ruin*, pp. 61–75. Written in 1812.

Soane, John. *Description of the House and Museum on the North Side of Lincoln's-Inn-Fields, the Residence of John Soane*. Privately printed, 1830. Held in Sir John Soane's Museum, London.

Soane, John. *Description of the House and Museum on the North Side of Lincoln's-Inn-Fields, the Residence of Sir John Soane*. Privately printed, 1832. Held in Sir John Soane's Museum, London.

Soane, John. *Description of the House and Museum on the North Side of Lincoln's Inn Fields, the Residence of Sir John Soane*. Privately printed, 1835. Held in Sir John Soane's Museum, London.

Soane, John. *Memoirs of the Professional Life of an Architect, between the Years 1768 and 1835. Written by Himself.* Privately printed, 1835. Held in Sir John Soane's Museum, London.

Soane, John. 'Soane's Note Books', 14 vols. Held in Sir John Soane's Museum, London.

Soissons, Maurice de. *The Holkham People*. King's Lynn: Woodthorpe Publishing, 1997.

Solkin, David. 'Education and Emulation'. In Solkin, *Turner and the Masters*, pp. 99–101.

Solkin, David, et al. *Turner and the Masters*. London: Tate Gallery, 2009.

Speck, William. 'Britain's First Prime Minister'. In Moore, *Houghton Hall*, pp. 4–19.

Steers, J. A., ed. *Blakeney Point and Scolt Head Island*. Norfolk: The National Trust, 1976.

Steers, J. A. 'The Physical Features of Scolt Head Island and Blakeney Point'. In Steers, *Blakeney Point and Scolt Head Island*, pp. 13–25.

Steers, J. A. 'Physiography and Evolution'. In Steers, *Scolt Head Island*, pp. 12–66.

Steers, J. A., ed. *Scolt Head Island*. Cambridge: W. Heffer & Sons Ltd, 1960.

Sterne, Laurence. *The Life and Opinions of Tristram Shandy, Gentleman*. Ed. Melvyn New and Joan New. London: Penguin, 2003. First published in nine volumes between 1759 and 1767.

Stirling, A.M.W. *Coke of Norfolk and his Friends*. London: John Lane The Bodley Head, 1908, 2 vols.

Stirling, Robin. *The Weather of Britain*. London: Giles de la Mare, 1997. First published in 1982.

Stobart, J. C. *The Glory that was Greece*. London: Sedgwick & Jackson, 1911.

Stobart, J.C. *The Grandeur that was Rome*. London: Sedgwick & Jackson, 1912.

Strauss, Susan, and Ben Orlove, eds. *Weather, Climate, Culture*. Oxford and New York: Berg, 2003.

Stroud, Dorothy. *Humphry Repton*. London: Country Life, 1962.

Summerson, John, ed. *Concerning Architecture: Essays of Architectural Writers and Writings Presented to Nikolaus Pevsner*. London: Allen Lane/Penguin, 1968.

Summerson, John. 'Soane: The Man and the Style'. In Dunster, pp. 9–23.

Summerson, John, and Helen Dorey. *A New Description of Sir John Soane's Museum*. London: Trustees of Sir John Soane's Museum, 2001, 10th edition.

Swift, Jonathan. *Gulliver's Travels*. London: Penguin, 2001. First published in 1726.

Taylor, Charles. *Sources of the Self: The Making of Modern Identity*. Cambridge: Cambridge University Press, 1989.

Thomas, Keith. *Man and the Natural World: Changing Attitudes in England 1500–1800*. London: Allen Lane, 1983.

Thomson, James. *Liberty, The Castle of Indolence and Other Poems*. Ed. James Sambrook. Oxford: Oxford University Press, 1986.

Thomson, James. 'A Poem Sacred to the Memory of Sir Isaac Newton'. In Thomson, *The Seasons*, pp. 241–252.

Thomson, James. *The Seasons*. London: John Millan, 1730.

Thornbury, Walter. *The Life of J.M.W. Turner RA*. London: Ward Lock Reprints, 1970. First published in 1861.

Thornton, Peter, and Helen Dorey. *A Miscellany of Objects from Sir John Soane's Museum*. London: Laurence King, 1992.

Tipping, H. Avray, ed. 'Four Unpublished Letters of William Kent – II. In the Possession of Lord Spencer'. *The Architectural Review*, vol. 63, May 1928, pp. 209–211.

Townsend, Joyce. *Turner's Painting Techniques.* London: Tate Publishing, 1993.

Townsend, Joyce, ed. *Turner's Painting Techniques in Context.* London: UKIC, 1995.

Townsend, Joyce. 'Turner's Use of Materials, and Implications for Conservation'. In Townsend, *Turner's Painting Techniques in Context*, pp. 5–11.

Tusa, John, with James Cornford, Peter Laslett and Colin Rowe. 'Critics or Conservatives: A Discussion of the Role of the University'. *Granta*, vol. 64, no. 1021, 4 June 1960, pp. 22–26.

Tuveson, Ernest Lee. *The Imagination as a Means of Grace: Locke and the Aesthetics of Romanticism*. Berkeley and Los Angeles: University of California Press, 1960.

Upjohn, Sheila. 'Town and Gown'. *The Architects' Journal*, vol. 155, no. 24, 14 June 1972, pp. 1322–1331.

Vanbrugh, John. 'From Letter to the Duchess of Marlborough (1709)'. In Mallgrave, pp. 230–232.

Van den Heuvel, Dirk, and Max Risselada, eds. *Alison and Peter Smithson – from the House of the Future to a House of Today*. Rotterdam: 010, 2004.

Varey, Simon. *Space and the Eighteenth-Century English Novel*. Cambridge: Cambridge University Press, 1990.

Vasari, Giorgio. *Vasari on Technique*. Trans. Louisa S. Maclehose. New York: Dover, 1960. First published in 1550 as *Le vite de' più eccelenti pittori, scultori e architettori* (The Lives of the Most Eminent Painters, Sculptors and Architects).

Venning, Barry. *Turner*. London and New York: Phaidon, 2003.

Vico, Giambattista. *New Science*. Trans. David Marsh. London and New York: Penguin Books, 1999. First published as *La scienza nuova* in 1725.

Vidler, Anthony. 'Air War and Architecture'. In Hell and Schönle, pp. 29–40.

Vidler, Anthony. *Histories of the Immediate Present: Inventing Architectural Modernism*. Cambridge, MA and London: MIT Press, 2008.

Vidler, Anthony. *The Writing of the Walls*. Princeton: Princeton University Press, 1987.

Virilio, Paul. *Bunker Archaeology*. Trans. George Collins. New York: Princeton Architectural Press, 1994.

Vitruvius. *The Ten Books on Architecture*. Trans. Morris Hicky Morgan. New York: Dover, 1960. *De architectura libri decem* was written in the first century BC.

Voogd, Peter Jan de. 'Tristram Shandy as Aesthetic Object'. *Word and Image*, vol. 4, no. 1, January–March 1988, pp. 383–392.

Wade Martins, Susanna. *Coke of Norfolk (1754–1842): A Biography*. Woodbridge: The Boydell Press, 2009.

Wade Martins, Susanna. *A Great Estate at Work: The Holkham Estate and its Inhabitants in the Nineteenth Century*. Cambridge: Cambridge University Press, 1980.

Waldheim, Charles. 'Landscape as Urbanism'. In Waldheim, *The Landscape Urbanism Reader*, pp. 35–53.

Waldheim, Charles, ed. *The Landscape Urbanism Reader*. New York: Princeton Architectural Press, 2006.

Wall, Cynthia. *The Prose of Things: Transformation of Description in the Eighteenth Century*. Chicago and London: University of Chicago Press, 2006.

Walpole, Horace. *Aedes Walpolianae: Or, a Description of the Collection of Pictures at Houghton-Hall in Norfolk, The Seat of the Right Honourable Sir Robert Walpole, Earl of Orford*, 1752, 2nd edition. London: British Library and Ecco Print Editions, 2013. First published in 1747.

Walpole, Horace. *Correspondence*. Ed. Wilmarth Sheldon Lewis. New Haven and London: Yale University Press, 1937.

Walpole, Horace. *The History of the Modern Taste in Gardening*. New York: Ursus Press, 1995. Written in the late 1760s and printed in 1771 but not published until 1780 as part of Walpole's *Anecdotes of Painting in England*. It was published on its own in 1785.

Warner, Deborah Jane. 'The Landscape Mirror and Glass'. *Antiques*, vol. 105, no. 1, January 1974, pp. 158–159.

Watkin, David. 'Built Ruins: The Hermitage as a Retreat'. In Woodward, *Vision of Ruins*, pp. 5–14.

Watkin, David. 'John Soane: Architecture and Enlightenment'. *Casabella*, 1998, vol. 62, no. 660, pp. 72–83.

Watkin, David. *Sir John Soane: Enlightenment Thought and the Royal Academy Lectures*. Cambridge: Cambridge University Press, 1996.

Watt, Ian. *The Rise of the Novel: Studies in Defoe, Richardson and Fielding*. London: The Hogarth Press, 1987. First published in 1957.

Weber, Susan, ed. *William Kent: Designing Georgian Britain*. New Haven and London: Yale University Press, 2013.

Webster, Helena, ed. *Modernism Without Rhetoric: Essays on the Work of Alison and Peter Smithson*. London: Academy, 1997.

Webster, Tom. 'Writing to Redundancy: Approaches to Spiritual Journals and Early-Modern Spirituality'. *The Historical Journal*, 1996, vol. 39, no. 1, pp. 33–56.

Whale, John. 'Romantics, Explorers and Picturesque Travellers'. In Copley and Garside, *The Politics of the Picturesque*, pp. 175–195.

Whately, Thomas. *Observations on Modern Gardening, Illustrated by Descriptions*. London: T. Payne, 1771. First published in 1770.

Wheeler, Dennis. 'The Great Storm of November 1703: A New Look at the Seamen's Records'. *Weather*, vol. 58, no. 11, pp. 419–427.

White, Roger. 'Kent and the Gothic Revival'. In Weber, pp. 247–269.

Wiedmann, August. *Romantic Art Theories*. Henley-on-Thames: Gresham Books, 1986.

Williams, Raymond. *The Country and the City*. Nottingham: Spokesman, 2011. First published in 1973.

Williamson, Tom. *The Archaeology of the Landscape Park: Garden Design in Norfolk, England, c. 1680–1840*. Oxford: Archaeopress, 1998.

Williamson, Tom. 'The Development of Holkham Park'. In Schmidt, Keller and Feversham, pp. 58–72.

Williamson, Tom. *An Environmental History of Wildlife in England 1650–1950*. London and New York: Bloomsbury, 2013.

Williamson, Tom. 'The Planting of the Park'. In Moore, *Houghton Hall*, pp. 41–47.

Williamson, Tom. *The Transformation of Rural England: Farming and the Landscape 1700–1870*. Exeter: University of Exeter Press, 2002.

Willmert, Todd. 'Heating Methods and their Impact on Soane's Work: Lincoln's Inn Fields and Dulwich Picture Gallery'. *Journal of the Society of Architectural Historians*, March 1993, vol. 52, no. 1, pp. 26–58.

Wilson, Michael. *William Kent; Architect, Designer, Painter, Gardener, 1685–1748*. London: Routledge & Kegan Paul, 1984.

Wilton, Andrew. 'Forward'. In Parry-Wingfield, pp. 4–5.

Wilton, Andrew. *The Life and Work of J.M.W. Turner*. London: Academy, 1979.

Wilton, Andrew. *Turner and the Sublime*. London: British Museum, 1980.

Wilton, Andrew. *Turner as Draughtsman*. Aldershot: Ashgate, 2006.

Wittkower, Rudolf. *Architectural Principles in the Age of Humanism*. London: Warburg Institute, 1949.

Woodward, Christopher. *In Ruins*. London: Vintage, 2001.

Woodward, Christopher, ed. *Visions of Ruin: Architectural Fantasies and Designs for Garden Follies*. London: Sir John Soane's Museum, 1999.

Wordsworth, William. *Lyrical Ballads*. London: Longman, 1802, 2 vols. First published in 1798.

Worpole, Ken, and Jason Orton. *The New English Landscape*. London: Field Station, 2013.

Worsley, Giles. *Classical Architecture in Britain: The Heroic Age*. New Haven and London: Yale University Press, 1995.

Yates, T. 'Mechanisms of Air Pollution Damage to Brick, Concrete and Mortar'. In Brimblecombe, *The Effects of Air Pollution on the Built Environment*, pp. 107–132.

Young, Arthur. *A Six Weeks Tour, Through the Southern Counties of England and Wales*. London: W. Nicoll, 1768.

Zimmerman, Claire. 'Photographic Images from Chicago to Hunstanton'. In Crinson and Zimmerman, pp. 203–228.

Zucker, Paul, ed. *New Architecture and City Planning: A Symposium*. New York: Philosophical Library, 1944.

Zweinger-Bargielowska, Ina. *Austerity in Britain: Rationing Controls and Consumption, 1939–1955*. Oxford: Oxford University Press, 2000.

INDEX